Spiral Up

Spiral Up

... and Other Management Secrets Behind Wildly Successful Initiatives

Jane C. Linder

✦AMACOM

American Management Association

New York • Atlanta • Brussels • Chicago • Mexico City • San Francisco
Shanghai • Tokyo • Toronto • Washington, D.C.

This publication is designed to provide accurate and authoritative
information in regard to the subject matter covered. It is sold with the
understanding that the publisher is not engaged in rendering legal,
accounting, or other professional service. If legal advice or other expert
assistance is required, the services of a competent professional person
should be sought.

A Note on the Sources: This book includes numerous case studies and
examples. In many instances the information is so specific and perhaps
surprising that the reader may wonder: "How can she know that?" The
information comes from years of painstaking research, including personal
interviews with many of the people profiled in the book. The facts are
beyond question; their interpretation, of course, is my own.

Library of Congress Cataloging-in-Publication Data

Linder, Jane C.
    Spiral up : and other management secrets behind wildly successful
initiatives / Jane C. Linder.
        p.   cm.
    Includes index.
    ISBN-13: 978–0-8144–0917–6
    ISBN-10: 0–8144–0917–2
    1. Success in business.   2. Management.   3. Organizational change.   I. Title.
HD31.L4744   2008
658.4′04—dc22

2007025759

Printing number

10   9   8   7   6   5   4   3   2   1

To Mont

Contents

Foreword

I am thrilled to introduce this wonderful book. Why? Many people say that I have been wildly successful, but it certainly doesn't feel that way to me. According to *Spiral Up*, however, it's not unusual for champions of working wonders to feel the same way I do. Let me explain . . .

My colleagues, Colin Angle and Rodney Brooks, and I started iRobot Corporation, a company that makes robots for both the military and the consumer markets. We developed the iRobot PackBot, a bomb-disposal robot for the military that has saved scores of soldiers' lives. When we get one back from the front lines of Iraq in pieces, we know we have made a big difference for an American family somewhere. The company also developed and commercialized the iRobot Roomba, the first practical and affordable robot for the home. Yes, it cleans your house. Through 2006, we have sold more than 2 million of them.

I didn't start out to be a bomb-disposal expert or a house-cleaning maven. Actually, *Star Wars* got me into the robot business. I was 11 when I saw the movie and was completely enthralled by R2D2. He was much more than a machine—he had character and personality. If you think about it, unlike the humans in the series who come and go, R2D2 starred in all six of the films.

At the time, I was hacking away on the family computer, a TRS-80, and I could see how machines could be programmed to do the things you want. I could control the motors in the computer's tape deck and request sensor readings from the key board. It wasn't hard to imagine having a camera system connected. Like others in this book who worked wonders, I reached for something well beyond my grasp.

Of course, at 11, I had no concept of how difficult it would be to build a real robot. That was probably a good thing, too. If I had known, I might not have been so eager to try.

Ultimately I went off to MIT where I learned about engineering and computers through a proverbial fire hose. Despite earning degrees in mechanical engineering and computer science, I didn't actually learn how to build robots in a way that was useful.

I reasoned that a research university was not the best environment for building practical robots; it would take a company. In graduate school, when the PhD student finishes her dissertation and leaves, the project dies. That means a lot of wasted energy. In a company, you can keep the team engaged, feed a portion of profits back into internal research and development (iR&D) and continue to develop the technology. If you want to devote your energy to making progress in the field—getting it right, as *Spiral Up* would say—that kind of persistence is essential. So I left the research lab to start iRobot.

We started with something familiar—making robots for people exactly like us. Other researchers had been calling the lab and asking whether they could buy our robots, so we concluded there must be a market. I must say that it was a very forgiving marketplace to cut our teeth on. If you send out a robot, and it doesn't work, the customer calls you. You might tell them that one of the resistor values is wrong, so they get out a soldering iron and fix it.

Working in our own backyard gave us the opportunity to develop the technology for a few years. We began bidding on government contracts to design the "next generation" robot for the military. What we didn't realize was that *this* generation didn't exist yet. No matter, we designed a wonderfully sophisticated, bomb-detecting, 6-legged walking robot called Ariel.

Instead of taking the baby steps that *Spiral Up* recommends, it was more of a "start at the top" approach. Not surprisingly it didn't work out very well. But we used Ariel to make some really cool videos to demonstrate our capabilities, and these opened the door to strategic partnerships with *Fortune* 500 companies. For example, we designed robotic toys for Hasbro under their brand, we developed an oil drilling robot for Baker Hughes, and we licensed commercial cleaning technology to SC Johnson. We learned something from every project we did and used it to develop our technology base.

Once we started using the *Spiral Up* approach with the military, our developments turned more practical and filled a real need the soldiers have today. For example, to locate caches of weapons the insurgents had stored in caves in Afghanistan, the U.S. military used to send in soldiers with ropes tied to them—to retrieve the bodies if bad things happened. We offered them an alternative—a PackBot that could clear caves and find weapons caches and booby traps without endangering a single person. Our troops quickly learned to send PackBot into the caves first.

Later, in Iraq, the military used our PackBot robots in the push to Baghdad, sending them into buildings to look for potential ambushes. To deal with nasty IEDs—improvised explosive devices—the military used to suit up a soldier in Kevlar and send him out to deal with the bomb. Now they are using PackBot to do that dangerous job.

On the consumer front, we never would have been able to launch Roomba, a mass market product, without the Hasbro experience under our belts. Of course we could build a cool robot for cleaning the floor, but the consumer wouldn't pay $2,000 for it. We learned from Hasbro how to pinch pennies on every electronic component, how to design for manufacturing and how to source from Asia. In addition to worrying about the price point, we also had to shift our mindset about the technology. When someone buys a Roomba, they are not buying it because it's a robot, but because it cleans. We had to tune our thinking to the customer's perspective rather than to the technical possibilities.

When you build things, you also have to be practical. At iRobot, we benefit by having lots of employees who have gotten their hands dirty—and not just in our engineering staff, but also in customer support, logistics, IT and finance. And when you have to design something tightly integrated—whether in robots or logistics—you have an epiphany about complexity: it is evil. Designers know how to keep things simple and build on them. *Spiral Up* will have more to say about the importance of simplicity.

One of the management practices that have made us successful is empowering small teams of passionate people. We let them make the decisions about the project and give them the time—and what *Spiral Up* calls "space"—to develop good ideas for the company.

For example, I didn't invent the Roomba; it was suggested by one of our employees. He pulled in a few other passionate colleagues and $20,000 in R&D funds and built a very simple prototype. It wasn't really a Roomba—it was much simpler—but we could see that it had potential. So we invited the team to take it forward.

One of the most important factors in our success has been getting small, passionate teams to believe they can make a difference—creating what *Spiral Up* calls the strong emotional field. That's what iRobot is all about. We figure out better ways to do things so people no longer have to do tedious or dangerous jobs. We are an evolving and learning organization—an open system in the best sense of the term. No one of us is smart enough to know where robotics will take us, so we make sure we stay flexible and learn from both the inside and outside. That way we can morph as the field develops. And people are constantly telling me that, no matter who they meet at the company, they can feel the energy.

Over the past 17 years since we started iRobot, we have gone through multiple stages. Some of our projects made money, and some didn't, but we used them all as stepping stones—to spiral up. Along the way, people told us: "You can't sell robots for a living." But that's exactly what we are doing. With *Spiral Up* in your hip pocket, perhaps you will work wonders too.

Helen Greiner
Co-Founder and Chairman
iRobot Corporation

Preface

This book began upside down.

I don't know about you, but I have always been captivated by the proportion of business projects that don't turn out the way people hope they will. Whether we're talking about strategic partnerships or IT implementations, total quality initiatives or corporate transformations, the statistics all seem to come out about the same: 65 to 70 percent of the projects fail to deliver the expected benefits.

Where I come from, getting 35 percent of the work right earns people a big red F. It's the kind of performance that losers turn in. It's not even close to acceptable.

Are the businesspeople you know losers? Are they poorly trained, lazy, or stupid? Are they taking drugs or drunk all the time? I just don't get it. How could the well-intentioned, smart, skillful, and energetic people who are everywhere in our organizations perform consistently at the same level as high school dropouts? This was the intriguing question that got me started on the idea of working wonders.

I usually try to follow my own advice and expose my ideas to a little sunlight very early in the process. I'm lucky enough to be surrounded by friends and family who are happy to tell me what they really think, and I learn the most amazing things from them. From their reactions, I can tell immediately whether or not I am on the right track. If their eyes light up, I'm on to something good. If their eyes dim, I'm heading into a sinkhole.

You can guess what happened when I approached my confidantes and enthusiastically described my plans to explore the anatomy of failure. Eye after eye lost its light. A good friend who provides perceptive feedback said, "You're right about all the failure, of course. I just don't want to read about it. I live with it every day."

That encounter set this book in motion. Instead of studying failure, I began looking for organizational initiatives that had been wildly successful. In stunning and immediate contrast to my earlier experiences, eyes lit up and people said, "I'd like to read that book."

It gets better. As I gathered data about more than forty wildly successful initiatives, some common characteristics began to emerge. In particular, it quickly became clear that the management approach for working wonders was radically different from conventional practice. I was lucky enough to have the opportunity to share some of my early insights with a group of MBA students in Elizabeth Teisberg's course on innovation at the University of Virginia's Darden School. The students capably laid out the steps for a well-managed project. Then we compared those steps with the management approach in a wildly successful initiative. The two were completely, utterly different, and the room shimmered with a palpable "aha."

That day I clarified the purpose of this book: to encourage initiative champions to try an unconventional approach. I am convinced that uncommon success will result.

And it gets better. I originally began the work on this book in 2002. The words "what took you so long?" should come to mind. Suffice it to say that there were a few setbacks. I suppose they were no worse than the normal slew of distractions, rejections, and obstacles that any book project might face, but I was lucky. In every wildly successful example I was studying, champions were telling me about how they used adversity to push them forward and how they never gave up. It worked like my own personal support group. So I never gave up.

I owe these champions a huge debt of gratitude, both for spurring me on and for sharing their stories. You'll meet them in the book, so I won't name them here. I only hope I have done them justice, because they are truly amazing.

These accolades also apply to the champions who are not named in the book for one reason or another. Even though they remain in the shadows, their accomplishments light our world. Jack French and Linda Neshamkin stand out in this regard. Alex and Ellen Sturtevant were kind enough to take me inside the world of debate.

My research colleague, Donna Stoddard, made all the difference in developing the AIRNow and Coplink stories. We're both grateful to Valerie Gregg and Larry Brandt of the National Science Foundation for supporting our work and to Steve Powers for his invaluable assistance in the research. Sean Shine, Paul Duff, Dave Regan, and a number of other out-of-the-ordinary people at Accenture willingly shared their time and their perspectives. Al Jacobson and Susan Cantrell came through every time, no matter what kind of help I needed. What would I do without their energy and their buoyant spirits?

I reserve special thanks for my editor, Adrienne Hickey, who never gave up on me.

Finally, and perhaps most importantly, I thank my family for their honest, gracious, and unqualified support. They are everything to me.

Spiral Up

CHAPTER 1

Concrete Slippers or Helium Hightops

The Management Secrets Behind Wildly Successful Initiatives

You won't be reading about Jack Welch in this book. Or about any other rock star CEOs, no matter how stunning their insights or accomplishments might be. This book is about everyday heroes who have stepped outside the practice of conventional management to produce initiatives that are wildly successful. In a phrase, they have worked wonders. We're going to be looking closely at their stories to understand what makes these initiatives so different from so-called best management practice and what it takes to pull them off.

We'll start with the assumption that most managers are neither inept nor venal. The vast majority are well-trained, well-intentioned, hard-working solid citizens. They have internalized the lessons of good management: how to get things done through people. But oddly enough, when these fine people set about managing their organizations' initiatives, the results are, well, mediocre. That's the mystery. For the most part, the people are very good, but the results of their initiatives are no better than ordinary—and sometimes worse.

Wildly successful initiatives play out much differently from abject failures. But that's not really the comparison I want to focus on. Instead, I want to draw the distinction between amazingly effective initiatives and the mass of undistinguished projects that makes up most of our collective organizational experience.

When we actually look at the numbers, we see that the average initiative rates about a 3.5 on an effectiveness scale of 1 to 5.[1] Sure, some projects famously end in failure, but most initiatives fall in the boring middle. They do not achieve quite what their managers promised, but neither do they fail completely. There are many reasons for this, not the least of which is that organizational incentives make it difficult to admit that things have gone awry and that it's time to apply the brakes.[2] So managers keep going and get somewhere, ultimately declaring victory almost regardless of the results.

Wildly successful initiatives stand in stark contrast to ordinary projects like this. Let me offer a few examples to whet your appetite. We'll talk about these in more depth as we go on.

David Rose and Ambient Devices

David Rose, the CEO of Ambient Devices, started his professional life as an interface designer for museum exhibits and educational computer games. Among other assignments, he worked with Lego to make its Mindstorms "computerized building blocks" approachable and fun for kids. His unique experiences resulted in an abiding disdain for the way most computerized gear relates to its owner. He recalls,

> My dad has always used a barometer. Every morning he walks out of his bedroom with a towel around his waist; he taps the barometer to see weather trends. Then he takes a shower. It is a beautiful antique device. It never frustrates him—he doesn't have to change the batteries or upgrade it. Contrast that with a new computer that you have to replace after two years. I wanted to create simplicity, not more complexity. I wanted to find a way to package computing

power into elegant devices that people can scatter around their homes like clocks and barometers.

Rose launched Ambient Devices to make headway on his aspirations. For the company's first product, he developed the Ambient Orb. This simple, elegant product glows colors to reflect the current state of the Dow Jones Industrial Average, the wind speed at your favorite sailing spot, progress against your daily fitness goal, or any number of other metrics that people want to track. The Orb has no complex interface; it's what Rose calls "glanceable."

Rose had gotten this far before. He had convinced brilliant developers to take pay cuts to work with him. He had raised money and convinced leading-edge customers to talk with him about prototypes. With the Orb, however, Rose faced some additional obstacles.

He knew that in order to make devices that were "Zen simple," he needed to take the computers completely out of the picture. He recounts,

> We needed a relationship with a telco [telecommunications company]. I built a growth-oriented business case aimed at big telcos for a constellation of Ambient devices at home, at work, and on the customer's person. I told them they could net big increases in their average revenue per user with small subscription fees, and increase stickiness and loyalty from customers. Unfortunately, they wouldn't pay any attention to us.

So Rose went outside the United States to innovative companies like Docomo in Japan. He also used his personal network to get in through the back door of the U.S. telcos. He won consulting contracts with their research organizations to develop the prototypes he envisioned.

Prototypes notwithstanding, Rose still needed a service partner to broadcast the information that the Orb would pick up and display. Without a partner, the Orb would be nothing more than an inert desk object. The telcos' doors were closed, but the telcos weren't the only game in town. Rose hit on the idea of using pager, rather than cellular, technology in the orb. He explains,

> The pager companies are intrigued by doing new things with old technology. They have better coverage, penetrate into buildings, and are super cheap. Instead of costing us $80 for cellular technology, we engineered the Orb's communications chipset to cost $10. And we built a protocol that runs right on top of the pager protocol to keep it going continuously. The pager companies are ecstatic. They are doing all the customer service and providing all the bandwidth for the entire country, and they are doing it all for a share of the revenue.

Getting space on retail shelves presented another hurdle. Rose and his fledgling team called Brookstone and Sharper Image buyers and shared product sheets with them. Bang; more doors slammed. But the Hammacher Schlemmer buyer took a different view. He featured the Orb on the front page of the company's catalog. Within a few days, the Brookstone buyer was ringing up Rose. He sighs, "The retailers wanted to feel like they found us, and not the other way around."

Orbs are now stocked in Brookstone stores around the country as well as being available over the Internet and in the Hammacher Schlemmer catalog. Sales have taken off, but for Rose, that's only the beginning. He has an even higher aspiration for a large family of simple devices. He explains,

> We found that, when people started using the Orb, it had a huge influence on behavior. People checked their stock portfolio and traded stocks three times more often than they had before. But as we know, trading stocks that often doesn't usually produce good returns. So we asked ourselves what awareness application would be useful for the world. That stimulated a raft of new ideas. We've thought about monitoring home water use to help conservation. And we have imagined a device at the bus stop that tells riders

when the bus is coming to encourage more people to take public transportation. We could monitor pollen count for asthmatics—the real-time data to do this already exists today in most cities in the United States.

By any measure, Rose has launched a successful company and a successful product. As the Orb begins to improve the way people work and live, it has reached well beyond even Rose's original aspirations.

How Do Wildly Successful Initiatives Differ from Ordinary Projects?

Wildly successful initiatives do not look anything like "best practice" projects. To make sure we're talking about the same thing, we need a definition. I use two tests. First, a wildly successful initiative is one that produces breathtaking results. Second, from a process perspective, such an initiative seems virtually impossible at the start, and even after it has succeeded, people say, "How did you do that?"

In conducting the research for this book, I identified and developed case studies of 46 highly successful initiatives across a wide range of venues. I looked at product and service innovations, entrepreneurial start-ups and corporate transformations, public-sector programs and nonprofit ventures. I conducted more than 145 in-depth interviews. Three of the examples were researched in collaboration with Professor Donna Stoddard and Research Associate Steve Powers at Babson College under a National Science Foundation grant to explore successful initiatives in government.

Despite their diverse settings and circumstances, wildly successful initiatives have common characteristics. In particular, they sport a unique management approach that I call *working wonders* that sets them apart from conventional best practice. Many good managers would consider this contrarian approach wrong-headed or even destructive. In fact, it opens the door to the upside.

Working wonders means orchestrating five interrelated dynamics (see Figure 1-1). They make a difference, make space, get it right, energize people, and spiral up. Please do not mistake these for components or modules of a wildly successful initiative. That's entirely the wrong way to think about them. These are open systems, much like the systems in the human body. We can look at each one individually, but we must remember that they are inseparable.

As we explore these critical dynamics, we are going to meet the people involved in working wonders. They are all managers, but that term does not do them justice. Throughout the book, I'm going to call them *champions*. Some have founded start-ups; others work in the

Figure 1-1. Managers Invoke Five Critical Dynamics to Work Wonders

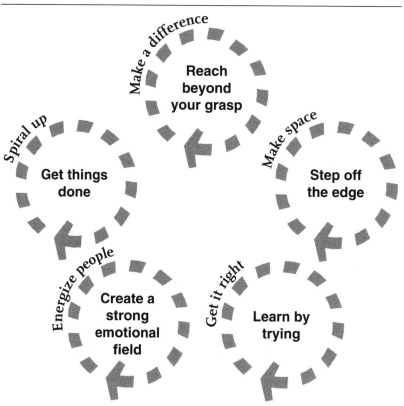

government or for nonprofit organizations; still others have traditional jobs in big corporations. Every single wildly successful initiative has multiple champions. When I use the term *champion*, I am speaking about all of them.

Make a Difference

Wildly successful initiatives reach beyond their grasp. They produce stunningly good results that make an impact. When you tell people what you accomplished, they say, "Wow!" even if they are your teenage children. Wildly successful results are substantial, surprising, and important. Whether no one ever dreamed of these outcomes before or most thought them impossible, working wonders profoundly affects people.

Ultimately, every wildly successful initiative finds at its core a deep sense of purpose. It succeeds by igniting wildfires of meaningful work. The conventional wisdom says that successful projects should have crisp, clear goals that are, most importantly, achievable. This will persuade the organizational stakeholders who must support the initiative to buy into it. But most successful initiatives involve a leap of faith of some sort—a clear vision of the way things should work without the faintest idea of how one is going to make this happen.

In the early 1990s, Zachary Duff, then a project manager at a small company known for high-tech breakthroughs, expressed this sentiment as he accepted a client's challenge to develop a virtual reality simulator for underwater mining equipment. Previous groups had tried and failed, and some key people in the client organization believed that the task was technically impossible. Duff recalls,

> You have to be willing to jump. If we had waited until we knew we could do it, we never would have done it. We said to ourselves, "We might be able to do it, so let's go ahead." But the customer wanted us to guarantee that we could do it. So we said, "If we can't do it, no one can." We had enough swagger to believe it, and it turned out to be true.

Because the client could not afford a supercomputer, Duff and his team linked up many small computers to create one of the first commercial "massively parallel" systems ever built. Ultimately they saved the client millions of dollars in testing costs and, more importantly, enabled it to lock in the market before competitors could get there.

Make Space

Wildly successful initiatives grow and develop in unpredictable ways. In fact, one of the reasons they seem to be so successful is that they are managed outside of control. Their leaders believe in a nonlinear path and work to enable it.

There are a thousand ways in which projects can fail. When executives tighten their managerial grip on people, tasks, resources, and status, they may reduce the likelihood that their initiatives will run off the rails. But this approach strangles their chances of working wonders. To venture into the upside, executives must loosen their direct hold and engage a much more powerful set of forces.

If you were a senior foreign trade ministry official in the South American country of Colombia—resented around the world for its illicit drug trade—how would you tackle the problem of stimulating economic development through legitimate exports? Stop and think for a moment. You're accountable. Where would you start? Would you offer incentives to entrepreneurs? Would you invite in foreign companies to set up local subsidiaries?

Olga Patricia Roncancio Mendoza began in 1999 by creating spaces. She and her colleagues at the Ministry of Foreign Trade (MFT) believed that to succeed in global markets, Colombian entrepreneurs had to improve the distinctiveness and value that their products provided. Roncancio Mendoza and her team had some ideas about how that might happen, but they realized that governmental controls would not spark anything. They had to take a different approach.

Roncancio Mendoza recalls,

We decided that we needed a special space to establish a dialogue between the government and the private sector. We called the space "export competitiveness discussions." We designed an experience to put all the private-sector entrepreneurs—the suppliers, the producers, the sellers, and the exporters—together with academics and government policy makers. We wanted everyone in the value chain to participate.

The team got an earful of problems and suggestions from the private sector directed toward the Columbian government and how it could help them be more successful. After this initial session, the MFT team created a matrix to organize the problems and identify possible activities to solve these problems. One of these activities was to connect the entrepreneurs in Colombia's cosmetic sector with the entrepreneurs in the medical plant industry in order to produce natural cosmetic products for world markets.

At the time, the medicinal plant growers were concentrating on breaking into the supply chains of large pharmaceutical companies, with little success, and the cosmetics sector was limited largely to domestic sales. Furthermore, the businesspeople treated each other as adversaries. Some entrepreneurs had never even met their counterparts in companies that had been their suppliers for years.

Roncancio Mendoza and her team continued to push open the space. "We put the two sectors together to create a dialogue between them. We worked like a bridge between two similar interests. The principle was to create more value-added in the products."

To begin to build relationships among competitors and overcome skepticism during the early meetings, Roncancio Mendoza worked with Hartwell Associates to seed the discussion with a case study of a successful collaboration in Peru's asparagus industry. Independent asparagus growers had been cut off from world markets because they lacked a refrigerated warehouse to keep their produce fresh until it could be shipped. No single grower could afford the expensive facility.

Through an initiative facilitated by the government of Peru, the growers were able to form a consortium to build and operate the warehouse. Their share of the world asparagus market grew dramatically as a result.

The Colombian entrepreneurs began to talk to one another. "At the beginning it was a fierce time," Roncancio Mendoza explains. "They talked at length about all their small problems. Sometimes they didn't think at all about the future or the innovation or research needed to develop new products." But the discussions did highlight specific obstacles that the MTF team could work to resolve. For example, the cosmetics entrepreneurs used alcohol as an ingredient in some of their products. Alcohol was controlled by Colombia's regional governments and taxed heavily as a beverage, making it completely unaffordable as a raw material. Over two relentless years, the MTF team harangued its colleagues in the regional government, eventually convincing it to give up its alcohol tax revenue to enable a more competitive cosmetics industry.

In time the meetings expanded so that all the people related to the opportunity were sitting at the same table. They ultimately included, in addition to the MTF and the entrepreneurs, academics from research centers related to cosmetics, the health minister, the customs services, and the central planning department. More importantly, as the collaboration continued, its character changed. It evolved from a mare's nest of fierce adversaries to a productive, problem-solving team.

Ever watchful for good business, the team headed for the cosmetics industry's sweet spot: high-quality, healthy products made with natural ingredients. The marketplace's resounding welcome drew the team members forward and even increased their willingness to collaborate.

As a result, eleven small enterprises named the Colombian Beauty Group are now marketing a new line of natural cosmetics for men in Mexico.

Roncancio Mendoza and her team opted for a circuitous, bursty, serendipitous, and uncontrolled approach to this promising result. She reports enthusiastically, "It was a beautiful experience—to show that you can do your job, but in a different way. We are more creative now. It was a practice to find the resolve and the road ahead."

Champions of wildly successful initiatives carve out the space to experiment and relentlessly learn by trying to accomplish what they have in mind. In a complex and unpredictable open system, this is the manager's version of the scientific method; it is anything but deterministic. One executive calls the approach "ready, aim, steer."

Get It Right

The people who participate in wildly successful initiatives search for answers and learn incessantly until they break the code. Remember when your primary school teacher gave you credit in arithmetic for following the right steps, even if you arrived at the wrong answer? That practice still exists in organizations today. If we follow all the written and unwritten rules, check all the boxes, and tag all the bases, we get credit for a good effort, even when the results are not what we had hoped for.

I'm not making this up. Just look at ISO-9000. This very important certification does not demand that an organization operate effectively or produce good results. It requires only that the organization have a specified process and actually follow that process—regardless of how well it works. Wildly successful initiatives don't make this mistake.

Champions of wildly successful initiatives insist on finding the right answers to the hard questions. They place priorities where they belong, recognizing that implementing the right solution is ten times more valuable than a solution that is only "good enough."

Consider the example of a successful executive in one of the world's most renowned consumer goods companies. Let's call it Unigamble. This executive believed that his company could gain a great deal of benefit from improving manufacturing reliability—the percentage of time that the equipment was operating as it should. At the time, despite successful initiatives to measure reliability consistently and improve performance, many plants were stalled at 65 to 75 percent. He asked his organization to achieve at least 85 percent, and he required all new operations to reach that level in the second month. He set this extremely aggressive goal, then he gave his people the latitude to go meet it.

A pair of engineers in the diaper business took the challenge personally. They were well aware of the existing research on reliability, but the accepted theories did not jibe with their everyday experience on the manufacturing lines. Something was wrong. Operations had hit a plateau of improvement. No matter how hard the engineers tried, they could only get the manufacturing lines to be up three-quarters of the time at most.

Working from the middle of a very large company, the engineers had two problems. First, the predictive simulations that reliability experts provided just weren't working for them, but continuing to operate intuitively wasn't going to get them to the next plateau. Second, in the absence of a good model, the company was awash in competing ideas about the right approach. Since there were no hard numbers on which to base these proposals, politics took over. In the engineers' view, a negotiated compromise was an unacceptable substitute for a valid, mathematical proof.

The engineers knew that their theories were incomplete, but one thing they did have was a wealth of data on machine reliability. Every stoppage was recorded, with detailed coding to indicate why it had taken place. They had thousands of recorded incidents, but no effective framework for analyzing them.

The engineers set out to try to make sense of the extensive data they had gathered in the plant. Their explorations ultimately led them to Los Alamos National Laboratories, where scientists were working on the predictability of nuclear weapons systems for the U.S. military. Lacking a real-world operations environment in which to test their mathematical model, however, they had never demonstrated its efficacy.

Through what one engineer calls a "courageous process," the two organizations joined forces and pooled their intellectual property—the data from one side and the mathematical simulation from the other. Over the following year, the team developed a categorically new reliability simulation—one that actually predicted failure in a manufacturing environment. This model found that machine stoppages interact. Even the smallest hiccup could start a chain reaction that would breed more stoppages. The model predicted that eliminating every small stoppage, instead of concentrating on eliminating the catastrophic failures, could substantially improve performance.

Why was getting it right so important? For the first time, the engineers were able to make accurate predictions of the value of particular improvements so that operating executives could make good investment decisions. This opened the door to reliability improvements that dropped more than a billion dollars to the company's bottom line.

One engineer remarked, "The first thing we did was to clarify the business impact of running the manufacturing process well. It sounds easy, but sometimes the truth gets lost in the accounting data." It seems that the practice of management has ramped up its emphasis on process over the past three decades, and this tidal wave of focus has almost swamped the other fundamental foundation—getting the right answer.

Getting it right doesn't stop at the intellectual solution. If the right answer can't be communicated to the people who must implement it, it has little value. As a result, the word *simple* finds its way into every story of working wonders. Unigamble's engineers used a homey little analogy to make their new approach easy for everyone, from their management colleagues to the machine operators in the factory, to understand. They talked about the family vacation. They gave operators a new view of manufacturing downtime by likening it to all those little stops that families make on a road trip.

One engineer explained, "The reliability of repairable production systems is like taking a cross-country trip with your family and predicting when you will get to Grandma's. People want to know the reliability of your car, the probability of an engine failure or a flat tire, and the chance you will run into construction. When you think about it, the number one failure mode with a car full of kids is the bathroom and gas stops. Conventional reliability science treats all those bathroom stops as independent events. They aren't. When we stop to get gas, if we all go to the bathroom, we don't have to stop again in 20 minutes. That way, you take advantage of the stop to be resetting as good as new. It turns out that's radically different from resetting a piece of equipment as good as old."

In another example, Intel's future-of-technology research organization—which is staffed with anthropologists and social scientists, not engineers—recently had an epiphany. A team that was nominally studying trends in home music usage found itself pondering a very different concern: how families were going to take care of aging parents. The team concluded that technologies that were already in the home, such as televisions and telephones, would form the foundation of a personal care network. If Mr. Johnson needs to be reminded to take his medicine, that message should come to him through the telephone, not through a personal computer or PDA. Why? Because Mr. Johnson already knows how to use the telephone. With this simple interface, he will actually get the message and take his medicine. As a result, the more complex technology underneath will become useful.

Leaders of wildly successful initiatives recognize that simple is the doorway to usable. And if a "solution" is not usable, it just isn't right.

Energize People

Wildly successful initiatives boast a strong emotional field. Have you ever walked into an office area, a call center, or a plant that seems on fire with excitement? It looks different; it sounds different; it even smells different from ordinary places of business. The emotional intensity is palpable.

Of course, emotional intensity is only part of the tapestry; it does not, by itself, guarantee success. But an initiative will never be wildly successful without it. Champions in highly successful initiatives create an emotional environment that engages and energizes people. This fuels the work they must do to take on challenging issues and, like a powerful magnet, draws others into the field.

Engagement really matters. Research tags it as one of the few identifiable workforce characteristics that is statistically associated with company profitability.[3] A study by ISR Research, based on information about 360,000 employees in 41 companies, indicates that engaged employees are two to three times more productive than average and ten times as productive as those who are not emotionally involved in their work.[4]

Two features of the strong emotional field stand out. First, it's not brought to you by Pollyanna. We'll talk about this in more depth in Chapter 9, but a strong emotional field takes advantage of the full range of human feelings—from fear and anger to hope and joy. Champions help people harness these feelings to produce directed action by shaping the way they interpret what's going on. For example, our Unigamble reliability engineers were given a target that some would have considered unattainable. They had exhausted the sources of ready answers. Ever-present politics undermined their ability to get things done. *They* weren't personally on the hook to solve the problem. Unigamble at the time was incredibly insular, so working with an outside organization—even one as reputable as Los Alamos National Labs— was considered heretical. Yet these engineers interpreted the situation as inviting, in a challenging sort of way. They interpreted the obstacles as signals to try harder, in spite of having to take personal risks to do so.

Second, the kinds of experiences that energize people change as an initiative progresses. In the early, discovery-oriented phase, people get juiced from possibilities and new ideas—the "aha" factor. As the initiative progresses through pilots and implementation phases, the source of energy shifts toward getting things done and demonstrating results. At this point, discussions about new concepts or alternative approaches actually *deenergize* the initiative.[5]

Our linear, almost mechanistic mindsets for managing ordinary projects don't address the emotional components or the way they change over time. And by the way, have you ever been part of an initiative that was linear? The norm is bumps and turns, sticking points and setbacks that evoke strong feelings in the people involved. An executive from Nike, for example, described a strategic initiative driven by the company's most senior management to streamline the firm's idea-to-profit cycle. At the end of a year's intensive investigation, the hand-picked, up-and-comer team presented its findings to the board and was greeted with skepticism and resistance. A few of those high-potential people quietly went back to their day jobs, but most of them decided to leave—opting for companies that valued their contributions.

In contrast, champions of wildly successful initiatives use community recognition and public visibility to fan small sparks of interest into hair-on-fire motivation. The heroes in working wonders are made, not born. Leaders spend their time giving others credit for accomplishments. They run internal contests to make winners and help team members earn external awards as well. They fuel their engines, and those of their teammates, not with financial incentives, but with public acclaim. As a result, team members feel that they belong to something important. These feelings increase commitment and build momentum.

How did the EPA's Chet Wayland get local and regional air quality engineers to volunteer their time to the AIRNow project? He asked them to apply for it, and he gave them a vision of what success could mean to their agency. They did not just receive new monitoring equipment; they "won" a grant. Wayland highlighted these accomplishments in his annual air quality conference, an occasion to give participants credit for "their" initiative. When Wayland himself takes center stage, it is to acknowledge people's efforts, to applaud their progress, and to celebrate their results.

When Rose describes what he finds satisfying about developing products like the Ambient Orb, he does not talk about revenue or profit. He says instead, "It is very satisfying to build a company where each team member is a huge contributor—all stretching and growing."

Conventionally managed projects are frequently staffed with seasoned veterans—individuals who have implemented the same type of software or brought the same kind of product to market before. Wildly successful initiatives are littered with first-timers. Make no mistake, these initiatives include some extremely competent people. But two counter-conventional characteristics stand out. First, team members are often self-selected, rather than drafted. Second, they are plowing new ground, not familiar furrows. Choosing to take on a challenge one has never faced before adds creativity and energy to the process. And this shows up in the results.

Consider the example of Toyota's production crisis in 1997. Its manufacturing organism in Japan was humming along, producing 15,000 cars a day. Relying on its famously well-tuned supply chain, it held only three days of inventory ahead of the line. Then there was a devastating fire; a supplier's factory that was the sole source for a critical brake valve burned to the ground overnight. Toyota had no backup supply and no secondary supplier in the wings, and building a new plant with a full complement of specialized tools and equipment would take at least six months.[6]

How could the company avoid a financial and marketplace disaster?

Toyota turned to its network of suppliers to find a solution. At Toyota's behest, the engineers, managers, and manufacturing experts from more than 200 companies went to work simultaneously to find a way to restore the flow of brake valves. With little chance of simply replicating the process that had been destroyed, these problem solvers worked through their interpersonal connections to coalesce naturally around ideas that might have a chance of working. The groups that emerged—some of which brought together firms that were head-on competitors—pulled in guidance from the original brake factory and from Toyota itself. Using the tools and expertise they had at hand and patching together solutions on the fly, they designed at least six totally different production processes.

Within three days, the new production lines were picking up

speed, and within a week, the cobbled-together scheme was turning out enough brake valves to support Toyota's prefire schedule. Toyota's vaunted manufacturing expertise notwithstanding, its management knew that a structured approach could never avert the crisis in time. Instead, the company counted on the wealth of everyday talent and resourcefulness that lay quiet in its supply network and invoked it by requests rather than directives. This approach opened the space for Toyota's manufacturing partners, linked by a rich web of affinity, to volunteer their own energy and will to design workable solutions.

Champions of wildly successful initiatives actively manage the emotional field throughout the initiative to keep passions lit—inclusively taking as much oomph from adversity as from victory.

Spiral Up

Wildly successful initiatives take a long time to play out. Or as Mont Phelps, the CEO of NWN Corporation, quips, "It took me years to become an overnight success." Ordinary initiatives always have an explicit end. They need to fit within an organization's attention span. Declaring victory allows the team members to move on to their next assignment with honor. For some companies, the ability to focus withers in less than a year; others can sustain a project for as long as five years. We all know how this works. If the project takes longer than the organization's ability to concentrate, people on the project move on to other assignments, budgets get pulled, capital allocations dwindle, and folks just lose interest.

Wildly successful initiatives do not seem to wear this straitjacket. Leaders and team members don't gather up their winnings and move on. Instead, they extend their work into new areas. So the project scope evolves, and the acolytes either stay involved or hand the project off willingly to another team that can take it forward. This unusual approach maintains focus on the predictable and critical but often overlooked effort that follows implementation. It also takes advantage of the initiative's momentum to scale the next peak.

Of the 46 examples I studied, the median initiative duration is almost seven years. Even more telling, two-thirds of these initiatives have no end in sight. In order to extend the value of its manufacturing reliability solution, Unigamble has packaged its know-how for distribution and sale. If we count from the beginning, that initiative will be turning seventeen this year. The AIRNow initiative to make air quality information public is still going on after ten years. Motivated by its success with one pollutant, the nationwide team has turned its attention to others. The Stansylvanian revenue agency, which we'll meet in Chapter 4, after more than ten years of effort, continues to plan new releases that add to its capability. The digital simulator that Zack Duff and his team built has been extended to many more types of "smart" construction machinery, serving their customer well for fifteen years.

I sometimes use the word *patient* to characterize these initiatives. For example, our Unigamble engineers spent about ten years altogether achieving the reliability target they were shooting for. In many cases, the same individuals who began the initiative are still pushing it forward years later. That in itself is unusual in an organization environment, where the norm is constant human shuffle.

Chet Wayland, one of the architects of the U.S. Environmental Protection Agency's AIRNow initiative, which we'll explore in Chapter 8, explains the duality this way:

> Deep down, we had a vision to bring air quality information out of the shadows. We knew that if people around the country could see the situation, they would be more energetic about improving it. But we didn't let the vision get in our way. We were happy with all the small steps. We didn't want to lose sight of our progress just because we didn't reach our ultimate vision in the first year. Our goal was to pull together real-time air quality information for all fifty states, and we had no plan except to build from what we had.

Spiraling up implies more than just duration. Wildly successful initiatives progress through plateaus. To paraphrase David Brower's "think globally; act locally," we would say that for working wonders it is necessary to "think possibilities and act practicalities." And in some cases, those practicalities are extremely prosaic. We'll meet Dr. Hsin-chun Chen in Chapter 10. In order to begin to work on a problem that was worth his time and attention, he asked his artificial intelligence laboratory to spend two years building a very ordinary data warehouse for the Tucson police department. As he had known, this first plateau was an essential foundation for what came later. Without it, he and his team would not have been able to see all the possibilities in front of them. It gave them a view of a much broader horizon.

Patience and plateaus imply a long-term perspective and the willingness to push ahead no matter what. That's an accurate picture of these initiatives. But these descriptors do not quite capture the sense of urgency—occasionally even crisis—that infuses the initiatives. Paradoxically, they are both relentlessly driven and confidently enduring.

When the city of Sydney, Australia, began work on its stunning opera house in the late 1950s, the building was intended both to stimulate the arts and to give the city its signature icon. More than 230 architects participated in an anonymous design competition that stipulated no cost limit for the construction. At least one knowledgeable member of the panel that selected Jørn Utzon's progressive design suspected that it would be unpalatably costly to build, but he held his tongue so that the vote would pass. The Labour government at the time agreed to pursue the project only with the proviso that no existing public funds could be used, so the organizers implemented a lottery to provide AUD $100 million over fourteen years of construction. The comments of celebrated architect Frank Gehry qualify the accomplishment as a highly successful initiative: "Utzon made a building well ahead of its time, far ahead of available technology, and he persevered through extraordinary malicious publicity and negative criticism to build a building that changed the image of an entire country. It is the first time in our lifetime that an epic piece of architecture has gained such universal presence."[7]

Creating Wildfires of Meaningful Work

As you can see, wildly successful initiatives can come in small packages or large ones. With apologies to 7-Up, this book highlights the "un-management" practices that champions use to work these wonders. Rose's Orb does not solve world hunger, but it's a working wonder all the same. The point is, champions can choose an arena—or a playground, if you prefer—that fits their own passions and abilities.

Champions orchestrate the five dynamics described earlier to fuel the hard work that goes into accomplishing their unthinkably challenging initiatives. With the right touch, champions use the working wonders approach to lift initiatives off, produce meaningful results, and ultimately develop a self-sustaining momentum that makes the initiatives virtually unstoppable.

Should managers use this approach for everything they do? In a word, no. Some initiatives are never intended to break new ground. Their leaders deploy them to achieve a specific, well-understood objective. For example, when Intel needs to expand its manufacturing capacity, executives use a formula that they call "copy exactly." They replicate an existing, working plant down to the detailed layout and processes. No innovations, no improvements, no deviations. While they might call the entire copy exactly approach a wildly successful initiative, the project to build each new plant doesn't deserve that name. It does exactly what it set out to do.

To consider working wonders, managers must first ask themselves whether they are seeking routine results or have set their sights on what could or, perhaps, should be. Depending on how they answer, they should manage everything differently. Managers must understand that they have this choice. When they indiscriminately use accepted, legitimate, conventional rules of project management—demanding a clear project scope, asking for detailed and disciplined task plans, and drafting "been there; done that" experts for the staff (among other rules)—they put their projects on the "avoiding failure" path. Many of them don't even know that there's another way. And the approach that makes so much sense for routine projects guarantees that they will never see the upside on other types of projects.

Anyone can work wonders. Nothing in the approach requires a particular type of experience or set of resources. What is required, however, is a willingness to rethink the practice of management from the ground up. Although this is considered illegitimate by the conventional wisdom, many superb executives already do work this way. That's why, when I ask executives to tell me about their wildly successful initiatives, I get one of two answers: "I never had one like that" or "Which one do you want to hear about?"

Beware, though; working wonders is addictive. Executives who learn how to manage this way will be ruined; they will never again be satisfied with standard management practices or the results that these produce. To start on this path, you will want to:

◆ *Decide at the outset whether you would rather reach for a big impact or simply avoid failure.* This is not a gratuitous comment. It's a legitimate and valid decision. Most organizations will want to avoid failure in implementing Sarbanes-Oxley, for example. But executives who hope for the upside while managing for the downside will never get what they want.

◆ *For initiatives on the high road, legitimize the contrarian approach.* Do not hobble yourself with the best practice strictures that make so much sense for no-fail projects. Loosen the laced-up processes that strangle exploration and drain energy, and welcome your team to an un-management experience.

◆ *Build your organization's strength for working wonders repeatedly.* Start with people. Since managing these initiatives requires a distinctive way of working, look for executives who have several "unthinkable" successes in their experience. Move executives who have embraced this approach to arenas where you have high hopes.

CHAPTER 2

Locked in Lima

An Oil Refinery at Risk Creates a New Future

In 1991, on Jim Schaefer's first day in a new assignment as commercial manager for BP's Midwest and Gulf Coast refining, wholesale, and crude oil system, his boss paid him a visit. Dropping a thick folder full of studies on Schaefer's desk, Michael Press, senior vice president for U.S. downstream operations, remarked, "Headquarters has looked at every option for reversing the twenty-year decline in profits from the Ohio refineries. Every single study shows that further decline is inevitable. That may be true, but I want you to take one more look at the situation before a decision is made to shut one of these refineries. You're the most entrepreneurial person I know in BP; if anyone can figure out another answer, you can. I'll give you whatever support you need."

Press could have accepted the studies as conclusive, but he was not satisfied. He had worked with Schaefer in the past, and he knew that if a more optimistic alternative existed, Schaefer would find it.

However, Schaefer had some doubt about how open the people at corporate headquarters would be to radical suggestions because of their limited experience in refining. He recalls, "I probably knew before anyone else at BP that they were likely to close one of the Ohio refineries.

How? I just had to look at where they came from." Schaefer was sitting at "one of those canned culture meetings" when the facilitator invited no-holds-barred contributions. Never hesitant to speak out, Schaefer raised his hand and suggested that BP spin off the Ohio refineries and take back a supply contract. "The room went silent. Not a single thing was written on the flip chart," Schaefer sighed. "It was clear that the facilitator had been briefed about what counted as a 'good' idea."

Reflecting on his role in keeping the 100-year-old Lima, Ohio, refinery from being shuttered, Schaefer emphasized, "What tears at my heart is seeing facilities that are in danger of closure and communities that are going to be crushed by job loss—when I know that the people there can save the facility if we allow them to. It's a big driver for me." In the end, Schaefer, a host of Lima managers and supervisors, union leaders, and even unwitting BP—headquarters executives heroically allowed the people at the refinery to create a future for themselves.

The Writing on the Wall

Entrepreneurs had struck oil in Lima, Ohio, in 1885 as part of the region's drilling boom. In 1886, Standard Oil's acquisitive CEO, John D. Rockefeller, began stockpiling Lima oil and built a refinery and a pipeline to Chicago. His gamble paid off handsomely, but by the early 1900s, the Lima oil field was played out, the Standard Oil monopoly had been fractured into 34 pieces, and Texas gushers were attracting wildcatters' attention. The Lima refinery—one of the largest in the country, with a capacity at the time of 10,000 barrels a day—continued to thrive as one of the "queens of the fleet" for Standard Oil's Ohio spin-off, Sohio.

In the late 1960s, according to one historian, Sohio gasoline sales in Ohio exceeded those of the nearest five competitors combined, and the Lima refinery boasted a "pacesetter" performance record— profitability per barrel in the top quartile for the nation.[1] The reconsolidation of the oil industry also began in earnest when BP bought an interest in Sohio, ultimately moving to 100 percent ownership in 1987.

BP eventually acquired two other offshoots from the original Standard Oil family, Amoco and Arco, bringing it to $240 billion in highly profitable revenues in 2005, the second largest oil company in the world behind Exxon (see Figure 2-1 for BP financial results and Figure 2-2 for historical operating statistics).

In the early 1990s, however, when Schaefer took on commercial responsibility for the Midwest and Gulf Coast refining system, the outlook was not nearly so sanguine. Schaefer spent sixty days gathering facts about the situation. He identified several root causes for the Ohio refineries' declining profitability that were outside BP's control, including global market pricing and lack of access to advantageously priced crude oil. He found one factor, however, that he believed he could reverse: The Ohio refineries were currently running at about 85 percent of their optimum run rate, well below their stated capacity of 270,000 barrels per day.

Driven by BP's performance metrics, BP's Midwest retailing organization had been systematically closing BP gas stations that failed to meet the company's hurdle rate for profitability. Headquarters experts had modeled the impact and had estimated that most of the volume would find its way to another BP outlet because of high customer loy-

Figure 2-1. BP Historical Income Statement Statistics

Year Ended	Revenue ($ mil.)	Net Income ($ mil.)	Net Profit Margin	Employees
December 2005	239,792.0	22,026.0	9.2%	96,200
December 2004	285,059.0	15,731.0	5.5%	102,900
December 2003	232,571.0	10,267.0	4.4%	103,700
December 2002	178,721.0	6,845.0	3.8%	115,250
December 2001	174,218.0	8,010.0	4.6%	110,150
December 2000	148,062.0	11,870.0	8.0%	107,200
December 1999	83,566.0	4,686.0	5.6%	80,400
December 1998	68,304.0	3,260.0	4.8%	96,650
December 1997	71,782.9	4,079.7	5.7%	56,450
December 1996	76,601.8	4,370.3	5.7%	53,150

Source: Hoover's.

Figure 2-2. BP Operating Statistics

	1994	1995	1996	1997	1998
Crude oil and natural gas production (net of royalties)					
U.K.	471	446	458	437	518
U.S.A.	897	867	859	869	841
Other	565	560	586	624	690
Crude oil production					
(thousand barrels per day)	1,933	1,873	1,903	1,930	2,049
U.K.	1,048	1,057	1,335	1,423	1,258
U.S.A.	2,589	2,515	2,650	2,513	2,401
Other	1,853	1,913	1,932	1,922	2,149
Natural gas production					
(million cubic feet per day)	5,490	5,485	5,917	5,858	5,808
Total production (thousand					
barrels oil equivalent per day)	2,880	2,819	2,924	2,940	3,050
Group refinery throughputs[a]					
(thousand barrels per day)	2,815	2,958	2,804	2,855[b]	2,698[b]
For BP Amoco by others	9	10	8	12	13
Total	2,824	2,968	2,812	2,867	2,711

[a] Includes crude oil and other feedstock input to BP Amoco's crude distillation units both for BP Amoco and third parties.
[b] Includes BP Amoco share of the BP/Mobil joint venture.

Crude oil and refined petroleum product sales	thousand barrels per day				
Crude oil	3,576	3,764	4,589	4,433	4,588
Refined petroleum products	4,315	4,463	4,454	4,674[c]	4,802[c]
Total oil sales	7,891	8,227	9,043	9,107	9,390

[c] Includes BP Amoco share of the BP/Mobil joint venture.

Estimated net proved reserves of crude oil[d]	millions of barrels at 31 December				
Developed	4,509	4,618	4,696	4,975	5,318
Undeveloped	2,281	2,369	2,629	2,637	1,986
Group companies	6,790	6,987	7,325	7,612	7,304
Associated undertakings (BP Amoco share)	1,953	1,912	1,869	1,995	2,013

[d] Net proved reserves of crude oil and natural gas exclude production royalties due to others.

Average realizations

North Sea	$/bbl	15.7	17.0	20.4	19.1	**12.7**
Alaskan North Slope	$/bbl	14.8	16.7	19.7	19.0	**12.6**
U.S. natural gas	$/mcf	1.7	1.4	1.9	2.2	**1.8**

Further analysis is contained in *BP Amoco Financial and Operating Information 1996–1998 (see page 88).*

Source: 1998 BP Annual Report (restated to reflect the merger with Amoco, announced July 3, 1998).

alty. So, from a retail-only perspective, closing smaller stations improved results. As volume declined, however, the refineries' results looked worse and worse. Schaefer summarized, "In isolation, this decision seemed smart, but no one was looking at the business as a whole. From an overall perspective, it was a very poor decision."

To begin cross-functional discussions to remedy the decline, Doug Farris, the refinery manager, and Schaefer launched what they called the Maumee mission—quarterly offsite meetings at Maumee Bay State Park at which managers from the retailing, refining, wholesale, and pipeline business units could hammer out the issues. Farris and Schaefer opened the first meeting optimistically: "Despite the pessimism that surrounds us, there's a chance that we can turn around 20 years of decline." A lively discussion of a new strategy and the challenges culminated in a melee of enthusiastic support. Schaefer asserted: "I believe that, even though our proven capacity is only 270,000 barrels per day, we can achieve 300,000 barrels per day without a major investment. We'll do that with a new strategy and by capturing the brainpower of our employees. It will give us $15 million in savings." Infected by the opportunity, others jumped in with savings commitments of their own. When the energy subsided, their collective response to headquarters's call for $7 million in cost savings over the next three years added up, instead, to a commitment of $60 million.

The Chicken *and* the Egg

Schaefer recognized that it would be difficult to convince the BP leadership to keep operating an unprofitable refinery, but he believed that volume increases held the key. Furthermore, he knew that the turn-around would have to be accomplished with no major capital investment. He recalled, "There was potential for enormous improvement, but I didn't know quite how we would achieve it. I thought that if we could improve the demand side first and, in parallel, get the refineries ready to operate at higher levels and at lower cost, it could work. It was a leap of faith."

Schaefer took an unprecedented step. To increase demand from 250,000 to 300,000 barrels a day, he called on BP's rivals in the Ohio market, Ashland and Marathon Oil, both of which were supplying their retail outlets with product transported from the Gulf Coast. Schaefer demonstrated that he could sell them his refinery products more cheaply than they could buy these products from their own sources. In one remarkable day, he signed contracts with competitors that increased his refineries' demand by 30,000 barrels a day, and he knew he could expand further. Schaefer remarked,

> This kind of cooperation with competitors was highly unusual—giving them a way to make more money. They were paying a pipeline tariff to move crude up from the Gulf Coast, so I was able to lower their cost a little. But BP actually received 80 percent of the value in the deal. It helped stabilize prices and kept us from having to sell on the spot market. So it made them happy, and it made me very happy.

With demand on the rise, the challenge shifted to optimizing the refinery. A victim of sustained lack of investment that had left the unionized workforce feeling understandably skeptical about management's motives, Lima was struggling to find a way to get people to work together. When Doug Farris retired in late 1993, Schaefer stepped in to accelerate the improvement program.

Engaging More Brains

Just four months after Schaefer took over the Ohio refineries, BP headquarters management paid a visit to Ohio. Headquarters was asking each refinery to be in the top quartile of performance with low mainte-nance costs. With Lima below the median at the time, Schaefer ap-peared in front of the august group to present his plan for achieving the goal. "I'm going to reach the top quartile by *increasing* maintenance spending," he stated flatly. His colleagues in the room burst into laugh-ter. Schaefer continued, "I want you to allow me to spend $7 million more than is in my maintenance budget early in the year. If you will permit me to spend that as fast as I can, I will recoup that $7 million—and more—by the end of the year, and you will not see any difference."

The headquarters managers agreed. Schaefer later confided that he would have gone ahead with his plan even if they hadn't—he would have shouldered the risk personally because he believed strongly that he could energize the refinery employees to deliver. He emphasized that his direct supervisors in the United States were always very sup-portive and had agreed to help him with their London superiors in his bid to get Lima ramped up to the new higher run rate. But results had to come quickly. "If you wait for senior executives to pass judgment on all the things you want to do," he said, "you'll never succeed. I had to remove any micromanaging as an obstacle."

Schaefer also took his strategy and his improvement agenda di-rectly to the workers in the refineries—more than 400 people in Lima alone. These were often very challenging audiences. Schaefer had asked for a spot on the agenda of his manager's weekly 7 a.m. meeting with the maintenance workers, some of the sharpest and most senior people in the plant. The manager eagerly agreed. When Schaefer met him a few minutes before the appointed hour outside the room where the workers were gathered, however, the manager said very directly, "You are facing a challenge." Through the closed door of the room, Schaefer could hear the steady thrum of fists pounding on tables, keep-ing the beat to a loud chant: "We want the show to start. We want the show to start." Schaefer reassured the manager that he had handled tough groups like this before and walked through the door. If anything, the intentionally intimidating pounding and chanting got louder as Schaefer walked to the front of the room. He said confidently, "The show is about to start *now*! Let me tell you why it's going to be worthwhile for you to hear this and how we are going to change this place." The room quieted, and Schaefer reviewed his new strategy and what it would mean for them. The workers engaged, asking many good, tough questions. "The hourly employees had a strong culture, and they sometimes ignored management, with some justification," Schaefer remembers. "But by the end of the session, I had their buy-in. They had been looking for fresh meat to chew up, and they expected to run me out of the room with their intimidation tactics. But they ended up thanking me for giving them some hope."

At a session with another group, Schaefer reviewed the new strategy, then he characteristically asked for "questions, comments, and insults." Schaefer recalled,

The first question was from a guy I later found out was a perennial troublemaker. He stands up and says: "We've heard all this crap before." I was a little surprised that that was the first question, but I fired right back. "No, you haven't. This is new crap. Apparently you didn't listen carefully enough. Let me tell you why it's new. I will go back over the four main points. This is why it's different." The questioner was stunned, since his "class clown" tactics had always generated murmurs of approval from his compatriots in the past. This time was different. After I gave my reply, the rest of the audience started asking all these really good questions, such as what would it take, how would it work, how can we help you. If I had planted that guy in the audience, it couldn't have worked better. All the employees who normally sit on the fence swung their weight toward the new strategy that day.

Abhorring micromanagement, Schaefer also resolved to remove *himself* as an obstacle to the people running the refinery at Lima.

I knew that going above me to headquarters on some things would be time-consuming and unproductive, so I decided to avoid going up. I assumed that the people below me felt the same way about me, so I said, "Don't come to me with ideas for what you *want* to do. I'll be more impressed if you come to me with ideas you have already implemented. You know the details of this operation better than I do. As long as your projects follow the payback and safety guidelines we've agreed on, just go ahead and implement them as quickly as possible."

To put teeth into his unusual approach, Schaefer promised to fund every single improvement employees wanted to make that would pay back in a year or less. In his frequent lunch meetings, he said,

I have ideas about what could make the plant better, but I'm more interested in having you work on what's bugging *you*—the things *you* have passion for. Those are the things we are going to do. I'm not going to get involved in making the decisions about which specific improvement investments to make. You just keep bringing the projects, and if they meet the payback criteria, they'll be funded.

In Schaefer's mind, this radical change in approach would demonstrate that management trusted the workers' judgment and was serious about improvement, it would shorten the decision cycle, and it would engage the brains of everyone at the refinery.

In addition to meeting with employees in big groups and small and providing a 15 percent gain share, Schaefer also chaired a monthly meeting with the section supervisors at Lima, at which he asked each supervisor to submit at least one improvement that he had made in the last thirty days and at least one that he was planning to make in the next thirty. Lima's most successful supervisors, however, had achieved their positions by preventing potentially disruptive changes, rather than embracing them. Schaefer reiterated his request for two months running, and for two months he received no submissions. The third month, one of the most influential supervisors in the refinery presented one idea that had been implemented. The next month, Schaefer received two submissions, and the snowball started rolling. By the end of Schaefer's tenure at the refinery, the stack of monthly submissions was so thick that he barely had time to read them all.

In another example, Schaefer and Dan Simonelli,[2] his handpicked Lima refinery manager, were discussing a recent reorganization that they had implemented at the plant as part of a corporate reengineering effort. Schaefer said, "I'm worried about some of the things I'm hearing from the operators. Because of the organizational change we made, we are having more trouble transferring information across shifts. That part of the change may have been a mistake, and I want to challenge whether or not we did the right thing." Simonelli wholeheartedly agreed that that aspect of the change was a mistake and asked how soon they could switch back. Schaefer replied, "Immediately. And remember, just because I put something out doesn't make it right. If it's wrong, I need to hear that from you, not through my lunches with the operators." Simonelli, who had become accustomed to deferring to Schaefer's predecessor, immediately raised his leadership game. "He was a new man," Schaefer grins.

The Manufacturing Game

Schaefer was not the only manager who was pushing hard for change (see Figure 2-3 for selected biographical sketches). Paul Monus, an engineer by training who was a senior project manager in BP Chemicals, got infected with the "proactive maintenance" bug. In his search for a credible theory that he could use to drive operational improvements, he encountered systems dynamics. That led him to Winston Ledet and the Manufacturing Game (see Figure 2-4).[3]

Ledet had spent years and more than $30 million at DuPont benchmarking maintenance and plant performance. The evidence pointed to one incontrovertible conclusion: If you eliminated defects in the manufacturing process, you could drop billions of dollars to the bottom line. Ledet's research pointed toward a new mindset for managing maintenance, however: not reactive maintenance or even preventive mainte-

Figure 2-3. Biographical Sketches of Selected Individuals in Alphabetical Order

Dave Berger

Dave, a native of Mansfield, Ohio, moved to Lima in 1977 to become the executive director of Rehab Project. The agency achieved national prominence for training programs for male and female prisoners who renovated single-family homes. He worked in that position until August 31, 1989, when he resigned to campaign in the general election for the position of Lima's mayor.

He was elected and was sworn into office on December 5, 1989, for his first term. During that term and continuing through his current fifth term, the Berger administration successfully managed the city's economic development challenges, implemented community-oriented policing, renovated the town's schools, launched programs to revitalize both neighborhoods and the downtown area, and through a public and private partnership created the Central Point and Liberty Commons industrial parks. Additionally, the Berger administration facilitated positive community dialogues on race and diversity through a program entitled Study Circles. His most recent initiatives have focused on economic development in the field of nanotechnology, specifically the manufacture of carbon nanofibers and related products.

Dave earned both an M.A. and a B.A. in philosophy from the Catholic University of America in Washington, D.C.

John Browne

The Right Honourable Edmund John Philip Browne, Baron Browne of Madingley, group chief executive of BP since 1995, was born in Hamburg, Germany, to a British Army officer and a Hungarian Auschwitz survivor. He was educated at the King's School, Ely, and St. John's College, Cambridge, where he earned a first class bachelor's degree in physics; he later obtained an M.S. from Stanford Business School. In May 2003, he was awarded an honorary Doctor of Engineering degree from the Colorado School of Mines.

He was knighted by Queen Elizabeth II in 1998, and in 2001 was named as one of the "people's peers," taking the title Baron Browne of Madingley, of Cambridge in the County of Cambridgeshire, and becoming a crossbencher (independent member) in the House of Lords.

Under his leadership, BP recovered from its slump in the mid-1980s and shook up the staid oil industry. From 1997, Browne challenged the

(continues)

Figure 2-3. Continued

oil industry's rejection of global warming and sought to recreate BP as a "green" energy company. Browne has stated that the right to heat, light, and mobility is crucial for people everywhere and that he sees his company's mission as finding ways to meet current needs without excessive harm to the environment, while developing future, more sustainable sources of energy. He has promised that BP will cut its emission of greenhouse gases by 10 percent by 2010.

In August 1998, Browne announced a $57 billion merger with Amoco. Later acquisitions of Arco and Castrol kicked off a round of industry consolidations that saw the creation of today's oil "super majors." In April 1999, Browne oversaw the acquisition of a controlling stake in Solarex, a solar energy company, for $45 million; this and further investments of over $1 billion made BP the world's largest producer of solar energy. The company also invested in wind power.[4]

Dan Simonelli

Dan began his career at BP Chemicals, Lima, in 1965, where he held various operational and technical positions. In 1984, he became plant manager at BP's Green Lake, Texas, facility. He joined BP Oil's refining department in 1987 as operations manager at the company's Alliance refinery. After an international assignment, Dan returned to Lima in June 1993 as the site manager and became the refinery manager in November 1996. He served in this capacity until August 1998, when he was named refinery general manager for Clark Oil USA's Port Arthur, Texas, refinery. Dan earned a B.S. degree in chemical engineering from Ohio University and completed the Tuck executive program at Dartmouth College.

Paul Monus

As part of the Pacesetter facilitators' network, Paul spent 1996 through 1998 working at BP Oil and BP Exploration delivering Manufacturing Game and systems thinking workshops. Paul previously held positions as manufacturing manager, process technology manager, and area superintendent for other BP departments. He has also designed and started up plants in Japan and Switzerland. Paul earned a degree in chemical engineering from the University of Minnesota.

Jim Schaefer

Jim has a chemical engineering degree from Catholic University of America and an M.B.A. from Harvard Business School. Jim joined

Sohio/BP in 1981. In 1991, he was named commercial manager for the Ohio and Louisiana Midwest and Gulf Coast supply system, and in 1993 he assumed responsibility for the Lima and Toledo, Ohio, refineries. He was named a vice president in BP USA in 1996. His strategic and operational insights led to major profit improvements in BP's mining, chemical, and refining operations.

After leaving BP, Jim made rapid profit and productivity improvements in a variety of industries, both as an executive and as a consultant. He has received corporate, union (United Steelworkers), university, and community awards for his efforts. He now heads the Shelburne Group, Inc., a profit-improvement consulting firm in Cleveland, Ohio.

---

nance, but proactive maintenance. In short, the effective operating manager focused on eliminating the need for maintenance rather than on fixing things faster. To communicate this surprising new approach, Ledet invented a game. With DuPont's blessing, he launched a start-up in 1994 to help other large companies master the art of proactive maintenance. On behalf of BP's chemical plant, which was immediately adjacent to the refinery in Lima, Monus became the first paying customer for Ledet's signature two-day workshop in February 1994.

Monus recalled,

> Without knowing quite what the game was or whether it would be possible for us to do what these world-class plants were doing, we hired Winston to teach us about managing maintenance. My plant manager and the operations guys didn't want to participate, so I had to "Trojan horse" them into it. I asked them if they would be comfortable having their employees know more than they did about how to manage maintenance effectively.

Throughout 1994, as Schaefer provided funding for improvement projects in the refineries, Monus and Ledet repeated the game six more times to help managers and supervisors—mostly in Chemicals—adopt a new mindset about effective operations. These initiatives began to

Figure 2-4. The Manufacturing Game Description

The Manufacturing Game workshop is an innovative "high-touch, high-tech" learning lab using accelerated learning technology. It is a strategic simulation of a manufacturing plant. It is a powerful tool for teaching the principles of systems thinking, high-commitment and high-performing teams, planning, and defect elimination in a total quality environment. The Manufacturing Game is particularly useful for revealing:

◆ Organizational breakdowns caused by "local" or functional perspectives
◆ The challenges of reversing the "momentum" of past practices within an organization
◆ How the structure of a system drives its behavior
◆ The tendency of feedback loops to amplify or diminish the actions and responses of management
◆ Breakdowns caused by operational and informational delays in the "system"
◆ Our tendency to focus on what is measurable rather than on what is important to make our decisions
◆ The actual steps for transforming a mediocre facility into one where production, quality, and teamwork are sustainably increased even as the resources required for operation are ultimately reduced.

The Manufacturing Game is a hands-on learning experience where participants work together in teams of three to six players. Team members make assessments about the operation and performance of their departments and the organization, make requests of and promises to one another, and make increasingly proactive decisions about production, strategy, planning, inventories, manufacturing, effectiveness, maintenance, and the allocation of scarce resources. The Manufacturing Game experience provokes participants into exploring their mental models and thinking systemically; it encourages collaboration through team learning and enhances communication.

These workshops create a profound change in beliefs and commitments about defect removal, and lead to an immediate action plan for dramatically lowering defects in the participants' processes. This is the paradigm shift needed for an organizational change effort to work. Typical improvements have been 40 percent fewer failures and a third lower costs within a short time frame.

Source: www.manufacturinggame.com.

converge when Monus pulled Simonelli into one of the sessions. Monus had previously worked for Simonelli, and he argued, "I know this workshop seems strange, but just trust me and give it a try."

Simonelli went along and dragged several other Lima refinery supervisors with him. "The game hammered them," Monus remembers.

> Our experienced senior supervisors were not great performers. They just couldn't make the plant do what they thought they could, so they had to rethink their approaches. That frustrated them, but it also intrigued them. They got receptive and listened to the front-line workers in a different way. When playing the game, you lose your title and credentials as you try to decide where that poker chip will go. And if you screw up, everyone will know.

With Simonelli's support, Monus set up a workshop at the Lima refinery in early 1995, inviting both supervisors and operators. The environment was tense. For years, management had pinched pennies when it came to winterizing the plant, and as the temperatures dropped, everyone had the previous year's big freeze on their minds.

A bout of unusually cold weather in the Midwest had forced operators to brave temperatures of 20 degrees below zero to blast steam onto the refinery pipes to keep them from freezing. The operators had pulled Lima through, but a Chicago-area refinery had frozen solid. One of the largest plants in the country, it sat idle for six weeks while gas prices spiked, oil companies struggled to deal with the unplanned outage, and union leaders redoubled their complaints about poor management practices.

Concerned about being "brainwashed," the Lima plant's suspicious union leadership mounted a mass protest against the Manufacturing Game. The leaders' formal, written policy was to resist any management attempt to improve operations. But Simonelli stood staunchly behind the effort, telling the union that it would have to call a strike to keep its members out of the workshop. The union stewards ultimately allowed their members to attend, but told workers not to play.

The game allows the participants to "operate" a refinery however they please and see how their decisions affect the refinery's performance. Then participants are given the chance to revise their thinking to try to get better results. "We were betting that the game would liberate people's potential and create some new thinking," Monus explained, "even if we had to invoke authority to get the workers there. We used diversity and inclusion as our secret weapon." Monus lined up as diverse a group as he could find, including folks from Alaska and Australia. He offered the game as a professional development experience to the public school teachers in town—who just happened to have the workers' children in their classes. He even arranged to pay for their time. He brought in a benchmarking professional from Solomon Associates and two Darden School professors that he knew.

Monus chuckled.

The first activity in the workshop is to go around the room, introduce yourself, and say why you are here. A union guy went first—he sat there with his arms crossed and said his name and "I don't want to be here." The next person said, "I'm Mrs. Smith from Lima South Middle School, and this is fantastic." The next union person says, "I'm Joe X, and I don't want to be here." The next person says, "I'm Mr. Z, the benchmarking expert of Solomon Associates, and I'm here to learn." The next person says, "I don't want to be here," and so on. The union guys were embarrassed and mad as hell, but they didn't want to look like jerks in front of these people, so they played. At the end, the head union guy said, "I'm glad you are finally listening to us about how to run this place." It was a miracle. We never expected to see such a huge change in attitude in two days. It wasn't the only time it happened, either. Over and over again, as workers experienced the dynamics that were affecting them and the refinery, they realized that the key problem was not management, it was the defects. These created both the safety problems and the conflicts between people.

Monus and Ledet ran two workshops a month for the Lima refinery throughout 1995, ultimately exposing 80 percent of the plant employees to proactive maintenance. The participants in each game spent the second day of the workshop forming action teams. Under the banner, "Don't just fix it; improve it," each of these teams identified an important problem that they felt could be solved in ninety days, and went to work on it. They tapped their collective, intimate knowledge of the processes in the refinery to root out and correct defects so that these would never surface again.

This approach made some people in management decidedly uncomfortable. To honor the efforts and contributions of the union workers, managers had to allow the teams to be self-directed. Although each team included a supervisor who linked back to management, the workers were responsible for choosing the problem that they wanted to work on and for driving corrective action. One manager commented, "The action teams felt they had the power to fix things, and they were given money and authority to make changes."[5] Another confided, "I'd get frustrated because the team would just seem to wander around and not get anywhere. But I bit my tongue, and then, out of nowhere, we'd take an amazing step forward. Frankly, I was surprised at the results."

The refinery operators were clearly engaged. "Many people here have a strong church background," one explained, "which translates directly into their work ethic." Another continued, "There's a sense of not only working for the company, but also working for your family. If you don't perform, you are letting somebody down." A maintenance supervisor summarized, "It may take a thousand little ideas to get that one that will lift you up to the next stage, but you have to listen to each little one or you will never get the big one. You have to develop trust and listening abilities—and we did, both workers and management."

The Butane Action Team

In one of Ledet's March 1995 workshops, Lima refinery management asked an action team to take up the problem of contaminated aviation gasoline emergencies. If the Dayton airport, Lima's customer, were to find any contamination in aviation gasoline for any reason, then the Lima refinery was responsible for providing an instant emergency replacement. Such an episode was estimated to cost the company $100,000. But the action team had no interest in that issue. Monus recalled, "They just kept bitching about safety. They said: 'We are all going to die because management doesn't care about safety.'"

Instead of discussing contaminated aviation gasoline, the team was talking about the refinery's huge pressure vessel full of butane. Butane was used as a blending stock component for making gasoline. In the hot summer months, the butane warmed up, and the pressure inside the sphere got dangerously close to the safety valve setting. If the valve opened, workers worried, the sphere would spew out butane. One spark could ignite the cloud, and they might die. While they had expressed their concerns in the past, no one in management seemed to be taking the issue seriously.

To demonstrate its concern—and to get the action team back to working on contaminated aviation gasoline—management commissioned an engineering study. It concluded that, for $400,000, foam could be applied to the outside of the pressure vessel to keep the summer heat from penetrating. The study noted that a cooler designed to manage the temperature of the butane was already operating around the clock, so it recommended insulation as the appropriate secondary measure. Management agreed to spend the money to proceed with this solution.

However, when the action team met again a few weeks later, it did not buy into the fix. The team members concluded that the real problem was that the cooler was undersized for the job and that they would have to take matters into their own hands. They had no faith that management would buy them a bigger compressor, so they decided to "liberate" a heat exchanger to improve the operation of the existing cooler. On the night shift, they drove around the plant grounds and found a heat exchanger that was not being used. They "procured" it and hauled it back to the shop.

However, the "midnight maintenance" operators realized that they would be risking their safety if they simply hooked up the heat exchanger. What if the heat exchanger were unsuitable for butane? Was its pressure rating adequate? They decided that they should follow the plant's change management process. That meant that they had to find a maintenance supervisor they could trust and confess what they had done.

Instead of punishing them for breaking the rules, this supervisor did something novel: He listened. He researched the pedigree of the heat exchanger for them and confirmed that it had the right characteristics. He also informed his area manager, who, surprisingly, also listened and allowed the experiment to go on.

The conspirators put their heat exchanger on line, and it worked. What had begun as a small mutiny had turned into a collaborative, controlled experiment.

With the borrowed heat exchanger humming away, the compressor performed better, and the butane pressure dropped and stayed down. In the aftermath, it came to light that for the past eight years, concerned workers had been venting butane to the flare every summer to relieve the pressure, and that the same poor process design was having the same poor result in three other refineries. All told, the midnight experiment that broke a number of rules saved BP about $1.5 million per year in each of these refineries.

This small victory for the action team opened a floodgate of innovation. One manager recalled, "Once we put the second cooler in, the guy that was most adamant about the problem called me on the radio and said, 'This is great! This is the best thing that ever happened here.' Then he started coming up with ideas for additional improvements." An operator continued, "You do something like this and you don't want it to stop. You always want to try and top what you've done before."

Monus mused, "What made the difference between the eight years of being victims and that one day when they decided to take ownership of the problem themselves? What role did the game play? I don't know. All I know is that it did happen."

Lima on the Block

In June 1995, Lord John Browne took over as CEO of BP, fresh from a distinguished six-year tenure as head of BP Exploration, which was seen by many as the heart of the company.[6] He immediately began shifting the company's focus beyond petroleum to renewable fuels, planning to retain only enough refineries to supply 80 percent of the company's petroleum needs and to buy the other 20 percent. He began an initiative to close low-performing refineries.

Meanwhile, the improvement program at Lima was picking up momentum and beginning to show measurable results.[7] Pump failures dropped 35 percent, from 545 in 1994 to 355 in 1995. Mean time between pump failures jumped from the industry average of 13.9 months to 21.5 months, hydrocarbons lost at the flare were cut by more than half, and employee safety incidents dropped 32 percent in the same period. These tangible effects of proactive maintenance allowed the refinery to redirect its spending toward eliminating more defects, which had the potential to improve performance even further. The refinery was on a roll.

But headquarters didn't seem to be paying attention. In a curious exchange between Schaefer and one of London's global strategy experts, the headquarters guru pronounced that Lima could never be profitable, since it was physically impossible to increase demand to the level that Schaefer wanted, and that the Ohio refineries were incapable of running at that rate anyway. Schaefer replied, "Have you seen our performance statistics lately? We've already *exceeded* those goals."

Schaefer found the look on the expert's face especially telling. "He wasn't pleased," Schaefer remembers. "He was shocked and worried and walked away somewhat shaken. I knew at that moment that he and others in London must have told John Browne the same thing they had told me—that Lima could *never* be profitable. The headquarters types had reached the wrong conclusion, but they were highly unlikely to go back to Browne and recant their position."

When Schaefer received word that the Lima refinery was up for sale, he saw it as an opportunity for the plant to attract an owner that was more comfortable with refining. Yet the headquarters pronouncements during the 1996 sale process were troubling and counterproductive. For example, the company announced that it was seeking offers for its "unprofitable refinery in Lima," a damning characterization.

Going through the correct motions, BP entertained a series of bidders, including a team of its own managers who took early retirement to put together a proposal. Meanwhile, the refinery continued to improve its performance, cutting hydrocarbon loss in half again and reducing safety incidents by another 30 percent and pump failures by an additional 38 percent. Maintenance costs also continued to decline substantially.

BP Pulls the Rug Out

In November 1996, BP headquarters announced that it was rejecting all bids as insufficient and that the Lima refinery would be shut down, effective August 1998. Ironically, the plant's recent improvements in performance might have convinced headquarters management that it should not be sold cheaply to a competitor. The land would be cleaned up environmentally and converted to an industrial park. Schaefer's employment ended—the result of a mutual understanding that he had previously arranged with BP—and he absented himself from Lima to avoid acting as a lightning rod for conflict with London.

The announcement hit Lima like a punch in the stomach. "I have never seen so many grown men cry," recalled one manager. The operations manager railed, "What are we going to do now? Headquarters certainly won't give us any money for maintenance. But we have to run safely for two more years. What are we going to do to keep the people here from quitting and to keep them safe?" An answer emerged. The team at Lima decided to continue trying to improve in spite of the closure. "It was not logical; it was emotional," Monus explained. "Over the past few years, we had seen a way to get back to the refinery's historic excellence as the 'queen of the fleet.' We couldn't control BP or the buyers of refineries, but we could control ourselves. The threat of closure just galvanized our resolve to keep improving."

About a quarter of the 400 workers at the plant resigned to take jobs elsewhere in spite of a new 22 percent gain-sharing program that management launched. Senior maintenance people agreed to go from day shift back to rotating assignments and even to work in tandem with outside temporary workers, supervisory roles were reduced from eight per shift to only three, and front-line workers shouldered more personal responsibility for ensuring that things were done correctly. One manager recalled, "We found ways to work differently. It was like strike coverage, but we had to keep it going for two years. It was hard for people to swallow, but they were simply magnificent in putting the good of the whole ahead of their personal aims." To bolster morale, the team scheduled quarterly all-hands parties in the gym, with rock music and steaks on the grill.

One day, as the headquarters executive responsible for the plant closure looked out his office window, a crowd of boiler-suited employees began to gather around the flagpole in the parking lot. They took down the green BP flag and respectfully folded it up. Then they raised a new flag—a blue one with an oil derrick. They had decided that since BP was abandoning the refinery, "No one owns this place but us." The ceremony concluded, and everyone went back to work—except that every day thereafter, on every shift, the employees at Lima saw their flag and felt like owners.

While the plant did have a maintenance budget to cover some contingencies, the original Lima management quietly agreed to spend whatever was necessary to operate the refinery safely. "We didn't need to worry about being punished," one remarked. "What else could they do to us?" But in the event, the plant spent 25 percent less on maintenance than was budgeted. Failures simply were not happening. The refinery continued to make impressive improvements in safety and product costs as well.

The Community Pitches In

The refinery workers were not the only people galvanized by the closure announcement. Lima's mayor, David Berger, called a town meeting to launch the Refinery Task Force, a group of citizen volunteers. A thousand people attended during a sleet storm.

Berger had been meeting with Schaefer monthly for years as part of his normal, collaborative dialogue between town government and local BP management. When Lord Browne announced that the refinery would be sold in early 1996, or closed if no buyer was found, Berger began corresponding with Browne to let him know how important the refinery was to the city of Lima and asking to be kept informed. In reply to his offers to go to London to meet with headquarters management, Berger received only "patronizing responses."

In late 1996, Berger took a call from London informing him that BP intended to close the refinery. Berger dashed off a particularly blunt letter to Lord Browne, but was unable to influence the decision. Berger reflected, "This was the oil field where John D. Rockefeller made his fortune; he built this refinery more than 100 years ago. It's on the city's flag. The symbolism of this loss was really damaging."

With BP's decision now made, most Lima townspeople and other community leaders threw up their hands. Berger did not. He explained humbly, "I tend not to take no for an answer. The town has been facing economic setbacks for a number of years, and you have to go right at them. I have been fortunate that sometimes it works."

In late 1997, after successfully winning another term in office, Berger renewed his efforts to find a buyer for the plant. He got in touch with Jim Schaefer, who had moved on to a management role at another company, and together they began quietly working their way through

Schaefer's contacts. That led them to David Stockman, former budget director for the Reagan administration and principal in the Blackstone Group, an investment firm. Blackstone owned a big piece of Clark Oil.

In contrast to Browne and most oil industry pundits, Stockman believed that refineries would be in short supply some day, and he wanted to be holding those valuable assets. Stockman flew to Cleveland to meet with Schaefer and review the Lima refinery's track record at improvement (see Figure 2-5). Because of the sensitive nature of the discussion, it had the trappings of a spy thriller. Schaefer was met at the agreed hotel by an intermediary and ushered into a room. Stockman was brought in separately so that the two men would not be seen together by anyone.

Stockman asked questions for three hours, exploring the industry, the competition, and the refinery itself. Schaefer wasn't free to discuss financial results, but he painted as complete a picture as he could of the activities he had personally witnessed. One of Stockman's key concerns was whether the plant had reached the end of the line on performance improvements. Schaefer built the case for value—Lima's committed employees had demonstrated what they could do, continuing to improve plant performance against all odds. Prudent investments in additional capabilities, Schaefer argued, would only increase profitability. Stockman became convinced.

Structuring a successful bid was a bit more challenging. Berger and Schaefer knew that they had to make it look as if Stockman had discovered this opportunity all by himself—BP would slam the door in Stockman's face if headquarters got wind of their participation. From January through March 1998, they worked under the radar, suggesting possible sources that Stockman might be able to tap to find the information he would need to make a decision.

In early May 1998, three short months before the bulldozers were scheduled to arrive, David Stockman made the call to BP headquarters in London. According to Berger's sources, Lord Browne bristled, saying that he didn't want to discuss the matter. Stockman rejoined, "I am prepared to offer you $150 million in cash." Browne ended the call, but

Figure 2-5. Lima Refinery Performance Metrics

Lima Refinery Pump Repairs

Year	Failures	MTBF (months)	Cost ($000)
1991	643	11.9	2,250
1992	599	12.6	2,096
1993	599	12.6	2,096
1994	545	13.9	1,907
1995	355	21.5	1,242
1996	221	34.5	774
1997	168	45.4	588
1998	131	58.1	459

The Lima refinery's MTBF (mean time between failures) measurement went from the U.S. industry average in 1994 to the best in the United States by 1998.

Lima Refinery Hydrocarbon Loss

Year	Percent Loss by Weight
1990	1.40
1991	1.70
1992	1.55
1993	1.45
1994	1.30
1995	0.50
1996	0.30
1997	0.35
1998	0.30

The Lima refinery went from having the greatest hydrocarbon percent loss of all BP refineries in 1993 to the least in three years.

Employee Safety at Lima Refinery
Incidents per 1,000,000 man-hours

Year	Incidents
1991	40.8
1992	42.2
1993	36.4
1994	23.3
1995	15.9
1996	10.8
1997	10.9
1998	11.5

Cash Margin Enhancement, 1997 vs. 1994

Factor	$/Barrel Crude (95 basis)
Higher reliability	0.08
Hydrocarbon loss	0.27
Process optimization	0.22
Crude delivery and quality costs	0.05
Energy efficiency	0.06
Cost savings initiatives	0.07
Total cash margin enhancement	0.77

an hour later, another London executive called Stockman back with two conditions for proceeding: (1) The mayor of Lima would know nothing about the deal, and (2) the transaction would have to be complete by the end of June. If either condition were violated, all bets were off.

In June 1998, Clark Oil paid BP $175 million for the Lima refinery plus an additional $35 million for inventory. BP received not only the cash but also the ability to reverse its accounting accrual for the plant closure, severance, and environmental cleanup (a $300 million reserve, according to one executive), or more than $500 million in total. Clark Oil received a refinery that had achieved top quartile performance in maintenance. Clark's press release read: "The acquisition will increase Clark's total crude oil capacity to 540,000 barrels per day—an increase of approximately 50 percent. The Lima refinery will contribute $1 billion a year to the company's sales."[8]

Lima Earns a Future

The Lima workers were gathered in the gym trying to archive the story of the refinery so that the information about how they had achieved their improvements would not be lost to the world even if the plant were destroyed. David Stockman and the CEO of Clark Oil came striding in to make an announcement: "We have just purchased the refinery." The gym exploded in cheers.

As surprised as anyone at the last-minute reprieve, Monus stressed,

> The workers knew that they had earned this result. It was not just a business deal; they were all key players. They were locked in Lima; they couldn't leave. During a hopeless time, they kept a positive attitude and never gave up. That's what Stockman must have seen. They had maintained the plant in pristine condition in spite of everything. It was a jewel.

Epilogue

- Three days after BP sold the Lima refinery to Clark Oil, it announced that it was merging with Amoco.

- Clark Oil (subsequently renamed Premcor) was sold in 2005 to Valero Energy, a refining powerhouse in the United States. Lima remains one of its key refineries and has attracted significant investment from Valero.

- Ten development projects in the city of Lima that had been on hold because of the uncertainty of the refinery's situation went forward. The investments, which included a beautiful new downtown hotel, sparked a newfound energy in the city.

- The Lima refinery continued to improve, turning in about $1 million in profit per day in 2005. It often hosted delegations of executives from other refineries to help them learn how to achieve a similar high level of performance.

◆ Dave Berger successfully ran for a fifth term as mayor of Lima in 2005.

◆ Jim Schaefer was quickly hired by a specialty chemicals firm to run and improve its worldwide operations. Some years later, Jim launched his own consulting firm, the Shelburne Group, Inc., through which he has helped many firms achieve rapid improvements.

◆ Paul Monus remained with BP. After the Lima sale, he worked in Chemicals, the Exploration and Production business in the North Sea, BP Solar in Maryland, and BP Exploration and Production in Alaska, where he is currently based.

◆ Dan Simonelli moved to another Premcor refinery and created another wildly successful improvement program.

◆ In January 2007, John Browne announced that he would retire in July of that year, eighteen months earlier than had previously been planned.

CHAPTER 3

Secret #1: Reach Beyond Your Grasp

Linder: Mayor Berger, what made you decide to try to save the Lima refinery?

Dave Berger: We had been suffering for a number of years in Lima. We had had our share of economic setbacks. I tend to be a person who aggressively seeks solutions. You have to go right at those things. I have been fortunate that sometimes it works.

*   *   *

Linder: Paul, what led you to Winston Ledet and the Manufacturing Game?

Paul Monus: I have been an operating manager most of my career, first as an engineer, then as an area supervisor. I found myself in a place where I was trying to make big changes in a business, but I didn't know the theory. So I started looking for answers.

*   *   *

Linder: David, how did you come up with the Ambient Orb?

David Rose: All the other companies I knew were working on convergence devices—PDAs and cell phones with a million features. I was inspired by how much my dad loved his barometer. It was beautiful and easy to use, and it did *one* job very well. So I created a company that was on a mission for simplicity—not convergence devices, but *divergent ones.*

Champions of wildly successful initiatives reach beyond their grasp. That means that they set their sights on goals that they do not know whether they can achieve. It gets worse. They take on agendas that others have already failed at or given up on. And worse. Their colleagues and associates—sometimes even their significant others—tell them they are nuts even to try.

Dion Joannou, president of Nortel's North American business, describes an example from earlier in his career. Nortel is a $10 billion global communications company known for its technology innovation. At the time, Nortel was organized by geography. So the Nortel sales organization in Europe "owned" European clients, the North American group "owned" clients in the United States and Canada, and so forth. This kind of structure works well for clients that are also regional. But it is a disaster when the client wants to operate globally and asks its suppliers to treat every outpost the same way.

Despite having competitive products, Nortel had never been able to get any business from Vodafone, one of the largest telecommunications service companies in the world. Nortel spotted a glimmer of opportunity when telecom companies—and Vodafone among them—began upgrading their infrastructures to move to the latest-generation equipment. That gave Nortel the opening it needed, but Vodafone had asked for a global relationship that would also be responsive to the needs of its thirty-four local subsidiaries. It was clear that Nortel would need to break out of its regional mentality to win the business.

Nortel's vice president of sales for Vodafone knew that he needed someone strong to lead the charge, but no one wanted the nearly thankless job. Vodafone wanted consistency in worldwide pricing, and it wanted all of its subsidiaries to be treated the same way, from Italy with 20 million subscribers to Egypt with 1 million. Yet it insisted that suppliers also work through its centralized technology organization and coordinate all commercial agreements from a global perspective.

This would almost certainly mean that some Nortel regions would have to sacrifice revenue and profit for the benefit of the overall customer relationship. In other words, satisfying Vodafone would require active politicking across the Nortel regions to get them to focus on their collective customer instead of their own performance metrics.

Recognizing that he was heading into a maelstrom, Joannou signed up. Almost as soon as he set foot in Europe, one of his colleagues took him aside and said, "We've tried for fifteen years, and we've never managed to sell Vodafone anything." Joannou remembers, "In the beginning, I couldn't get anyone to join my sales team." The "smart people" preferred to sit out the first few rounds to see what would happen. Why wait? They lived on commission income, and they recognized that they would see precious little of it until the company broke the Vodafone code.

The story has a happy ending, but we'll save that for later. What's important here is that Joannou took a very untraditional approach to this initiative. First, it was more than important—Joannou believed that it was critical to Nortel's success. The company had been struggling for years to expand outside its North American base, and it needed credibility with a name account in Europe. Joannou saw Vodafone as the best reference account he could possibly have and the gateway to other clients.

Joannou was hungry for the business, so he took on an initiative that others ran away from. His colleagues were neither cowardly nor stupid; they spotted the setup. In order to win the Vodafone business, the lucky individual charged with that objective would have to both fight his way into a new account against entrenched competitors *and* fight his way through an internal Nortel organization that would throw up obstacles at every turn. The friction was palpable. By the way, as a commissioned salesperson, this individual was probably looking at a big pay cut for accepting the challenge.

Cracking Vodafone wasn't some fluffy, vague aspiration; it was a specific out-of-reach target. And at the start, Joannou had no idea how he was going to get the business. That didn't stop him.

Finally, he did not wade into the initiative by trying to line up all the Nortel factions that would ultimately have to buy in. He knew that would be foolhardy. He didn't wait for alignment—that lovely concept that makes traditional initiatives comfortable—he just carved out some space for an adventure.

What happened? In four months, Joannou and the maverick salespeople he was able to attract to his side had their first order from Vodafone. In twelve months, the relationship was profitable. Over the next two years, Nortel became one of Vodafone's major suppliers and leveraged that position to go from zero percent market share in Europe to double digits.

Reaching beyond your grasp is a nice idea; Joannou's nontraditional moves show us exactly how to go about it. These tenets appear again and again in our collection of wildly successful initiatives:

◆ Don't accept the common view; look at the situation differently.

◆ Don't aim for a target that's within reach; take a leap of faith.

◆ Don't set your objectives rationally; make them personal.

Let's talk about each one in more detail.

Don't Accept the Common View; Look at the Situation Differently

An ordinary initiative fits within the organization's (or society's) accepted mindsets and ways of working. Oh, it may ask people to learn a new technology or change the way they handle some process or other, but it doesn't embarrass people or ask them to abandon their important habits and assumptions.

In the case of Nortel, the ordinary approach to Vodafone would have been to have the regions continue to sell to their local subsidiaries independently. That would have maintained the hegemony of geography and, more importantly, the consensus that geographic leads were the power players in the organization.

Here's another prosaic little example that will illustrate the point. Let's say Lee is planning a meeting for a group of managers from around her company. The purpose is to have the managers share their plans for the coming year so that they can identify common issues and opportunities for coordination or even synergy. Lee has done this kind of thing before, and she knows it can be deadly dull—one talking-head presentation after another that no one remembers the next day. She thinks about ways she could make the meeting more engaging and effective. She's a bit of a maverick, so she decides to start the meeting off with an open discussion of a short case study, highlighting a real situation in the company that shows the impact of poor coordination. She's never facilitated a case study discussion before, so she's a bit nervous, but she's willing to try. She writes up the case study based on her personal experience with one of her colleagues in another region, laying out some of the conflicts and tensions fairly bluntly. Her colleague okays the case study as long as she agrees to change the names to make the story less personal. Because this is such an unusual approach, she makes sure she gets her boss's approval as well. He waters down some of the conflicts in the case study, saying that they're "just too inflammatory." Lee makes the changes and distributes the case study to all the managers who will be coming to the meeting. The day before the event, Lee's boss's boss calls and suggests that she shouldn't actually facilitate a discussion at all—after all, there will be fifty people in the audience, and that's too many for a good dialogue. He recommends that Lee present her own analysis of the situation, then ask for questions.

What happened here? Lee started off with reach. She recognized that the normal meeting format would never accomplish its objective. But by the time her novel approach had been worked over by her associates and her superiors, it had been crammed back inside their comfortable package—a talking-head presentation with a few minutes at the end for questions.

This same constricting process, whether on a small scale like this or across a much larger organizational expanse, takes place every day to make sure initiatives remain ordinary and comfortable. For Lee, well, she decided not to fight this particular battle, but she'll be reaching again on the next initiative.

Champions of wildly successful initiatives don't take the given wisdom as, well, given. Even when the experts agree that a conclusion is incontrovertible, champions are not satisfied. Even when all the gurus are going in the same direction, champions question whether it's right. They look for possibilities when others have stopped looking. And they take matters into their own hands.

When Jim Schaefer stepped into the role as commercial manager for the Midwest and Gulf Coast refining system, his boss handed him a bulky file full of years' worth of studies by BP's central planning experts. The planners had evaluated every option for reversing the twenty-year decline in profitability, and every study had reached the same conclusion: Decline was inevitable.

"It looked like something from Mission Impossible," Schaefer recalls.

> The folder was packed with all the negative news. All the options would slow the decline, but not reverse it. I thought it was most important to understand how we got into this situation. So I asked myself: "Does anyone understand why this decline happened? Are there any factors under our control?" I looked at this for thirty to sixty days, and I identified three or four reasons for the decline. I evaluated them in a different way from the way the headquarters planners had looked at them, and that opened new options.

Schaefer simply failed to buy BP's version of reality. He looked at the situation differently.

Paul Monus did the same thing when he scoured the landscape for a new way to manage maintenance, reasoning that there must be something out there that he didn't know. He knocked on the doors of well-regarded professors, including Peter Senge from MIT and Bob Kaplan and Dave Norton at Harvard. He found a graduate student from the U.S. Navy who was trying to go beyond total quality. Ultimately he found his way to Winston Ledet and the Manufacturing Game—complete with radical new assumptions about how to manage manufacturing effectively.

Don't Aim for a Target That's Within Reach; Take a Leap of Faith

In three-quarters of the wildly successful initiatives I have reviewed, champions said something like: "When I started into this, I had no idea how I was going to get it done." In other words, they committed to the initiative before making absolutely sure that they could deliver. What's even more telling, in many cases their friends and colleagues were telling them that they were crazy to try.

Good management practice would never advise this approach. Successful projects, experts tell us, should have crisp, clearly scoped objectives that are, most importantly, achievable. Smart project managers establish risk-adjusted doability before they do anything else. They do not make commitments until they have laid out an achievable scope for the initiative and detailed plans to accomplish it. They not only determine whether the objective can be achieved, but put stresses on their plans, looking at all sorts of difficulties to make sure they'll succeed no matter what. Many even ask critical stakeholders to sign off that they will fulfill their part of the bargain. The Project Management Institute's comprehensive handbook urges formal acceptance of a project's scope and explicit processes for controlling changes to it.[1]

Champions of wildly successful initiatives don't approach their work this way. First they commit to the initiative; then they figure out how to do it.

Champions obviously do not see their initiatives as impossible, in spite of the naysayers and the well-meaning skeptics. No one would take on a hopeless challenge. And they may well underestimate what they are in for. Whether through naïveté, inexperience, self-confidence, courage, or optimism, they see the potential for success where others see only obstacles. They take a leap of faith that they will be able to do what they have promised.

Because I am an American, my all-time favorite example of a wildly successful initiative is the founding of my country. I'm sure there are many versions of the story, but Joseph Ellis makes the point in *Founding Brothers* that no other country had ever succeeded in creating an inclusive, democratic government before.[2]

When the early American patriots declared war against England, they certainly had no clear plan for how they would run the country once it was independent. And if they had paid attention to the lessons of history, they might have concluded that the democratic form of government was utopian foolishness. Happily, they did not. Instead, they embraced democracy to "form a more perfect union, establish justice, insure domestic tranquility, provide for the common defense, promote the general welfare, and secure the blessings of liberty to ourselves and our posterity."[3]

Consider another historical example. Baby boomers will remember the Japanese plastic toys of their youth. In the decade following World War II, many of the Japanese products that found their way to the United States were cheap in every sense of the word. As a rule, they were inexpensive, insubstantial, inexpertly made, and obviously inferior to U.S. and European products. Some Japanese shared this view of their own products; it underpins the mission that Akio Morita used to galvanize Sony in the early 1950s. He gave his organization the following challenge: to be the company that was best known for changing what "made in Japan" means.

This goal doesn't sound like most corporate mission statements. You know the ones: serve our customers; reward our shareholders; be a great place to work. It's extremely personal and, we can imagine, quite compelling to proud Japanese workers. It's also expansive—a goal that asks for a leap of faith rather than a list of tasks.

Just for fun, you can try to match the corporations in Figure 3-1 with their mission statements. Looking on the Internet is cheating.

Leaps of faith and the blank slates they imply challenge people to reach for their own solutions. Recalling his youthful exuberance, Zack Duff, now CEO of his high-tech innovation company, recounts a leap that he made in his earlier days in the company. In the early 1990s, a large client invited project manager Duff to help develop a computer simulation that would enable the client to do a "dry run" of deep-water mining equipment. Instead of taking this expensive gear out into the ocean in order to test it, the client wanted to fool the system into acting the same way it would under real conditions.

We'll explore this story in depth in Chapter 6, but the multiple leaps of faith we see in this initiative will serve as a preview. Both previous suppliers and the client's own people had come up short, leading some of the client's executives to conclude that the task was technically impossible. "The customer wants you to guarantee you can do it," Duff remembers. "So we said, 'If we can't do it, no one can.' . . . If we had waited until we knew we could do it, we never would have done it."

Karl Schmidt, a software engineer on the project, remembers the leap of faith as well: "There was a question about whether we could do it because it was challenging and had never been done before. Perhaps we didn't know any better, but I don't remember feeling that we couldn't do it. We all felt that it was very doable; ambitious, but doable. We didn't have any notion that we would fail."

The client took a leap of faith as well. Duff characterizes her as a person of "great vision." "She took a tremendous risk hiring us to do this," Duff says. "No one had done it before—certainly not us. She got in the boat with us. Without her, it could not have happened."

There's much more to the story, but I won't keep you in suspense about the outcome. Duff and his team delivered what they promised—an all-digital virtual reality simulator for the deep-water mining industry—in a time frame that won the race to market.

Figure 3-1. Mission Statement Matching Game.

The following mission statements were taken from their respective companies' Web sites. See if you can match the company to its mission.

a. 3M Co. b. American Express Co. c. AT&T Inc. d. ALCOA Inc e. Caterpillar Inc. f. Coca-Cola Co. g. DuPont h. Exxon Mobil Corp. i. General Electric Co. j. General Motors k. Intel Corp. l. Merck & Co., Inc. m. Microsoft n. Pfizer, Inc. o. Walt Disney Co.	1. To make people happy. 2. To enable people and businesses throughout the world to realize their full potential. 3. To preserve and improve human life. 4. Sustainable growth: Increasing shareholder and societal value while reducing our environmental footprint. 5. To benefit and refresh everyone [the company] touches. 6. We provide the best value to customers. We grow profitably. We develop and reward people. We encourage social responsibility. 7. To be the world's premier company [in our industry]. To that end, we must continuously achieve superior financial and operating results while adhering to the highest standards of business conduct. 8. To be the world's most respected service brand. 9. To be the best company in the world—in the eyes of our customers, shareholders, communities, and people. We expect and demand the best we have to offer by always keeping [our] values top of mind. 10. We will become the world's most valued company to [end consumers], customers, colleagues, investors, business

partners, and the communities where we work and live.

11. Imagine, solve, build and lead—four bold verbs that express what it is to be part of [company name]. Their action-oriented nature says something about who we are—and should serve to energize ourselves and our teams around leading change and driving performance.

12. To delight our customers, employees, and shareholders by relentlessly delivering the platform and technology advancements that become essential to the way we work and live.

13. To be the most admired and valuable company in the world. Our goal is to enrich our customers' personal lives and to make their businesses more successful by bringing to market exciting and useful [company type] services, building shareowner value in the process.

14. None.

15. To solve unsolved problems innovatively.

Answers: a, 15; b, 8; c, 13; d, 9; e, 6; f, 5; g, 4; h, 7; i, 11; j, 14; k, 12; l, 3; m, 2; n, 10; o, 1

Don't Set Your Objectives Rationally; Make Them Personal

Business works on a norm of rational decision making. When we sit around the table and set our objectives, we expect the group to consider the situation reasonably, to at least acknowledge our biases, and to use clear, sound logic to arrive at solid conclusions. We'll probably have to explain our conclusions to higher-ups and investors, so we should base them on a grounded business case.

Business cases are almost always completely static. They say: "If we invest this amount and use these resources in the following way, we will achieve that and get thus and such value. Since that equation adds up to a good return, we should proceed."

Using this logic, not a single one of the wildly successful initiatives in my study would have gone forward. Not one.

Let me use the Lima refinery to illustrate. What was the business case for making the refinery more profitable? From a BP headquarters perspective, there was none—London executives were already strategizing about how to reduce refining capacity when Schaefer arrived on the scene.

His motivation was much more personal: "What tears at my heart is seeing facilities that are in danger of closure and communities that are going to be crushed by job loss—when I know that the people there can save the facility if we allow them to. It's a big driver for me. That's one of the reasons I push so hard."

Paul Monus didn't track down Winston Ledet because of a business case. Although Ledet showed compelling evidence that his Manufacturing Game could save Lima money, Monus had a bigger agenda. He wanted to awaken the people in Lima and help them learn to be successful again. "The thing in the way is management," he states matter-of-factly. "Managers have to go on their own personal journey to unlearn what they have been taught. I am the way I am because I had the chance to go out and talk to people. Many managers don't get that experience."

I disagree with Monus on one thing. I think managers talk to people all the time about one thing or another. That doesn't mean that they see those conversations the way Monus does—as treasure hunts for valuable new understanding. Monus took himself on a personal journey in order to make the kind of contribution he was avid to make.

Daring rescues, such as the one that Schaefer, Monus, Berger, and the twenty other heroes of the Lima refinery story undertook, represent about 18 percent of the wildly successful examples I have compiled. But taking an objective personally doesn't have to mean saving the world—or even one small corner of it. Personal passions come in different shapes, of course, depending on the people. Even a single initiative hooks different people in different ways—and the same people in different ways at different times. The diagram in Figure 3-2 shows four types of personal passions that seem to grab champions of wildly successful initiatives.

We've talked about a daring rescue. Let's look at the other three types.

Principled Action

Marvin Runyon, an ex-postmaster general of the United States, shows a passion for performance that illustrates just how noble the principled

Figure 3-2. Champions Take Initiatives Personally in Four Different Ways

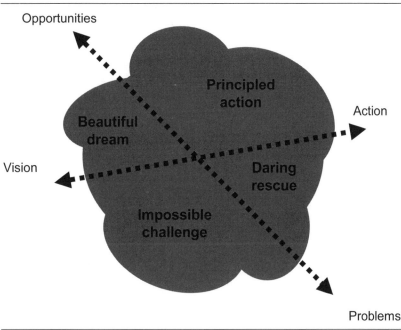

management role can be—if we take it personally. Runyon's appointment as postmaster general had been announced, but two weeks before he officially stepped into the role, he was asked to give a speech at the annual postal conference in Las Vegas. The audience of 8,000 would include postal employees and the Postal Service's most important customers.

The members of Runyon's marketing staff-to-be suggested that they write his speech for him, but he declined, explaining, "You can't do that. I don't know anything about the Post Office, and all you know are things about the Post Office. I have to write the speech myself." Stop right here and ask yourself how many executives would insist on writing their own speech in order to make it genuine.

He developed a fifteen-minute talk about management and business practices and intended to take questions from the audience for thirty minutes. The marketers recoiled: "You can't do that because you won't know the answers to the questions." He replied, "What better time is there to take questions? At least I will find out the problems." Take another moment; how many executives in your experience want to stand up in front of 8,000 people in order to listen?

In the event, the first question came from a small mailer located in Texas. She explained,

> I started putting mail together on my kitchen table, and I have grown a bit from there. Three days ago, I had a mailing to send off. I got to the post office a little after closing time, but I went to the back door, and I could hear the people inside talking to each other. I knocked on the door and said, "I have 100,000 letters that have to go out tonight." They said: "We're closed. Come back in the morning." What do you think of that?

Runyon said simply, "That will never happen to you again. I guarantee you that no one in the Post Office is going to do that again." He recalls, "The 2,000 postal employees in the audience heard that. People started to get the message quickly. It doesn't make you popular with your board of advisors or with Congress, but you're working for the government, and you should do the best job you can." Listen to what's personal here. Runyon made a personal commitment in a very public forum. Why? Because he felt accountable for doing the best job he could for the people of the United States—not for his direct supervisors or for the politicians who represented the public, but for the people of the country who counted on him.

Runyon's story of taking objectives personally doesn't end here. In 1995, he and his director of marketing, Loren Smith, were struggling to turn the Postal Service from an unreliable, bureaucratic supplier to a delivery service that could stand toe-to-toe with the best in the world. Smith argued that the organization needed a better image and that it should consider sponsoring cycling. Runyon was a bit skeptical, asking the obvious question: What does cycling have to do with delivering the mail? Smith explained that it was global—the second most popular sport in the world after soccer—and that the racers were more like mail carriers than, say, baseball players: They covered a lot of ground, they rode through every small outpost, and they never stopped for bad weather. Further, because the sport of cycling had yet to gain popularity in the United States, it cost only $1 million to sponsor a team.

Runyon agreed, and the Postal Service cycling team was launched. Runyon did not count on the backlash he would have to confront from his board of advisors and the Congress. They found the whole idea of marketing wasteful and irrelevant, and sports sponsorships particularly so. Runyon refused to budge. "Let them fire me," he said with characteristic directness. "I know I'm right."

In 1995 and 1996, Postal's cycling team worked toward slots in the sport's top-tier races, and in 1997, it earned its first invitation to ride in the Tour de France. At the time, Lance Armstrong was officially a member of the French team Cofidis, but he wasn't racing; he was very sick with testicular cancer. His part of the story is well known. As he recovered from his debilitating illness and decided to make a comeback in cycling, his French team cashiered him as "damaged goods." Lance's agent queried the other good teams—all European, of course—and couldn't find Lance a ride. When no one else would accept him, the U.S. Postal Service team added him to the roster.

Let's look at this from the sponsor's perspective. The budget for the year has been set and the athletes hired. Congress and the board of advisors are always cranky about spending on marketing, but those fights have already been fought this year. A phone call comes from the company that manages the team asking whether the Postal Service would be willing to add another athlete to the team—one who has been sick with near-fatal cancer for the past eighteen months. The rational business decision wouldn't take a minute to make, yet the Postal Service arrived at a different answer. One marketing executive recalls, "We decided to give him a ride. We said to ourselves, 'He's like us. He works hard; he gets hurt; he struggles to go on. He deserves a chance to do that, even if he never wins anything again.'"

Well, of course, Lance did win. He won the Tour de France seven times in a row—more times than any other racer. The marketing impact for the U.S. Postal Service was incalculable. When Lance appeared in public, he wore the USPS logo. When he raced, people around the world shouted, "Go Postal," helping to give the expression a new, more positive meaning. And wearing the words "United States" on his back compelled patriots across the country to take an avid interest in cycling.

No one in the Postal Service foresaw this outcome. They simply followed their personal principles. Things worked out pretty well.

Impossible Challenge

What hooked Zack Duff and his team was a little different. It was the challenge that lit them up. They wanted to wade into a difficult problem that others had given up on. These are very smart people who like being smart. They have spent their lives solving intellectual puzzles that most of us can barely understand, let alone conquer. You could hear the glee in Duff's voice as he said to his client, "If we can't do it, no one can."

Cambridge NanoTech, Inc., Jill Becker and Douwe Monsma's 2003 start-up, provides another example in this category. Becker and Monsma were colleagues in Harvard University's chemistry and physics departments, respectively—Becker a Ph.D. candidate and Monsma a postdoc. In the course of their studies on nanotechnology, they found that they had to develop their own tools to create the research materials they needed for their experiments. So they built an atomic layer deposition (ALD) system, which produced high-quality coatings that were only one molecule thick.

As Becker wrapped up her doctoral dissertation, she began looking for a job. Her search was complicated by the fact that her husband was planning to start work on his own graduate degree as she launched her career. They filled out applications and interviewed at companies and schools from Hamburg, Germany, to Boise, Idaho.

The stars never quite aligned. The places with the best graduate programs for her husband offered Becker the least appealing job opportunities. She wanted a challenge that she could sink her teeth into—something that made use of her world-class skills, but asked her to stretch as well.

Returning home from one particularly frustrating interview—at which the hiring company promised Becker that she would be considered for promotion from a lab technician's role after only three years—she and Monsma got together and started a partnership. They would manufacture affordable ALD systems for researchers around the world. At the time, no research-quality ALD tools were commercially available.

Although neither of the partners had any experience running a business, they suspected that they were smart enough to figure it out as they went along. They also had a few big arrows in their quiver. They carried a good brand: They had worked under well-respected and widely known professors at Harvard. They knew exactly what nanotech researchers needed and could talk to them as equals. Finally, as budget-constrained students, they had learned how to build tools frugally and time-efficiently by collaborating with good suppliers.

Three years later, Becker and Monsma have sold their tools all over the world. From the outset, they logged triple-digit sales growth and enviable profits each year. As 2007 opened, they hired their first employee and laid plans for taking on exciting new opportunities in consumer markets.

Beautiful Dream

Some other wildly successful initiatives begin with a beautiful dream. Champions envision a better life/company/situation and make it their personal business to build it. Public-sector and not-for-profit initiatives often start this way, although these certainly don't have a monopoly on dreams.

The dreams that launch working wonders are quite different from the vague good wishes that most of us have for the planet and society; they are very specific. For example, Olga Patricia Roncancio Mendoza, a Colombia ministry of foreign trade executive, had a beautiful dream for her country's commercial future. She wanted to help entrepreneurs in her country collaborate to develop unique and advantaged business models that would stimulate hotbeds of economic growth. In the process, she hoped that Colombia would build a reputation for hard work and innovation.

David Rose's Ambient Orb also came from a dream. For the company's first product, he developed an Internet-connected information object that is both effortless and elegant. The Orb couldn't be simpler; when the Dow Jones Industrial Average is soaring, it glows bright green. Developing glanceable information devices may not be your dream, but it gets David up in the morning. For him, it's personal.

Reaching in a Nutshell

Champions of wildly successful initiatives reach for what they really want. Ordinary projects may have stretch goals—aggressive deadlines or big savings bogeys—but this is different. Reach isn't just difficult; it's meaningful to the people involved. Reach doesn't just imply a long list of tasks; it implies uncertainty—having to take a fresh view and figure out how to proceed. Most importantly, *reach* is an action verb. Champions of wildly successful initiatives step out of the ordinary currents that move us along day to day and set off in a direction of their choice.

CHAPTER 4

The Connected Revenue Agency

Stansylvania's Tax Administration Learns to Love Change

Walter Matthews, assistant secretary of information technology, and Frank White, the commissioner of Stansylvania's[1] Revenue Agency (Revenue), chatted enthusiastically with the well-wishers at the Digital Media awards in January 2004. Their smart tuxedos and starched shirts could barely contain their pride as government and private-sector colleagues recognized Stansylvania's tax agency for its eRevenue System (eRS). Through fifteen years of effort—"Internet time" notwithstanding—Revenue had established one of the most effective and agile tax collection processes in the world. In fact, eRS was the highly visible tip of a proverbial iceberg.

Revenue

In the process of collecting and managing taxes, duties, and tariffs within Stansylvania, Revenue pulls in about $53 billion each year from 2.5 million business and individual taxpayers. It also administers the customs regime for the country and employs about 6,000 staff members housed in 130 offices throughout the republic. In 2005, Revenue guided its activities with two long-held objectives: to deliver high-quality customer service and to encourage voluntary tax compliance.

Headquartered in the nation's capital, Revenue is organized into two main units, each led by a commissioner who reports to the chairman of the agency: policy and legislation, and operations. The former collects the taxes and works with the legislature to set new tax policy and laws. The latter, working with taxpayers from offices distributed throughout the country, establishes what taxes are owed, audits taxpayers, and tracks down businesses and individuals that don't pay what they owe.

Revenue had only recently emerged as one of the most nimble and efficient tax agencies in the world. It did not achieve this position by accident.

The Data Study

"People outside the information technology organization don't understand what it takes to build an end-to-end process that works," Matthews emphasized. "Two-thirds of the effort is behind the scenes, and it doesn't happen overnight. We started in 1989." (See the timeline in Figure 4–1.) At the time, Revenue was one of the biggest computer users in Stansylvania—even larger than many of the country's banks. It boasted large mainframe computers and home-brewed systems that ranged in age from eighteen to twenty-five years. Like most organizations at that time, it built systems one by one with in-house staff and followed the best practices of the day—soliciting requirements, involvement, and support from the people in the organization who would ultimately use the system. Because these internal customers were siloed in separate, semiautonomous organizations, Revenue boasted one system for income tax, another for value-added tax (VAT), a third for employers' withholding tax, and so on. Not only did each mainframe system have its own input forms and payment processes, but each also had separate data files with taxpayer names, addresses, tax history, and

Figure 4-1. Timeline

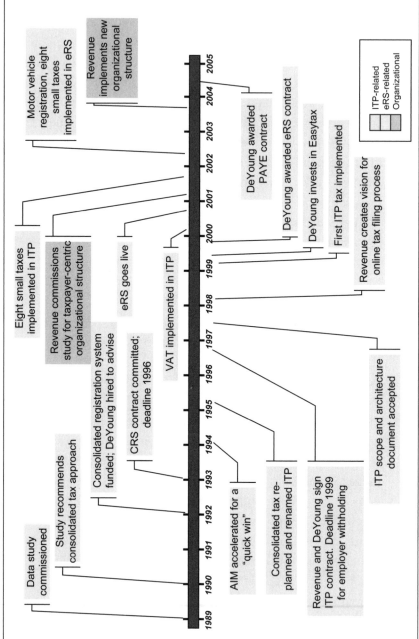

so on. The IT organization chugged away at improving these systems by automating manual processes, and most folks were content with the progress they were making.

As an unfortunate but predictable consequence of the organizational and systems silos, a taxpayer who wanted to change his address was required to make separate phone calls to all the relevant Revenue organizations (see Figure 4–2). One executive noted, "It was theoretically possible for a customer to get three knocks on the door in one month from three different people in Revenue who had come to audit him. There was no integration between the taxes and no communication between the parts of the organization." In fact, internal rivalries were more the rule than the exception.

The silos were certainly inconvenient for taxpayers, but some Revenue executives believed that they also undermined the voluntary tax compliance system. One remarked, "To get the largest VAT refund, a

Figure 4-2. How a Taxpayer Viewed the Stansylvanian Revenue Agency

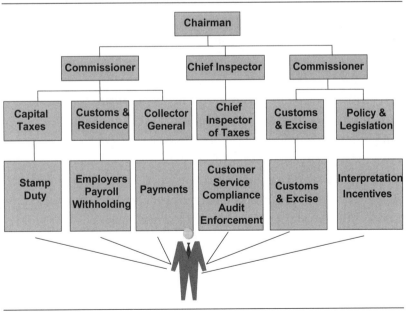

Source: Stansylvanian Revenue Agency.

business had every incentive to *overstate* its sales on that tax return. To minimize its income tax, it was better off *understating* sales on that document. If Revenue's right hand and left hand never checked with each other, we were subtly encouraging our business taxpayers to do both." Some of Revenue's departments were trying to arrange manual cross-checks in their payment processing, but these were time-consuming and error-prone.

Matthews recognized that the agency could do a much better job of managing taxes effectively. After spending more than a year haranguing his colleagues about dysfunctional organizational silos—with no effect—he decided that he could not just let things lie. He launched an unassuming, three-month information technology (IT) project in 1989 to review the agency's data. Matthews recalled, "We knew there had to be a better way to do things, but we had no pressing organizational problem to empower us as IT people to drive change. So I gave our project a neutral, nonthreatening name: the data study." The study's objective was to describe both a single data model and an architecture for integrating all taxes into a single, automated process.

Matthews tapped two in-house experts, Harold French and William Althouse, and brought in a small team of consultants from DeYoung and Company (not its real name), a global consulting firm, to help with the project.

French and Althouse had complementary skills. The organization recognized French as being a genius at IT architecture and strategy, but hopeless at dealing with people. Althouse was technically very capable, but was better known for his straight-from-the-shoulder interpersonal style. While he did have a tendency to say unpleasantly honest things in public from time to time, he was expert at negotiating, motivating his team, and setting a high bar for performance.

Describing the initiative's objective, Althouse explained, "Our overt purpose was to review the data structures, but what Walter really wanted was for us to stimulate debate and get people engaged." Althouse interviewed the key internal customers for the tax systems to understand their needs.

By early 1990, the team had translated Matthews's lofty ideas into a set of concrete deliverables, complete with a proposed five-phase implementation plan (see Figure 4–3). Althouse continued, "What came out was not a vision for IT, but a vision for Revenue and the entire organization. It put forward some very strong ideas, wrapped in the unassuming language of technology."

To move ahead, however, the team needed funding, so it began a three-year process of selling the project to the power players in Revenue—the chief inspector (CI) and the collector general (CG)—and to the Treasury minister. The financial justification promised a 2 percent improvement in tax yield by being able to shift the organization's attention toward tracking down the noncompliant. With 37 percent of Revenue's target collections in arrears, the goal seemed conservative.

Bringing together the CI and CG organizations—two "enemy camps," according to one executive—required deft interpersonal management. Althouse explained, "We knew it was vitally important to have them working together, so we constructed our plans to give a piece of cake to one, then to the other, and so forth." As another executive quipped, "The national game here is thumbing your nose at authority. If our internal customers wanted to do what we asked, everything would be fine. But if the boss told them to do something they didn't want to do, they were gold medal winners at blocking it."

In the midst of the process, the national borders in the European Union came down, freeing up a thousand customs inspectors who had been staffing those borders. Revenue leadership declared that there would be no layoffs, so these individuals had to be absorbed elsewhere in the organization.

By 1992, Matthews's team had secured funding and verbal support from the chairman and had selected DeYoung to support Matthews's in-house staff for phase 1 of the plan: building a common registration system (CRS). The first system in Revenue to use a relational database, CRS would provide a single source for common taxpayer data such as name and address. This seemed like an obvious improvement over having separate files in each department, but data ownership issues

Figure 4-3. High-Level Data Model

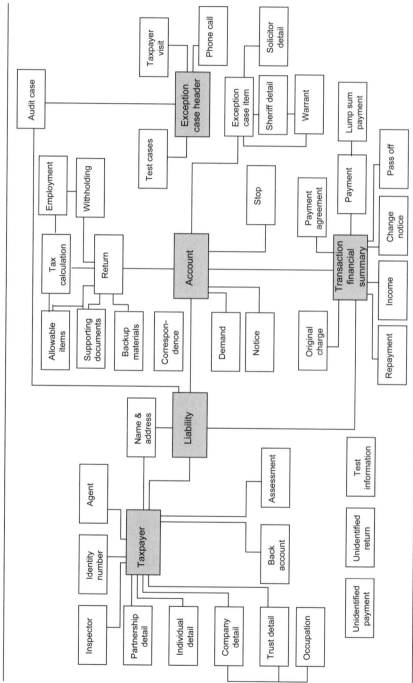

Source: DeYoung and Company

stalled progress. The people in each department who were responsible for that particular tax and all its supporting data dug in their heels. One executive said, "People in different departments thought they owned the data for their tax set, and they did not believe that anyone else would look after it as well as they did. The silo mentality was reinforced by the fact that the different departments had different pay grades and different cultures."

The management board also worried about a union backlash. The union could be counted on to fight against headcount reductions, even if a staff member's work had been completely eliminated. However, the dramatic expansion of the Stansylvanian economy at that time—with a ballooning workload for Revenue—offset this concern.

Ultimately, Matthews succeeded in convincing Revenue's chairman to issue a directive forcing all the departments to cooperate in developing a single taxpayer registration file.

Shifting Gears

In 1992, the government decided that it would decentralize the collector general's operation beginning in 1994, sending tax collectors out of the capital to offices in the provinces. This brought a new top man to the organization, and also an entirely new team, since 95 percent of the CG employees chose not to move and were reassigned as a result. Surprisingly, the new collector general turned to IT for help in implementing his agenda for change. Althouse recalled, "With Harold French's influence, we came to the same vision—an integrated approach. Now we had a business area buying in. It was our first bit of luck."

However, as Matthews's team marched the CRS project forward through its three-year plan, a sense of impatience grew among Revenue executives. While the data study had provided a well-grounded vision and the team was making progress, one executive privately noted, "All the benefits of CRS were behind the scenes. And at this pace, we were going to take twenty-five years to get to a system that would process multiple taxes."

Meanwhile, the team continued to struggle with its internal customers in the CI organization. "Magnificent indifference" was perhaps the kindest description of the CI attitude. One executive painted a harsher picture: "We were trying to roll PCs out to the organization as the system's desktop interface. One of the CI heads decided that PCs would never catch on and barred them from his department. And this was at a time when PCs had *already* caught on throughout most of the developed world."

In 1995, Revenue launched two parallel initiatives to shift the program into higher gear: integrated tax processing (ITP) and active intervention management (AIM). On the first of these, it initiated a back-to-basics project to relaunch the integrated tax system project. Naysayers still believed that it would be impossible to develop a single system that would process all the nation's taxes, but Matthews's team pushed ahead despite active and passive resistance.

In April 1995, Althouse presented his shiny new plan to the management board. Having paid personal visits to tax offices around the country to understand their practices, Althouse was able to assure the board that a single system was entirely feasible. It would also drop a very appealing financial benefit into the organization's lap. Althouse's report projected that ITP would reveal tax cheats instantly, leading to an immediate and positive impact on voluntary compliance. The net gain? An additional 1 percent per year in tax revenue—about $1.3 billion over ten years. With the board's eager agreement, Althouse issued a tender for the system.

By the end of 1996, Revenue had signed a contract with DeYoung to build ITP. DeYoung's blueprint for the system showed a clear departure from Revenue's previous approach. Instead of building the tax system function by function, it phased in the work tax by tax. In other words, when a tax was implemented in ITP, its entire process, from input to payment, would be automated (see Figure 4–4). The team placed a priority on employer withholding tax and set mid-1999 as the deadline for its completion in order to address Y2K concerns.

As its first formal step, Harold French and the ITP team took

Figure 4-4. Integrated Tax Architecture

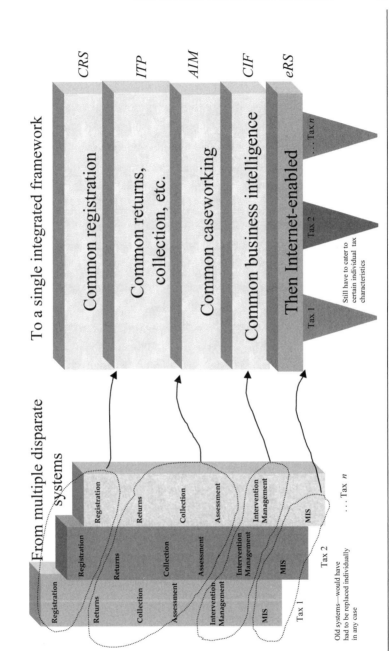

Integrated Tax System

To a single integrated framework

Common registration

Common returns, collection, etc.

Common caseworking

Common business intelligence

Then Internet-enabled

CRS

ITP

AIM

CIF

eRS

Still have to cater to certain individual tax characteristics

...Tax *n*

Tax 2

Tax 1

From multiple disparate systems

Registration

Returns

Collection

Assessment

Intervention Management

MIS

... Tax *n*

Registration

Returns

Collection

Assessment

Intervention Management

MIS

Tax 2

Registration

Returns

Collection

Assessment

Intervention Management

MIS

Tax 1

Old systems—would have had to be replaced individually in any case

Source: Stansylvanian Revenue Agency.

DeYoung's overall blueprint for integrated tax management through a grueling and inclusive evaluation process. Over nine months, they "ripped it apart and put it back together again," according to one participant. "We had to build a framework that would support not just withholding but also ten to twenty other taxes now and in the future. We asked ourselves a lot of fundamental questions and made some key decisions to ensure that the system would be generic." The team also used the intensive experience to engage and educate the business users about the architecture.

Lingering organizational rivalries and suspicions continued to challenge the effort, however. As one executive noted, "The concept of all working together was new. There were some awkward moments, but it just took time to work through them. And in any cross-organizational project, the lack of clear authority makes it difficult for the hard decisions to trickle up and be taken."

In late 1995, after relaunching the integrated tax processing effort, Harold French kicked off a second initiative, active intervention management. He hoped to take the heat off ITP by giving his internal clients something that they could use right away. His team slapped together AIM, a temporary system that would take advantage of the new consolidated registration file to target tax cheats. The collector general's tax compliance organization, which had ballooned through the addition of the more than a thousand customs officers who had been freed up when the European Union's borders came down, would be able to readily identify flagrant tax evaders.

By 1997, AIM was in place and working while the bigger ITP effort rolled forward. As French had hoped, CG was having great success at nabbing tax cheats, and no one was threatening to pull ITP's funding. One executive remarked, "This quirky little system, AIM, suddenly took off, and we got wonderful press. Meanwhile a team of seventy was working away on ITP in the background. The lesson we learned from the registration system was that it was going to take us time to agree to a generic set of principles for tax administration. AIM bought us that time."

Throughout, Althouse extended his hand to business-side colleagues at his level, so that they would bring their bosses' support along. He recalled, "It took a long time to win their trust. Sometimes we fought, but they saw complete consistency from us. They realized we were not trying to claim credit for things they did; we were just trying to do what was good for Revenue."

Matthews's IT organization pushed the integrated tax infrastructure forward from the ground up; meanwhile, others in Revenue had their eyes on the growing promise of the Internet.

eRevenue System

In 1997, Stansylvania was pushing itself to the forefront of the e-government world with an explicit goal of increasing Internet services, and Revenue led the pack. John Grenville, then Revenue's customer service manager, explained, "As the head of customer service, the objective of encouraging electronic filing sat on my desk. At the time, the view from above was that we should get people to send in their tax returns on diskettes."

Grenville and his team researched the approaches that other revenue agencies around the world were using for electronic tax filing and identified two alternatives: virtual private networks and the Internet. When his working party reached an impasse on the choice, he disbanded it and made the decision himself. He proposed a Web-based system.

"Internet usage in Stansylvania was low," he recalled, "so we were going to be out in front of both the country and the agency. During 1998, we did a lot of research and sent two papers to the management board of Revenue setting out our direction and the benefits we envisioned." While it would have been less controversial to opt for the more proven electronic data interchange technology instead of the Internet and to duck the question of digital signatures, Grenville reasoned that his more radical approach would pave the way for a completely electronic flow. The team anticipated that as a result, taxpayers' compliance costs would be reduced by 60 to 70 percent, filing would be faster, and Revenue would save staff costs. In 1999, with the board's approval, Grenville pressed ahead with a tender for a custom-designed, Internet-based electronic tax filing system.

Unlike the leaders of other IT projects in Revenue, Grenville hailed from the business side of the house. With just a little bit of rivalry in his soul, he set out to prove that he and his team could manage a far-reaching technology project just as ably as the agency's IT profession-als. The organization's first cross-Revenue core team—which included business users, a representative from legal, and individuals with IT expertise—was set on choosing a vendor by the end of 1999. Grenville stated enthusiastically, "I had a good team, and from day one, we set ourselves unrealistic and unachievable targets and said we were going to do it. We were doing the right thing, and I knew people would lose interest if we took too long. We were hell bent to get it done." To get the ball rolling, the team strained to issue its tender by early summer.

DeYoung and sixteen other companies prepared their responses. "DeYoung had been thinking about integrated tax systems since the mid-1970s," explained Ian Black, worldwide partner for government revenue organizations.

> We had concluded that electronic filing, by itself, was a waste of time. We believed that the big payoff was in real services for taxpay-ers, like the ability to see your entire relationship with the tax au-thority. We also saw a huge voluntary compliance benefit for Revenue. With the approval of our senior leadership, we had de-cided to develop the market by putting our own capital into a front-office system called Easytax. We knew Stansylvania was thinking about something like this, so we did our design and waited for its tender to hit. When it did, we went ahead and built a working prototype for the proposal.

Grenville's tender had not mentioned a prototype; it had asked bidders only for a proposal. Because of the tight restrictions on government procurement processes, Grenville and his team were unsure about whether they could even look at the demo they received in the DeYoung package, and they did not want to preside over a process that was biased in any way. When they named eight companies to the short list, however, they made it clear that they wanted bidders to include any prototypes they might have, along with their next response. "At the end of the second round, we were presented with seven proposals and one working system," Grenville recalled. "DeYoung won hands down."

In December 1999, Grenville advised DeYoung that it should begin the following January, and that the first release of eRS would be due in September 2000. Black said, "The schedule was crazy, but we decided to go for it."

In preparation, Grenville insisted on moving the team to a new building. Some people in Revenue had been sitting at the same desks for twenty years, and Grenville wanted to create a fresh start and a sense of newness. Grenville's decision to hire a consulting company to develop the system was also a radical departure from previous projects, and his colleagues in IT resented it. The rising level of conflict just convinced Grenville that speed was of the essence.

Despite the aggressive time frame, the team opted for a very inclusive process. It consulted with internal users in key Revenue departments and with a wide variety of prospective users in the business community—self-employed individuals, accountants, corporate tax departments, and others. "We recognized the danger," one developer noted, "that internal users would see the requirements from their own perspective, but not from that of the taxpayer."

During the early days of 2000, while eRS was being developed, Grenville worked with Revenue's legal representatives to introduce an e-commerce act in Stansylvania that would give legal standing to the digital signatures that eRS would require. On the technology front, he hired Wilmington Technologies, a security software firm, to implement eRS's public key infrastructure. He did not, however, allow the added complexity to shake his commitment to the September delivery date.

On September 20, 2000, after nine months of development, eRS went live. "It could have been a nightmare," one executive recalled, "but everything worked. The bosses were like helpless men in a maternity ward. Our team was putting the finishing touches on the system, and we were pacing about waiting for the delivery. To see everything come together on that evening, well, it was very special."

Revenue's plan for eRS's first year was to collect $82 million of the $38 billion total annual taxes paid. It passed that goal in the first six weeks. By the end of the year, eRS had collected $1.5 billion and was on its way to becoming an unmitigated success. With a small nudge from Grenville, the chairman of Revenue then set an almost unthinkable goal of collecting 50 percent of taxes online within five years. Remarked Black, "We knew we could deliver the benefits Revenue wanted because the online system would sit on top of a new, fully integrated tax processing system that the IT organization had been quietly developing in the background for more than a decade."

Connecting the Dots

ITP had been rolled out in mid-1999—just in time both to avoid any Y2K issues and to provide the end-to-end processing that made eRS more than just a slick e-mail system. With a new chairman who did not support ITP, the IT team counted itself lucky to have the immutable deadline that Y2K provided. Althouse explained,

> We argued that we should not invest resources in the withholding tax system because ITP would be ready in time. We quickly hit a Rubicon. The organization had to recognize that if ITP were not delivered, it would have no system at all. Faced with that possibility, the organization rolled in behind us and began moving heaven and earth to help us deliver. It was a completely different dynamic.

The 2001 introduction of the euro presented an additional opportunity for the IT team. It had to decide whether to hold tax data in Stansylvanian dollars or euros in an environment where the political experts predicted that the new currency would be late, if it were implemented at all. Althouse chose not to bother the board with the decision, but made the choice himself: euros. "The last thing I wanted," he pointed out, "was a major conversion effort one year after going live. It would have delayed the next tax and all future momentum. Besides, if I express a lack of confidence by sending a decision up the chain, then they develop a lack of confidence in me and in the project. A lack of confidence spreads."

Behind the scenes, the ITP initiative expanded in line with its long-term plan. At the same time, the eRS team adopted an up-tempo, twice-a-year release schedule, adding an appealing Internet front end within months to each new tax that was brought into the comprehensive ITP infrastructure.

Integration Ripples Out

Stansylvanian taxpayers flocked to file electronically. Electronic filing grew from 9 percent of the returns in 2002 to 40 percent in 2003 and 53 percent in 2004 (see Figure 4–5). And Revenue felt the ripples throughout its organization. Frank White, who was appointed Revenue chairman in 2001, asked himself whether the human organization should be restructured to focus on the taxpayer, just as the information systems had been. A consulting study on the "Revenue Organization of the Future" advised that regional revenue offices should no longer deal with a single tax. Instead, they should cover all the taxes that were relevant to the taxpayers in their territory.

White approved the design and, in October 2003, announced the restructuring. Through a tortuous process, management secured approval for this change from all of its unions. Ultimately, all senior management positions shifted from a functional to a regional focus, and this change trickled down from the regions to districts across the nation. According to one executive:

Figure 4-5. Total Monthly Returns Filed Through eRS

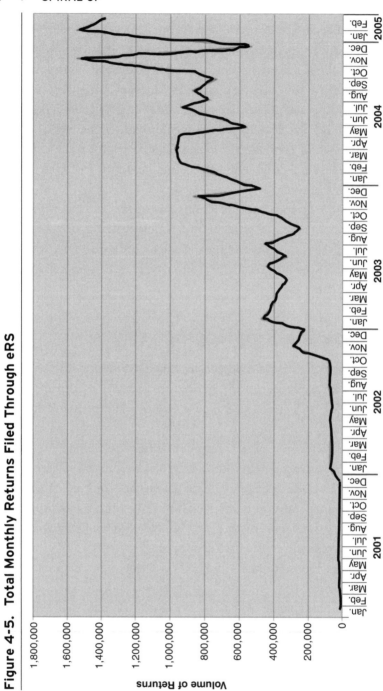

Source: Stansylvanian Revenue Agency.

The mandate that management had given for change in 1995 was not wholehearted; it was qualified. They wanted the ability to transform, but they wanted to stay in control of the process. They were waiting for the right time to set a true transformation in motion. By 2002, the system was working, the Internet was coming on, and they had an industrial relations environment in which change was more accepted. With all those ducks lined up, it became possible to push the button.

By early 2005, eRS included twenty-one separate tax returns, accomplished through eleven successful releases in three and a half years. These covered a broad range of business customers, including tax agents, solicitors, car dealers, the construction industry, individual businesses, and self-employed individuals. Each tax boasted end-to-end automated processing, courtesy of the integrated ITP back end.

The result was profound. ERS was chalking up e-government awards around the world. Revenue was processing double the number of transactions that it had a decade earlier with the same staff. Taxpayers were extremely satisfied with the new convenient services that Revenue offered. And improved tax compliance had increased tax receipts by 4 percent a year, netting the agency about $5.2 billion (€4 billion) annually (see Figure 4–6). The eRS team found itself hosting twenty to twenty-five visits a year from foreign delegations—a barometer of peer recognition in the public sector—that wanted to learn how they, too, could achieve this kind of performance.

Grenville's leadership of eRS earned him a promotion. In combination with ITP and the deeper infrastructure that Matthews, Althouse, and French put in place, it gave Revenue an efficient and flexible tax capability that separated Stansylvania from almost every other country in the world. The accomplishment was widely regarded as a triumph.

Reflecting on the reasons the initiative had been so successful, Althouse mentioned several factors:

We had a clear vision, and Y2K gave us a strong reason to succeed. Using the latest technology attracted people to our project. Perhaps

Figure 4-6. Improved Tax Compliance Cut Arrears from 37 Percent to 2 Percent

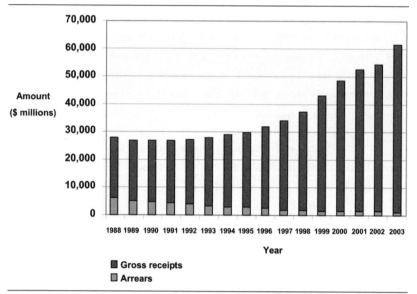

Source: Stansylvanian Revenue Agency.

most important was a huge commitment by three or four very clever people. These individuals came together by chance. No one did it with foresight. But the caliber of the team created a dynamic—the best people were encouraging and stimulating each other to create something profound.

Walter Matthews summarized the process:

When we started on the integrated tax journey, we were working in organizational structures and processes that hadn't changed in any significant way since 1922. Even though people recognized that these no longer made sense, no one knew how to change them. They certainly didn't imagine that renovating the information systems architecture would help launch us into the forefront of revenue agencies worldwide. But it has.

CHAPTER 5

Secret #2: Make Space

The science of conventional management is all about structure. We take our raw materials—money, people, technical know-how, time, and so on—and arrange them as neatly as possible into engines of progress. We articulate goals and priorities, clarify organizational roles and responsibilities, establish deadlines and metrics to gauge performance, then kick-start our motors and off we go.

Then it gets interesting. Diligent managers police their initiatives to make absolutely sure that nothing goes wrong. They watch budgets and timelines with cold, hawklike eyes and jealously guard against anything that would interfere with their agenda. This is a downside vigil. These normal management tactics—what some would even call "best practices"—protect against failure; they do not launch an organization toward unmitigated success.

When we do a very good job of putting our resources in order, we get exactly the results we intend. In fact, that's the whole idea. Crafting just the right machinery makes our initiatives efficient and predictable. However, these tidy, well-aligned initiatives are never wildly successful. Often they miss the mark by a mile.

David Rose, founder and CEO of Ambient Devices, explains this type of conventional management in terms of space—the space to experiment and explore. Before launching Ambient, Rose worked as the head of research for a famously customer-centric system design house. He recalls taking the company's CEO out to lunch to interest him in an innovative new system that Rose wanted to offer travel industry customers—real-time dynamic pricing for airplane tickets purchased through mobile phones. All Rose needed was three technologists for three months to complete the project. The CEO caught a bit of Rose's enthusiasm and gave him the go-ahead. Given to colorful language, Rose explains, "The CFO—I called him the Sphincter. He controlled the headcount, and when I asked him for the people I needed, he dug in his heels and blocked the whole project. I saw him as the channel for getting the resources, and it was completely choked up. There was no room to try anything."

Heading for the upside demands a different approach. Rather than having tightly ordered structures, wildly successful initiatives thrive on the exact opposite: open space. And the contrarian art of managing these initiatives involves deliberately creating that open terrain.

Remember how Jim Schaefer asked for cost-saving ideas in Lima? He didn't use the space-limiting approach of collecting ideas, ranking them in terms of ROI, and launching the ones that were at the top of the list. Instead, he told 400 refinery operators that he would fund every single improvement project they could come up with that would pay off in one year. He opened up a spacious umbrella and let them take it from there.

How was he able to make such an expansive offer? After all, didn't he have to live within his budget? Schaefer recognized that while he might overspend his budget early in the year, the accrued savings would bring him back in line by December. He asked his boss for the latitude to manage his spending in this way and got the nod. In other words, his boss agreed to ignore his budget irregularities in the first half of the year. He got the space he needed. Privately, he confided that he would have gone ahead even if his boss hadn't agreed. He was confident enough in his approach to take the heat, even though he didn't have the details of a single savings idea at that moment.

Rose figured how to create space, at least in part, from his experience with the Sphincter—because you can learn as much from a bad manager as from a good one.[1] He looks back on his big-company experience with a knowing smile and says, "I wouldn't handle that blocker the same way today as I did back then. Now I'd just do an end run—get people to work at night and on the weekends." In other words, Rose would liberate time and effort that folks like the CFO would never know existed.

What makes people use their free time to help out on Rose's initiatives? He shows them the space and invites them to jump in. To recruit top-drawer talent when Ambient was a risky start-up, Rose laid out the following very soft sell: "We may not make it. You won't have the resources, the support people, or the salary you're used to. We will have a huge challenge. But you, personally, will be able to make a difference." He reminds us that there is something deeply satisfying about being completely responsible for the success or failure of something.

Even in big companies, champions of wildly successful initiatives don't wait for their superiors to make space for them; they carve it out for themselves. Instead of petitioning senior management to formally support their initiative, they simply ask their bosses and colleagues to allow it to go on unimpeded. This is a very different request. They are not asking for top management attention, backing, or resources. They are asking only to be benignly ignored.

After months of trying to get formal buy-in for a taxpayer-centric approach in the Stansylvanian Revenue Agency, Walter Matthews shifted gears and carved out his own space. He crafted his initiative as an unassuming "data study," an effort that was totally within the bounds of his organizational authority. What was it really? It was a far-reaching vision for the entire Revenue organization. Through his clever positioning and Jobian patience, he lulled his colleagues and superiors into believing that his initiative was not worth stamping out.

Why Does Wild Success Flourish in Space Rather Than in Structure?

When managers parse initiatives into tidy structures, they are making a fundamental assumption—that they know how to produce the results they want. They are implicitly stating that the people on the team, the tasks in the plan, the resources in the budget, and the milestones on the schedule will take them from start to finish. And if they can just keep the train on the track and chugging forward, it will take them to the end of the line.

Champions of wildly successful initiatives harbor no such illusion. In fact, they are usually ready to admit that they don't have a clue about how to get from their starting point to the goal they have in mind. The goal itself may even be a bit fuzzy. They know they need to discover the path as they go rather than laying it out in advance. They need to bumble around a bit to learn the landscape and make choices as they go.

Are these explorers just lazy? Would they achieve their goals faster or better if they commissioned an expert project manager to sort out all the details for them? The short answer is: no. Chet Wayland and Phil Dickerson, the champions of the U.S. Environmental Protection Agency's AIRNow project, make this point explicitly. (We'll see more of Wayland and Dickerson in Chapter 8.) With no dedicated staff, no budget, and no regulations to force cooperation, they put real-time air quality data and daily forecasts into the hands of concerned citizens. Dickerson says, "People tell you to plan things in advance. But with AIRNow, if we had planned up front, I'm not sure we would have done as well. We would have come up with a different answer. As it was, we just had a spark that turned into a bigger and bigger fire."

Dickerson isn't alone in his point of view; other wildly successful champions like Stansylvania Revenue's John Grenville echo his statement. As Grenville got his eRS initiative underway, one of his subordinates came to him with a detailed task plan showing that it would take two years to complete the project that Grenville had promised in nine months. Grenville thanked the young man, threw the task plan away, and reiterated his commitment to the aggressive deadline. What these champions are saying is counterintuitive. It's not just that detailed, end-to-end task planning is unnecessary, but that it can actually be destructive. "Best practice" project planning would sabotage a wildly successful initiative by closing it in.

Make no mistake; using disciplined planning to keep a process under control is exactly the right approach in some situations. When the initiative's value comes from coordinating a lot of moving parts to make the result predictable, it's a boon. However, cramming an initiative into line has the opposite effect when the team will never reach its goal by marching straight ahead. Bumbling around does not guarantee that our heroes will be wildly successful. But making them walk through the well-worn ruts of past initiatives will guarantee that they won't be.

Consider Unigamble's manufacturing reliability initiative. A senior operations executive convinced himself that it was possible to break through the widely believed maximum. He threw down the gauntlet, asking his organization to achieve 85 percent, then giving his people the latitude to go do it.

In this context, latitude means looking the other way, even when your people are punching holes in the company's cultural norms. At the time, Unigamble was nothing if not insular. High priests of "not invented here" policed the company's borders so that no intellectual property could come in or go out. Yet somehow the engineers who were tracking down a new way to think about the problem ended up in a heretical collaboration with an outside organization. No one stopped them. Having the space to explore enabled them to find a solution they would never have invented by themselves.

It didn't end there. When our heroes had come up with a new way to manage machine stoppages, they had to prove it really worked. The crusty "if it's not broke, don't break it" manufacturing establishment would believe it only if they saw it. The engineers tapped their personal networks to find a plant manager who would "let an experiment go on under his nose." Having the space to experiment enabled them to demonstrate the merits of their approach. Without that opportunity, they would not have had the evidence to show that their unconventional approach produced better results than the other concepts being proposed.

What Makes Up Space?

Disciplined planning is only one of a whole raft of space-constricting tools that conventional managers use to ensure good results—emphasis on the word *good*. Performance measurement, capital and expense budgeting, risk management, and formal project reviews all fall into this category. The tools themselves do not squeeze people and activities into narrow channels, but the cramped, choking, downside way they are used often does.

Space is a mindset. I once asked a serial entrepreneur how he overcame the obstacles he faced in starting up his business. He chuckled and said, "One of the reasons I have been so successful is that I don't even *see* the obstacles. I see only the opportunities." Champions cultivate a spacious frame of mind for themselves and their colleagues using three essential elements and one other that helps. Wildly successful champions frame a big idea, nurture a sense of autonomy, and liberate enough time and effort to pursue it. The arrangement of physical offices can also contribute to a team's sense of space. Let's look at each of these.

Frame a Big Idea

We talked in Chapter 3 about reaching beyond your grasp. A big idea is roomy. It highlights what's missing even more than what's there, and those vacancies grab our attention like neon signs.

A big idea doesn't have to be esoteric or even wholly new to be powerful. In fact, simple big ideas work best. Matthews set his sights on making the Stansylvanian Revenue Agency *taxpayer*-centric instead of tax-centric. Rose wanted to create information delivery devices that were "Zen simple" to use. Unigamble's reliability engineers adopted a new "no stops" mantra instead of focusing only on the long outages. The snack food division of a large private food company doubled its revenue by concentrating on products that were composed solely of ingredients that consumers could pronounce.

What makes these ideas spacious? They click. People can see immediately how they offer new advantages. They are contrarian: They fly in the face of previous beliefs or approaches. You have to stop and think. And they introduce untapped opportunities. The crowded marketplace of a moment ago suddenly holds its doors wide open.

Working wonders are littered with big ideas that fly in the face of the norm. Schaefer's agenda to build volume by selling gasoline to his competitors broke with tradition. Mike Winch (discussed later in this chapter) had to counter the charge that self-checkout in a grocery store would invite thievery. Some would consider Matthews's concept of a taxpayer-centric revenue agency even more radical. Rose's belief in simple, beautiful information instruments certainly was a departure from the direction in which most technology companies were heading.

In some cases, the big idea and all the space it offers come out of a single word or phrase. The director general of the Belgian government's family allowances agency—the organization that provides aid to needy families—presented a new mission to his employees. Instead of providing citizens with the benefits they *asked for,* he pressed his people to give Belgians the benefits they *deserved.* This turn of phrase made a radical difference in the organization's mentality. For the first time, it became part of the employee's responsibility to understand what each family was entitled to receive and to make sure that that family got it.

Nurture a Sense of Autonomy

Picture yourself standing among a group of strangers on a street corner in New York City. You see two cars crash together, the airbags deploy, and neither of the drivers seems to be moving. What do you do?

According to Robert Cialdini,[2] the normal reaction is to do nothing. Only one-third of the people who find themselves in that situation would rush to help the drivers. In fact, the presence of other bystanders who are doing just that—standing by—seems to keep people from taking action.

Standing by is also the norm in everyday organizational life. How many people in Enron saw the wrongdoing and said to themselves, "It's not my job to fix this"? Champions of wildly successful initiatives cultivate a different mentality—stepping up instead of standing by. Their sense of personal responsibility and authority over what happens gives them a spacious sphere of action.

Remember the example of the compressor at Lima? It had been working poorly for years, but no one seemed to take the problem seriously. The supervisors didn't realize the magnitude of the issue, the plant manager wasn't aware of the true cost or the safety hazard, the engineers recommended a fix without getting to the bottom of the problem, and the operators worried about an explosion but didn't demand action. One day, the mindset of a few key workers shifted. They said to themselves, "No one is going to take care of this for us. We have to do it ourselves." The sense of autonomy that these workers *chose* to adopt carved out new space for action. Ultimately it led to a permanent solution to the problem, millions of dollars in savings for the organization, and a safer workplace for everyone. Paul Monus summarizes the point eloquently, "It was a huge success. An important problem was solved with no money after eight years of failed engineering."

Liberate Time and Effort

What was it that Rose said he would do, now that he is wiser, when blocked by someone like the Sphincter? He would go straight to the programmers and ask them to develop a new product prototype during their nights and weekends. He would claim time and effort that was otherwise not going to go to the company—so-called free time—by offering the individuals a chance to do something they found fun and exciting.

Mayor Dave Berger called on the townspeople of Lima to help convince BP headquarters to reconsider its decision to close the refinery. He launched the "visionaries task force" and asked for volunteers. One thousand people found the free time to participate.

One of Boston's successful biotechnology companies explicitly rewards its best drug developers by letting them decide how to spend the free time they cadge from other projects. The vice president of R&D explains,

> We decided it was a poor idea to give everyone the same amount of free time to spend on their pet projects. Some people wouldn't spend it as wisely as others. So our teams have to earn their free time. The best scientists get the official projects done efficiently, and they can pursue their passions with the time they liberate.

As we know, free time doesn't just come in blocks on nights and weekends. It sits in the leisurely conversations and idle moments of employees' routine workdays. That's what John Grenville was counting on when he asked his team to complete a two-year project in nine months. He knew that if he put the team on PST—passion standard time—it could get twice as much done as a formal task plan would suggest.

Find the Money You Need as You Go Along

We can't leave the topic of space without talking about money. Conventional management wisdom argues that successful initiatives need ample funding. This point of view translates into a whole litany of project budgets and periodic review processes that ensure that an initiative has an adequate financial runway.

Oddly enough, wildly successful initiatives do not seem to require this. Champions find the money they need as they go along rather than waiting until it is secured to begin. Often they make stunning progress with very little money. Both Schaefer's budget magic and the Lima compressor story illustrate how this works. Ambient's Rose provides another example. To create a working prototype of his innovative Orb, he needed some help from people and partners who expected to get paid. When he was unsuccessful at convincing the business development executives in a big telecommunications company to partner with him on the product, he went through the back door. He leveraged his relationships with the same company's R&D team and struck a contract with that team to develop the product on its nickel. Rose made sure that both Ambient and the telco would own rights to the product in the end, so he could take it to market with or without them.

Physical Space Lends a Helping Hand

When Stansylvania's John Grenville decided to go all out for an Internet-based e-filing project, he used every tool he could to create a gung-ho environment. One of these tools was the physical office space. He took his team off to its own building, segregating the group from other government workers both physically and mentally and signaling that this effort was going to be different from what these people had experienced in the past. He explains how he created a productive interpersonal environment by using physical space: "Some of our people had inhabited the same offices for a decade. I needed a different culture and work ethos for both my employees and the consultants working with us. I took us all to a separate building: our entire team, side by side, with no walls or dividers and no hiding from anyone."

What Does It Take to Make Space?

It's easy to spot ways in which managers shrink space for their employees. We see examples every day. I'm reminded of a CEO who, when discussing issues with his staff, responds to their ideas and suggestions by spitting out, "That's irrelevant." As a result, the people in his organization sit back and take direction, and he wonders why he seems to be the only one taking responsibility for driving growth.

Carving out space for a wildly successful initiative is just as easy.

Instead of clamping down on what people think and do, champions relax their grip. They set boundaries around the space by articulating the problem or goal and the time frames, they persuade people it's achievable, and they clear away obstacles.

Set Boundaries

Creating space doesn't mean setting up a complete vacuum. Picture a space-walking astronaut who becomes disconnected from his craft. That's what an unbounded or directionless initiative looks like as well. It's not a pretty sight.

An experienced entrepreneur and venture capital professional explains how debilitating this can be. Linda was hired by a highly regarded consumer electronics company to help it expand its business beyond its traditional stronghold in audio products. It gave her a "blank palette" and asked her to identify new business opportunities, building from the company's core technology strengths. The only rule: Stay out of the space that is already claimed by an existing business unit. Initially, Linda and her team found themselves wandering all over the map because the effort lacked boundaries.

As Linda's experience points out, to create space, champions must define boundaries. It's actually the fence around the corral that makes the space. Carol Pletcher, former chief innovation officer at Cargill, discovered this when she set out on a mission to improve innovation in the company, an international provider of food, agricultural, and risk management products and services and one of the world's largest private companies, with 149,000 employees in sixty-three countries. She began with a philosophy of inclusiveness, opening the innovation agenda far beyond the R&D department to make it everyone's business. Defying well-accepted frameworks, she also eradicated the distinction between disruptive and incremental innovations, remarking, "The company needs thousands of innovations of all sizes and shapes to stay healthy, and those labels just get in the way."

As part of her inclusive agenda, Pletcher and her team launched an effort to solicit innovative ideas from the company's employees. At first, this did not work out the way she had hoped. She recounts,

> We were trying to build the idea pipeline, so we opened suggestion boxes, both electronically and with paper. We thought we would just turn on the process and the good ideas would flow like a river. It doesn't work like that. We learned that to get good ideas, we had to ask people for suggestions in a specific target area with specific provocative questions. We are now developing multiple ways to do that.

Pletcher's example tells us that initiative space needs a boundary—a defined domain that lets us wander at will, but keeps us challenged and focused on accomplishing something of value.

How we set those boundaries matters a great deal, and Pletcher points us in exactly the right direction. By articulating a problem or an opportunity, but neither a solution nor a way of reaching a solution, Pletcher and her team created space for Cargill's employees to contribute their innovative ideas.

Schaefer did the same thing with his improvement challenge. He laid out clear parameters that helped employees choose the right ideas to pursue: Any project that improved operations and paid off within a year was fair game. Jim's boundary carried a deadline as well as a focal problem. This added a time dimension to the space he created.

A few years back, I had the opportunity to take on a challenging assignment for Tom Hennigan, then the CIO of a large consumer electronics company. His charge to me: "Fix management information." An ordinary boss might have said: "Make a plan to satisfy the information needs of the company's executives, and I'll review it with you," or even "Prepare an analysis of the management information gaps that the company must close." Instead, Tom asked for exactly the result he wanted, knowing that neither one of us could say precisely how to get there. His clearly stated outcome set up the boundaries for our work together.

Persuade People that the Problem Can Be Solved

Our friends at Unigamble highlight the second critical ingredient for creating space: doability. People who decide to take on the challenge of trying to solve a hard problem must believe that a solution is possible—usually in spite of what their colleagues and supervisors may say to them. Unigamble's vice president of operations did not set his aggressive goal for manufacturing reliability lightly. He first satisfied himself that achieving 85 percent reliability was entirely possible—difficult, but doable. That belief in the potential for a positive outcome opens the door for people to give it a go.

Despite everyone's best intentions, wildly successful initiatives often experience a darkest hour—a point when the project looks impossible and the team loses confidence. It seems almost silly in retrospect, but Texas Instruments's project to invent the integrated circuit went through this. Management had decided to pull the funding and reassign the team because it had concluded that the initiative would never produce anything. In a characteristic moment of courage, the project leader demanded to be allowed to continue. Through his own force of will, he held off those who would have cancelled the project until his team could deliver.

Confidence in the team's ability to solve the problem doesn't come from a rational consensus; it's a matter of belief. When that faith wavers, champions take steps to restore it. They spur each other on. As Rose says succinctly, "If you're a pessimist, you'll never pull it off."

Remove Obstacles

Leaving energy and motivation aside for the moment (we'll take those up in Chapter 9), are we saying that all we need to do to create space is identify a challenging, solvable problem (but not a solution) and set a deadline? There's one more ingredient. We also have to get rid of the blockages. These can be people (such as the Sphincter), old habits like Unigamble's insularity, rules and regulations, physical barriers, personal fears, and sometimes even the deadlines themselves.

One way to clear obstacles from the path is to experience a crisis. Cargill's Pletcher explains, "When we have a crisis, we are quite remarkable. At that moment, all the normal barriers just melt away." She punctuates her point with a stunning example:

Cargill routinely buys cotton from farmers in Zimbabwe and takes it to the world market. But Zimbabwe had gotten itself into a liquidity crisis—its "cash and carry" economy had no currency to fuel it. It was almost June, the time the farmers needed to sell their cotton, and Cargill couldn't get any currency to pay them. Neither could it pay by check because the farmers couldn't turn checks into currency either. There was no currency. Commerce in the area was grinding to a halt. Prospects looked grim, both for the cotton farmers and for Cargill.

Cargill's people in Zimbabwe connected with the folks in the corporate treasury to break down the barriers. Cargill Corporation partnered with the Reserve Bank of Zimbabwe and printed its own currency—bearer checks backed by money that Cargill had deposited in the bank. Cargill bought cotton with the bearer checks and gave the farmers a currency that they could use to buy other goods and services.

So let's imagine ourselves in a global corporation. One day we say to ourselves, "Let's invent a new currency for our business in XYZ-land." What obstacles would be in the way? Whose job would that be? Whose approval would we need? What laws would we have to observe? How would we legitimize it with the XYZians? Actually, there are so many obstacles that the whole idea seems foolhardy. Except, perhaps, in a currency crisis, when, as Pletcher says, these barriers melt away.

Harold French and William Althouse used a crisis masterfully to clear out the obstacles to Stansylvania's integrated tax system. In fact, they call it one of their key success factors. As pressure to address Y2K concerns mounted, they let their colleagues know that they had a simple choice—either finish the new system on time or endure the humiliation of being unable to collect taxes. Althouse explains:

In 1997, I fought for an agreement that we would not put resources into our legacy withholding system to make it Y2K compliant. At the time, our business users were not committed, perhaps not even interested. I argued that our new integrated tax processing system (ITP) would go live before our old employer withholding tax system fell over. We made the decision on a low-key basis, and our business users did not fully understand the significance.

We quickly hit a Rubicon. We couldn't go back. Now the organization was facing the fact that if ITP were not delivered, we would have no system at all. Think of the hassle and the bad publicity if we could not operate. We were within eighteen months of having no system at all to collect $1.8 billion (€1.4 billion) of withholding tax. At that point, we saw the organization roll in behind us. People began moving heaven and earth so that we could deliver. Our best friend was 1/1/2000.

But what if we want to clear away blockages *without* waiting for a crisis? That's a little harder, but champions do it all the time.

An approach we see again and again is a simple conditional close. Borrowing this technique from Sales 101, our champions present the following proposition to people who might otherwise get in their way: "If I promise to [fill in the blank], will you leave me alone?"

You'll recognize this approach in Schaefer's arrangement with his boss to overspend his budget early in the year, but make it up later. The reliability engineers also struck this kind of deal with their friendly plant manager when they needed a pilot to prove their solution. National Savings and Investments, an arm of the U.K. government, provides an even more visible example.

When Peter Bareau, a pin-striped Lloyds banker, took over as the CEO of National Savings and Investments (NS&I), he knew that he had a turnaround on his hands. NS&I, a captive savings bank that the U.K. government uses to help fund its treasury, had suffered from underinvestment for years. Part of Bareau's charge was to ask the hard questions: Does this agency add value? Should it even exist?[3]

Bareau commissioned a premier consultancy to answer these questions and, if the answers were positive, to measure the actual value that

NS&I created. With that gutsy move, Bareau created his own high-stakes report card. He demonstrated that, at the time, his organization contributed £100 million in net value to the government. This gave him the basis for his conditional close with the Treasury and the U.K. public: "If you would like this to continue or even increase, give me the latitude to make it so." They did, and he proceeded to radically transform NS&I.

No Room to Fail

Change management experts routinely advise managers to give their employees room to fail as a way to encourage them to take risks. They joke that the champion of a failed initiative should not be fired because the company has just paid handsomely for her training. Using this logic, we might imagine that providing a nice soft landing in the event of failure would be a good way to make space.

It doesn't seem to work that way. Champions of wildly successful initiatives resist failure keenly; they live in an environment that is anything but safe. Often, they are "all in," to use the Texas Hold 'Em vernacular. Mark Walsh, the media darling CEO of the Internet-based business-to-business (B2B) media and transaction company Vertical-net, describes how his team's unwillingness to fail created more space than a soft landing would have:

> In the late 1990s, we were flying high. Everyone wanted to emulate what we were doing. When the air came out of the Internet bubble in 2001, companies all around us were declaring bankruptcy. We were on the edge, but none of us wanted to say that we were in a dot-com that went out of business and go on with our careers. We just did not want to fail. We became foxhole buddies. It created an "us vs. the world" attitude, a sense of commitment, and a belief that, no matter what, we would all win or lose together. It was the psychic underpinning of our energy.

Walsh and his team converted Verticalnet into a purchasing analysis software and services company that remains viable today.

Making Space with Customers

While we've been concentrating up to now on making space for ourselves and our colleagues to be wildly successful, our customers and business partners are also part of the mix. For an initiative to succeed, they must also recognize the unmet need or entertain the unusual new solution. In short, they need space too, and the same principles apply.

A few years back, for example, an innovative training director at a large commercial bank—let's call him Frank—was extremely frustrated with his organization's transactional approach to selling. He believed that the bank would have far more success winning commercial clients if it took a more strategic, relationship-oriented tack. Sales growth wasn't on Frank's personal scorecard, but that didn't matter; he wanted to make the bank successful.

Our hero started in his own backyard by developing a strategic training workshop for the bank's loan officers. He had the space, remarking, "The higher-ups didn't really ask us to do it, but they didn't stop us. We figured that one day they'd wake up and appreciate it. So we created courses that were driving in the right direction." At that time, bank executives viewed their employees strictly as lenders. Frank's workshop was intended to help these individuals make a mindset shift and begin working with their clients as financial advisors. This meant that the banker would have to understand all the bank's products and when each was appropriate. Plus, in order to compete strategically, the bankers could not afford to wait for clients to come to them and ask for a proposal; they had to find a way to proactively uncover financial opportunities that customers themselves might not have recognized.

Frank approached several friends who had solid customer relationships and asked if they would allow their clients to be guinea pigs for his training workshop. He personally guaranteed them a good result.

He divided the trainees into teams, each one focusing on a live client, and gave the teams three weeks to come up with an innovative proposal based on their strategic review of the client's business situation and objectives. During those three weeks, Frank and his trainers provided strategy basics, diagnostic frameworks, analytical tools, case studies, and readings. In addition, other experts from the bank put themselves on call for questions from the teams.

The result? The bank's would-be financial advisors found business opportunities in the spaces between clients' existing loan activity. By taking a strategic perspective, they helped clients to see the opportunity space as well. Some clients accepted the proposals as presented. Others said no, but found the lenders' approach so helpful that they engaged the bank in other ways.

Moving from a bank to a supermarket—from one mature industry to another—we find another wildly successful champion in another unlikely role. When Mike Winch was the CIO of Safeway UK, a grocery chain, he invited both business partners and customers into his space. He had originally joined the Argyll Company, a start-up that aspired to build a global food and drinks business. The leadership reasoned that the company could get some advantage from information technology if it applied that technology better than its competitors, so it gave Winch free rein in using the technology to drive the business forward.

When Argyll subsequently acquired the U.K. subsidiary of Safeway, it adopted the latter's solid brand name. Winch, accepted by his colleagues as the most strategic member of the executive team, continued to innovate with information technology. He stressed, "It wasn't about what products we sold or what technology we could implement, but how we could make food retailing a better business."

In the early 1990s, when bar codes hit the food retailing industry, grocery chains began to understand what products had been sold and for what price. Safeway's competitors were beginning to use bar coding to cut labor costs by eliminating the practice of putting a price on each individual package. Winch had a different goal in mind. "My focus was on using technology to understand consumers and interact with them—while they were in the store—in ways that would improve our business," he summarizes.

Hand in hand with the bar-code technology expert Symbol Technologies, Winch launched a project called Shop and Go. He invited Symbol Technologies to the party to bring the handheld bar-code terminals—which most companies were using for managing inventory in the warehouse—out of the back room. Winch points out,

> Customers hate the checkout. When we ask them to draw a picture of our store in a focus group, they always draw the checkout in black. If someone sees a long queue, they don't stay as long in the store, and they don't buy as much. I wanted to improve that part of the experience through self-scanning.

With Symbol, Winch and his team created a handheld bar-code device that was intended for the customer to use—that is, for a casual user, not a full-time stock picker. The device had three big buttons: add an item to the basket, take one away, and calculate the total to pay. As customers went through the store and shopped, they would scan items in, then pay their total at the end.

Early on, Winch was just trying to move the customer-loyalty needle. He wanted the system to break even financially, but to pay long-term dividends by bringing the customers back. Some of the other executives in the company vehemently disagreed with his approach. Naysayers argued that customers would steal food and that the resulting "shrinkage" would more than offset any benefits the system would provide. Because of Winch's personal credibility, however, he was able to fend off the pessimists, at least until the pilot results came in.

Winch recalls,

> We worked out a few kinks in the first few pilot stores. Ultimately, the customers loved it. It gave them a sense of control. They could go through the store faster if they were in a hurry, or more slowly

if they were putting together a complex menu. They liked the fact that they set their own pace.

Did the project break even? In fact, the results were better than even Winch had hoped. Customers who used the Shop and Go system increased their spending by 10 percent. In the competitive food retailing industry, an improvement of 1 percent was hard to achieve, so this result was substantially above average. And it gave Winch the air cover to push his initiative to the next plateau.

Winch expanded the self-service concept to allow Safeway to interact with customers any time, anywhere. He explains,

> We already had a loyalty card, and we kept every transaction, so we knew a lot about our customers. We knew about their previous purchases, their shopping patterns, and how they responded to promotions. We wanted to open a dialogue with them while they were shopping, but we didn't want to limit that conversation to when they were actually in the store. We envisioned them on the beach, ordering groceries that they could pick up on their way home after a holiday. When we did Shop and Go, the self-scanning technology already existed. For this project, there was no obvious solution around at the time.

Once again, Winch reached out to technology partners. He asked IBM if it would be interested in working with Safeway to bring his ideas to life. He explained, "One of the groups I got close to was IBM Research. Most people misunderstand what it does. IBM Research actually does research; it invents things. That was particularly exciting for me—to work with people who are doing things for the first time."

Winch convinced IBM to put together a research team to work on the new vision of retailing that he had laid out. It was the first time IBM had worked directly with a retailer. The team was also one of the largest IBM had ever pulled together, driven by the diverse technologies that the initiative required. "These people are usually off inventing disk drives or something," Winch quips. "They normally don't relate to businesspeople. And you can't just tell these scientists to go research something. You have to give them some kind of vision to motivate them. I talked to them about the things we could do that would have huge benefits."

Winch knew that Safeway could not afford to fund the IBM research alone. He struck a deal whereby IBM would invest its scientists, and Winch would invest the time of a few of Safeway's commercial people. Safeway would have exclusive rights to use whatever the team came up with for two years. After that, IBM could market it to other companies.

Over twelve months, the team members produced a practical solution that implemented Winch's vision; they called it Easi-Order. Safeway's best customers would be given—for free—a modified Palm Pilot, engineered so that it could read bar codes. Once a customer entered his or her customer number, the system would use its extensive data-mining technology to produce a recommended shopping order based on the customer's previous purchases. What was even more convenient, all of this "shopping" could be done from the customer's kitchen in the evening. Mrs. Jones or Mr. Smith could be sitting in front of the telly or keeping an eye on junior while they looked over the list and made any changes they had in mind. One shopper liked to buy a month's worth of paper products in one go, but to select her own fruit at the store. If she hadn't bought a particular product recently, she would just spell it out free form or swipe her PDA over the package in the cupboard.

About 70 percent of the customers accepted the suggested list as it was given. While they were going through their shopping list, however, the Easi-Order system made some additional observations and recommendations based on what it knew about them. For example, if it noted that the customer had selected fish and a particular wine, it might suggest an alternative wine that would be an even better complement for that type of fish. "We weren't intrusive," Winch cautions, "and we didn't try to get people to switch products. We just made gentle suggestions." Sophisticated data mining behind the scenes also made a difference. Winch remarks, "We don't present meat promotions to vegetarians or baby products to pensioners."

When they finished their list, the customers would simply select a time to come by to pick up their groceries. With a quick telephone download, the customer's shopping was done. One sixty-year-old man, whose wife was severely disabled, called the system a "godsend." Since he had to organize his life around hers, he found it especially difficult to get to the supermarket. The system enabled him to get through the shopping quickly and still attend to her. In a pointed letter to the customer service department, he said, "If you ever change it, I'll never shop with you again."

Other customers found the Easi-Order system to their liking as well, but for an unexpected reason. Gary Anthes writes in *Computerworld,* "Two pilot customers say they have become friends with the clerks who process their orders—something that wasn't possible previously when they saw a different checkout clerk each time they shopped."[4]

Once again, some of Winch's colleagues on the leadership team had been reluctant to support the initiative. They had difficulty accepting the amount of change in the way the stores operated that Winch's ideas would entail. Before the fact, even the most articulate business case was insufficient to convince the conservative element in the company that his experiments would pay off.

Thanks to scanners, however, the company had excellent, detailed information about who bought what in the stores, and Winch was again able to prove the naysayers wrong after the fact. He grins,

> We could not only calculate the direct increase in revenues, but we went further. IBM's industrial psychologists interviewed hundreds of customers to find out how they felt about the system and about Safeway as a result. It was amazing. No matter how much the researchers criticized the system to a customer, they couldn't get a negative response.

Ultimately, 12 percent of the customers using Easi-Order bought a product they had never purchased before. In addition, the system measurably increased loyalty, primarily among the chain's best customers—those 20 percent that provided 80 percent of the profits. Winch remarks, "We began to change our relationship with the important customers who were crucial to our success."

Unfortunately for Winch, Safeway shoppers, and Safeway shareholders, this wildly successful initiative did not make Safeway UK a wildly successful enterprise. The company was sold to Morrison's, which, as a result of integration challenges, sold off or closed many of the Safeway stores. IBM, however, broke open a new market space for itself. Six years later, it has a substantial business in the retail sector. Among other exciting technologies, it markets a handheld, work-from-anywhere, bar-code-capable "personal shopping assistant," backed by extensive data mining, as part of its grocery store of the future.[5]

How Can Champions Make Space for Themselves and Their Initiatives?

Scratch the surface of most business interactions (and relationships, for that matter) and concerns with control will come oozing out. When people feel responsible for getting things done through others, they immediately begin looking for ways to ensure that they are not disappointed. They tend to grab the reins directly: You work for me, I determine your compensation, don't do anything without my approval, let me tell you how I want to proceed, and so forth.

To work wonders, managers will want to try a different approach:

To Make Space for Yourself

◆ Move toward hospitable parts of your organization where executives guide performance with a light touch. There's no need to put the Sphincter in your path if you can avoid him. Work for superiors who trust you.

◆ Notice when you're stuck; it means you need more space. This is easy for goal-oriented people. You're stuck whenever you're not moving forward—when you're spinning your wheels or revisiting the same ground over and over again.

◆ Name what's in the way. It might be an emotional issue: You're afraid or angry or disappointed. When you conclude that something outside your control is the obstacle, think again.

◆ Find a new way of approaching your goal or problem. Turn it upside down or inside out. Ask people who will tell you the truth to give you their perspective. Listen to them. Strike a bargain with your colleagues that gives you more runway.

◆ Attract help. Share your ideas and let others pitch in. Know what you would ask for if you had another pair of hands.

To Make Space for Your People

◆ Ask your team for an outcome. Let the team members figure out how to achieve it.

◆ Instead of directing people to do what you think they should, listen for their offers to contribute. If no one volunteers, let the silence stand or move on.

◆ Instead of overseeing the work your people do, make yourself available to help. Let them come to you, and when they do, listen and ask questions.

◆ Allow some civil disobedience and misalignment—let your team members earn free time and do things that are not on your agenda. Having complete strategic alignment sterilizes healthy organizational evolution.

◆ If your people come up with something that works, accept it, even if it isn't quite what you would have done.

CHAPTER 6

The Bigger Dig

Unconventional Scientists Break New Ground in Underwater Mining

The managing director of United Construction Equipment's Advanced Machinery Analysis Division ignored April's pounding rain as he and his chief quality officer strode across the parking lot. A no-nonsense executive with a penchant for action, Ben Erikson had just returned to Denver from an unnerving meeting with the company's senior leadership team. (The names and context of this story have been disguised to protect the privacy of the individuals involved.)

Headquarters strategists had just delivered their conclusions from a six-month intelligence study about the looming competitive threat from the Japanese. It was 1990, and United Construction Equipment's (UCE) dominance in the industry was under attack. UCE produced a wide range of cranes, earthmovers, and mining equipment for working in some of the most demanding environments in the world. With double-digit growth, worldwide 1989 revenues of more than $18 billion, and a healthy bottom line, UCE had been the company to beat for the past decade.

Unfortunately, several strong Japanese equipment companies had

UCE's highest-growth markets directly in their crosshairs. Among other things, the Japanese were working on a line of highly advanced products for the ocean-based mining industry, an emerging opportunity in UCE's traditional stronghold. The UCE competitive intelligence team had got wind that one Japanese firm was collaborating with a leading Tokyo University researcher to develop a system known as the MX. With an expected go-to-market date in mid-1993, this underwater mining system would boast sophisticated computer guidance and control systems that would not only direct the sea-floor drilling and extraction machinery, but also help topside operators keep the system humming in very challenging environmental conditions.

Entrepreneurs had been experimenting with sea-floor mining since the early 1960s, focusing on precious metals and jewelry-quality gems. A few had struck pay dirt. Several working diamond mines, now owned by De Beers, had resulted, but these were all in very shallow water. The promise of mining in deep water had never been realized.

The MX's promised features would permit underwater mining at the same depths that offshore oil rigs had plumbed for years, making deep-water mining economically viable for the first time. The MX would send sound waves into the ground, listening for the reverberations and interpreting them digitally. This would allow it to determine where and how to dig, targeting the richest deposits and guiding the drills appropriately. It would also sense and counteract the deep-water pressure and turbulence that, over time, could bring the equipment to a standstill. Since the most promising fields were in areas that were rife with volcanoes and undersea earthquakes, stabilizing the system vastly improved its productivity and its life. The system's potential customers were already laying plans for new diamond and gold fields.

UCE had its own answer to the MX under development, but the program had hit some serious snags. In a recent setback, UCE's "smart" underwater extraction system, dubbed the Mole, had performed miserably in its first in-water test. In a way, Erikson's team had been responsible for the failure.

While UCE had mounted an aggressive development program to

leapfrog the MX, it had not put the same effort and resources into its testing facilities. One of three UCE testing centers, Erikson's Advanced Machinery Analysis Division (AMAD) had the responsibility for telling the Mole's developers whether their latest build was going to perform when it hit the deep water. Unfortunately, AMAD was still relying on test simulators that were better suited to earlier generations of equipment. In short, the Mole had a substantially higher IQ than the laboratory systems assigned to put it through its paces. It had sailed through the prelaunch physical that Erikson's team had administered, but it floundered badly when it got out to the UCE test mine off the coast of Papua New Guinea.

Progress on the development program had slowed measurably as a result. In the most recent executive meeting, UCE's CFO had actually proposed that the company cede the underwater mining space to the Japanese and concentrate on other markets. Instead, the CEO asked the La Jolla testing center to assume primary responsibility for the Mole, leaving Erikson's group to back it up if necessary. Further, he allocated $50 million to La Jolla to develop a more capable laboratory simulator.

Erikson was seething. As he strode across the parking lot, he turned to his CQO, Lee Skelton, and said, "I know those guys in La Jolla. They're just going to throw money at the problem. If we don't get our own testing lab up to speed and win back that work, the Mole will be dead in the water. Find a way."

Scratching the Surface

Skelton knew that she had to start with a clean sheet of paper. She pulled together a small group of AMAD experts and explained the challenge. The Mole was the most complex undersea system that UCE had ever undertaken. The developers would race to pull together a new build and schedule another in-water test. Each test needed weeks of time to get the mining rigs and operators into place on the ocean and burned through another highly visible $100,000. After the "good" failures, the equipment would be hauled back to the lab for autopsy and repair. And if the testers were unable to retrieve all the pieces, there was hell to pay. Not only did they lose some of the data they desperately needed in order to understand what went wrong, but they risked having their latest technology fall into the hands of the ever-watchful competitors.

"We need a high-fidelity, real-time simulator that will test this extraction system," Skelton emphasized, "without its ever leaving our lab." Further, the simulator had to be good enough, ultimately, to take the place of much of the expensive, time-consuming, and destructive in-water testing. AMAD had used other simulators to test systems in challenging environments, but these had not achieved the realism and accuracy that Skelton was after. Furthermore, some of AMAD's simulation experts had concluded that a true real-time simulation was impossible to achieve with current technology. Finally, AMAD would have to build the simulator without asking the corporation for additional capital. That capped the budget at $1.5 million—Erikson's discretionary funds.

"At that first meeting," Skelton recalls, "some people were optimistic about our ability to build a real-time, high-fidelity simulator in the time frame I had in mind, and others gave it little chance of success. When the next meeting came around, I didn't invite the pessimists." She says dryly, "My team and I weren't chosen at random. Erikson and I had worked together in the past, and he knew what he was getting when he asked me to take this on."

The team members aimed high when they set their aspirations for the first fully digital "Sim-Mole" (see Figure 6–1). If they could pull it off, this tester would be fast enough to fool the smartest mining system into operating just as it would in water, and it would be flexible enough to adapt to just about any environmental condition that the Mole would encounter.

Skelton and her AMAD experts started by doing their homework. They approached the leading companies in the field—IBM, Cray, Honeywell-Bull, and Digital Equipment—to explore the potential of working together on the Sim-Mole.

In 1990, the Cray was the only computer that was *potentially* fast enough to simulate both the real-time underwater environment and

Figure 6-1. Sim-Mole High-Level Requirements

◆ *Modularity.* The Sim-Mole was to be constructed modularly to allow it to improve over time as technology improved, and also to enable it to analyze mining systems of increasing complexity.

◆ *Any acoustic environment.* It should be able to recreate any underwater and petrologic environment more accurately and realistically than any other current undersea simulation.

◆ *Detailed target models.* It should simulate a variety of gem and ore targets in detail to provide critical performance information as the drill heads home in on the veins.

◆ *Hardware—online and emulation.* The Sim-Mole must be able to operate either by emulating the Mole's systems or by linking directly to them.

◆ *Flexible architecture.* The architecture should be flexible enough to support other undersea equipment and systems.

◆ *Usability.* To facilitate training and operation, the Sim-Mole must have user-friendly interfaces for setup and operation, for real-time monitoring, and for postrun data archiving and analysis.

---

the reflected acoustical signals that the drill heads used for guidance. However, it was quite expensive: $25 million. Digital Equipment was in the process of developing a new parallel operating system for its Vax minicomputer, and Honeywell-Bull had built a digital simulator using mainframe technology. Skelton's team visited both companies to take a look.

Not completely satisfied with what she had seen, Skelton continued to search. She found an alternative at Galactica, a small company that had recently been spun off from MIT. Galactica's founders had famously worked with NASA on its lunar vehicles. Galactica's technologists had struggled to develop a simple, effective, and lightweight guidance system that fit within the program's payload parameters. The result was a parallel-processing node of the company's own design called Roots. The Roots node broke new ground by enabling small, inexpensive microcomputers to be connected together to share computing tasks. With the Roots architecture, the lunar vehicle was able to handle its heavy computing load without a heavy computer. In addition to its penchant for breakthroughs, Galactica had a reputation for being able to deliver.

The First Cut

Skelton knew Galactica. She had worked with Zachary Duff, a young Galactica physicist and project manager, on a past project, and the two had great mutual respect. Skelton called him.

She didn't waste Duff's time with small talk. "I need you to do a study for me. I've only got a few thousand dollars, and I need good answers fast." Skelton asked Duff if he would conduct a three-month study that would answer a few "simple" questions:

◆ What was the processing load the Sim-Mole would require?

◆ What computer architectures might be able to handle that load?

◆ Could the Sim-Mole be built for the amount of money that AMAD had budgeted?

◆ How long would building it take?

As Skelton requested, Duff and a Galactica colleague began with open minds about the best architecture for the Sim-Mole. Ultimately, the team considered three primary architectures: a supercomputer, a Digital Vax with array processors, and Roots.

Duff presented his conclusions to Skelton in February 1991: The project was both doable and affordable. Furthermore, Galactica would be happy to take it on. Recalls Duff:

> When we started the study, Lee didn't have any idea what to do, and neither did we, so we looked at all the options. We concluded that the only architecture that had any chance of working was one based on Roots. Most of the established experts in this arena said our approach could never work. We thought, "If we can't do it, no one can." We had enough swagger to believe it. If we had waited until we knew we could do it, we never would have done it.

The Galactica study laid out recommendations for addressing the knottiest problems in the Sim-Mole design. If the simulator had to fool the Mole into operating the same way it would in the water, it would have to provide feedback to the system's environmental, geologic, and petrologic sensing systems that looked just like the real thing. This turned out to be rather complicated. When the system sent a ping into the ocean floor in search of diamond-bearing rock, it "listened" carefully for the signal to reverberate with a pattern it recognized as its target. But this very smart system also expected its signals to carom around the geologic formations, bouncing off underground layers and traveling at different rates of speed through different materials. Finally, the system's signal interpreter could be looking for up to 200 "highlights"—each one with its own peculiarities—to home in on the richest area for drilling.

In addition to guiding the drill heads, the Mole's control system had to constantly monitor its environment for turbulence, which could come from a variety of sources, including distant earthquakes, volcanic activity, and even the Mole itself. Unless the system proactively counteracted the normal forces, the relentless vibration dramatically shortened the productive life of the pumps that shuttled the gem-laden slurry up to the surface. It also had to stay vigilant for more violent upheavals that could damage the pipes that connected the Mole to the surface.

To do its job, the Sim-Mole had to feed the sensors all of these data as fast as the system could swallow them. Even a Cray would be challenged to calculate all the echoes, vibrations, and reverberations necessary to give the Mole's signal processor a complete meal every few milliseconds.

Galactica's architecture took a different tack. Instead of limiting itself to computers that processed one calculation at a time, it proposed a massively parallel structure. Roots nodes would link together hundreds of low-cost microprocessors, all of which could be working on different parts of the problem at the same time. Of course, developing the hardware and software to coordinate this computing hydra would require a few additional breakthroughs. First, the programming aces of the 1990s had no generalized method for writing the parallel-processing code that the Sim-Mole would require. Duff remarks, "Even today, this is a real art."

Second, the parallel structure of the system meant that there would be hundreds of little operations, each one moving at its own pace and communicating when it had something to say. Unlike most computer systems, this architecture did not guarantee delivery of the relevant information bits in linear lockstep; it was nondeterministic. In other words, the team planned to build a system with tight time constraints out of an ensemble of asynchronously connected processors. Duff recalls, "More than anything else in the initiative, this is what people attacked. They said this approach would never work. We said it would."

Hardware Poor

In February 1991, shortly after receiving the results of the Galactica study, AMAD decided to proceed. Duff stepped into the role of project manager for the Galactica team and moved his office to Denver.

Skelton set a brisk pace for the initiative. While she did not announce a firm deadline for a demonstration prototype, she asked the team to work as quickly as possible. "We did not have an explicit end date planned," Skelton recalls. "We just worked our butts off."

Unfortunately, Skelton informed the team that it would not have access to actual Mole hardware to use in developing the prototype. The product development program simply didn't have any extra equipment available, and its own scientists and engineers had first call on every available unit. The Sim-Mole team would have to be satisfied, at least in the short term, with building its simulator to work with a software emulation of the system.

For her part, Skelton put together a handpicked AMAD team that included some of the organization's best geologists and undersea extraction experts. These individuals would be responsible for the emulation software and the geologic and environmental models.

The thirty-year-old Duff had never managed a team larger than three people, but he immediately began trying to attract the best talent he could find. He went looking for high-level skills in software engineering, signal processing, underwater acoustics, computer hardware design and development, and graphical user interfaces. Duff recalls,

> The team had some of the best people in AMAD, and their domain expertise was critical. To fill out the team, we went looking for hot-

shots in programming and signal processing. Some of them were already working at Galactica, but most were right out of school. It's hard to find people that good. Somehow we did. It was a whole spider web of connections that brought these particular people together. By luck or by talent, we built an extraordinary team.

Skelton continues, "AMAD had some excellent people, but we weren't tied into the Ph.D. programs as well as Zack was. Moreover, I never met anyone who could spot scientific and engineering talent as unerringly as he could. The Galactica folks were all under thirty, astoundingly smart, and thrilled to be working on something that had never been done before."

Karl Schmidt, a software developer with a background in biology, was one of the first to arrive. Duff had been trying to pull him into Galactica for a year, and the challenge of the Sim-Mole project proved irresistible. From that small kernel, the team expanded quickly. Ultimately Duff found himself managing twenty talented scientists and engineers, split 50–50 between AMAD and Galactica employees. The team went to work gathering up bits of existing software from the product development program they thought they could use.

Within a few weeks of kicking off the initiative, Skelton and Duff began holding a weekly Monday morning meeting to drive progress. Each person on the team had five to ten minutes to report on what he had accomplished the prior week, any issues he encountered, and what he was planning to do in the coming week. Skelton said simply, "I managed decisively. We had to find the roadblocks and clear them away."

Duff compartmentalized the work into big pieces and gave each one to a small team to deliver. He defined the interfaces among the modules and set the time budget for processing, then got out of their way. He emphasizes,

Too much planning is not good; it takes your energy away from executing. You have to know what you're trying to accomplish and what it will take to make the system work. But then you have to hand over control to your people and take yourself out of the loop.

We could never have succeeded if everyone had been waiting for me to make the decisions.

Early on, Duff began to suspect that he might have underestimated the difficulty of the task. He remembers,

I very quickly learned that even though I was good technically, I wasn't going to be able to build the Sim-Mole by myself. It required too much specialized knowledge. Paradoxically, that may have been one of the secrets of our success. I concentrated on doing the two most important things I *could* do: First, shield my people from the pressures of the customer so they could concentrate, and second, learn which members of my team I could trust to deliver. The people with the intellect, the ability to perform under pressure, and the discipline got responsibility for a piece of the work.

Karl Schmidt recalls,

There was a great sense of urgency on the team, and it quickly became obvious who the performers were and were not. If someone was having trouble and someone else was in good shape on her own piece, some of the work would get reassigned. The more aggressive engineers would try to prove their value by carving out bigger pieces for themselves.

This approach to assigning the work helped Duff and Skelton contain the natural rivalry between the Galactica and AMAD staff members and among the technologists on the team. Schmidt remembers the internal competition as intense, but productive. "We all wanted the system to work, and we wouldn't succeed if we didn't do something about the tasks that fell behind. This was one simple way to find the best person to do each part." Arguments between strong personalities on the team about how to tackle a particular problem were common. Skelton and Duff would sometimes let these fester just a bit to make sure the team got to the nub of the issue. Then they'd step in and make a decision.

Duff also spent a fair amount of time getting the team's chemistry right. He stresses, "Even though many of the team members' skill sets overlapped, it was also true that different people had different talents. You can't just form a team of smart people; you have to get the right people in the right roles."

Duff didn't wait for all the modules to be fully engineered to ask the team to begin piecing the system together. The team members began integrating skeleton code modules almost immediately to make sure the simple parts worked. "First we defined the pattern of reverberations we expected in a rich deposit of diamonds," Schmidt explains. "Then we saw what the Mole would do with that signal, but without including all the normal noise. As we added more and more functions, we knew what parts of the system were already working. That's how we did it—a piece at a time."

Duff continues, "You can't let the vision get in your way. If you always measure yourself against the ultimate goal, you'll go crazy. You have to break it down into smaller, simpler pieces and make sure you make progress every day."

Checking In

One Wednesday in June 1991, four months after the initiative kicked off, Erikson called Skelton into his office. Just to make sure the effort was on track, he informed Skelton, he had asked a panel of independent experts to critique the decisions her team had made. She had until Friday to pull together her side of the story.

After subjecting the team to a day of grueling questions, the experts reported that they couldn't disagree with the direction. With that assurance, Erikson and Skelton settled into a routine of informal status reports. This often translated into a pointed question from Erikson when he ran into Skelton at the office coffeepot in the morning: "When can we see something?"

One morning in early February 1992, Skelton replied, "What does your calendar look like for Thursday?"

At 6:00 a.m. the morning of the demo, Duff, Schmidt, and a few of the Galactica folks put the finishing touches on the current Sim-Mole version—one that worked. By 10:00, the AMAD executives had congratulated the team on its accomplishments. If they noticed a few baggy eyes, they were polite enough not to mention it.

Skelton was thrilled: A working simulator gave the initiative momentum. "If word had gotten out about what we were doing," Schmidt remarks, "someone in headquarters might have objected. After all, it was no longer our primary responsibility." Skelton knew that once it was working, no one could get in the way.

Coincidentally, and even more importantly, the manager of the Mole development program called Skelton with good news. He had freed up a system that he could allocate to the Sim-Mole initiative, and it was on its way to Denver. Within a few days, the team could set its software emulation aside and begin putting the simulator through its paces on a real system. Since running against software emulation gave the team no way to verify the simulator's performance, this was a coup for the project. With a real Mole in the tester, the simulator's output could be compared with actual in-water test results to prove its validity.

Hardware Rich

Duff and the team went back to work. They had to tie the Mole hardware into the Sim-Mole processor so that the two could communicate. That step alone took several months of work. They were still "maturing" the modules to make sure they could deal with a variety of environmental conditions, geologic formations, and ore and gem targets. And the team had set its sights on developing a highly engaging user interface—like riding on the nose of the remote control drill head.

Now that they had actual in-water test data for the system in their lab, they had a new way to spot hidden glitches in the code. As a result, some of the modules that had been "finished" found their way back onto the to-be-done list. The Monday morning meetings continued, and if anything, the second year's stress levels ratcheted up another notch. Disinclined to demand a specific deadline, Skelton gave the team another target instead: Get the simulator to deliver a high-fidelity, verifiably accurate test.

Schmidt, who personally wrote much of the code in the system, remembers the software development process as "CMM level one, at best, if CMM had been in use back then."[1] The team had sketchy documentation on the Mole, what its signal processor was looking for, and what it would do with the data once it got what it wanted. To make progress on the simulation, individuals had to do the best they could to track down that information. "We were a bunch of heroes working in chaos," Schmidt summarizes.

This didn't bode well for putting the pieces of the system together into a single working unit. The practices that facilitate software integration—version control, rigorous interface definition, disciplined debugging, and unit testing—were rudimentary. Big egos and short timeframes intensified the challenge. Schmidt recalls one team member from Harvard who was fond of saying, "I write bug-free code." He would defend his work as being perfect, without even bothering to check it, until Schmidt could provide unassailable proof that the bug was in his section of the code. This environment made integrating the system particularly stressful and, according to Schmidt, quite satisfying when things worked.

Some members of the team couldn't stand the heat. For example, there was the professor. He had been extremely successful in an academic role, but he found his head spinning at the pace that Skelton and Duff set for the team. After two weeks, he returned to the ivy halls. Then there was the individual who had difficulty working with others. After railing about his peers in one of the Monday morning meetings, he found himself without an assignment. He left shortly afterward.

Not all the glitches in the system were caused by software; the hardware components also created their share of excitement. Schmidt recalls one deadline-driven all-nighter spent scouring the code for a mysterious intermittent error. Ultimately it was tracked down to a poorly seated board in one of the processor backplanes.

In another minor crisis, a line in the cooling system sprang a leak, and Freon flooded the space under the raised flooring, threatening to ruin all the wiring. "I've never seen so many brilliant people on cleanup duty at once," Skelton laughs.

Throughout the high-intensity development effort, the distributed architecture continued to hold up. When the team ran into a tough computing problem or needed more storage, it hooked up more equipment. The first working version of Sim-Mole linked more than 140 processors together.

During 1992, the team pressed to complete the Sim-Mole. Skelton never relaxed her relentless weekly drumbeat of commitments, punctuated by late-night calls to Duff when something struck her as critical. The team faced down software bugs and hardware malfunctions. Schmidt muses, "I don't remember any notion that we might fail. We all felt it was doable, even though some other very smart people had tried and failed."

In early 1993, Duff scheduled a full system test. The room was abuzz. Loud cooling fans tended the banks of Sim-Mole processors lined up against one long wall; the Mole itself sat in front with thousands of wires coming off it in all directions. Running the simulation had not yet been automated, so fifteen members of the team sat poised at their computer screens, waiting to launch their part of the process manually. When each was ready, he raised his hand. When the hardware engineer saw all hands up, he took a big plug and connected the simulator to the Mole. Displays lit up and the room went quiet, except for the sound of the Mole's signals probing for a deposit of diamonds. Ping . . . ping . . . ping. . . . It found a pattern it liked, turned its drills toward the mineral vein, and headed for the deposit. It worked!

Meanwhile, the Mole's stabilizers were reacting to the turbulence simulated by the tester. Both the drilling equipment and the pumping modules responded with thousands of microadjustments to the waves of vibration they believed they were encountering.

Duff recalls, "At that point, the interface was a big kludge, but the system worked! The room erupted with jubilation. Lee and I had been having 'success parties' all along to celebrate hitting our milestones, but none of them compared with the party we had that night."

In bringing the Sim-Mole to life, Duff faced one final hurdle. The

Mole development manager couldn't understand why running the same simulation twice would produce slightly different results. He thought: It's a computer; it should reach the same answer every time. Duff explains, "Because of the distributed architecture, the system had no 'ground zero.' You couldn't find the state of the environment in any one of the processors at any one time. It was spread all over the place." Duff finally won the day by pointing out that the simulator was exactly like in-water testing—no two in-water runs would ever be precisely alike either.

In the spring of 1993, the development program manager visited the lab. He was fresh from an unsatisfactory experience with the expensive but low-fidelity La Jolla tester. He handed Skelton a stack of computer paper and made a simple request: If your simulator can replicate these runs, we will look to AMAD for the rest of our laboratory testing. Skelton recalls, "Our final exam only took a few days. The program office was satisfied, and we were satisfied that we had made a useful tool. Of course, that was only the beginning."

A Useful Tool

In December 1993, UCE's senior executive team approved the Mole "smart" extraction system for sale. UCE's Japanese competitor had run into some snags of its own and was not able to bring its MX to market until the following spring. By that time, UCE had sold and installed several units that were paying off handsomely for clients. One client had located a new deposit of diamonds that promised to yield more than 200,000 carats a year. With this kind of success story to intrigue them, UCE's customers were lining up to see the Mole in action.

Skelton and Duff's Sim-Mole team was testing a Mole 1.0; thirteen years later, the Mole development program had reached version 8.0. The program continually advanced the system and enhanced its capabilities, and the Sim-Mole simulator kept up. It expanded to include the ability to test more than two dozen other types of "smart" equipment for UCE.

In the years since the Sim-Mole initiative began, its original distributed architecture has stood the test of time. As computer technology advanced, the lab swapped out less powerful gear and replaced it with the latest capabilities. It put the additional computing power to good use, improving the Sim-Mole to include deeper water and Arctic environments, comprehensive analytical tools, and more simultaneous test options.

On the financial side, the savings have mounted. Before Sim-Mole, an underwater mining system might undergo 100 in-water tests during development, at an average cost of about $100,000 each. The first system developed with Sim-Mole support used 500 simulator runs at $500 each and cut the number of in-water tests by 85 percent. So the cost of testing went from $10 million to under $2 million.

More importantly, the rate of product development increased substantially. UCE spent four years developing the Mole. Subsequent releases with new features and capabilities popped out annually thereafter. In addition, UCE had won kudos and new sales in the building industry with its new high-rise/high-reliability "smart" construction crane—developed in record time with Sim-Mole 3.0. Driven by its industry-leading product development, UCE's revenues and profits doubled over the next five years. The Japanese competitor never got traction in UCE's market.

Galactica went on to develop several other wildly successful products for UCE and other clients. Schmidt summarizes his experience: "I have worked on and off on the Sim-Mole over the years, but building it for the first time was the best. Doing something no one had ever done before with unproven hardware and no blueprint, well, that was something."

Duff, now CEO of Galactica Technologies, continues,

> You gain a tremendous amount of confidence managing an initiative like this one. At its conclusion, you may not know all the ways to succeed, but you know one way. Despite the fact that the system seems complex, our philosophy was to make it as simple as possible. We used the simplest solution that would do the job. And, I was responsible. I ran the team that built the system. But I didn't make it happen. It was an amazing team.

CHAPTER 7

Secret #3: Get It Right

Try this. Put all the business books in your library into two piles. The first pile is for books that tell you what to do. For example, acquiring companies in related businesses produces higher returns than acquiring unrelated companies. Or, for retailers, serving customers through a single serpentine line produces higher satisfaction than running multiple independent lines, even with an express lane. Or, on the personal front, if your Myers-Briggs profile is INTJ, look for a career in pathology.

The second pile is for books that tell you how to manage your organization, regardless of what you have decided to do. These are the process books, and they are full of advice about how to lead, how to diversify your financial holdings, how to evaluate your R&D projects, and so on.

How would those two piles compare? If your library is anything like mine, you have far more wisdom from experts about how to implement a particular decision than about what to do in the first place. For example, you can probably find twenty books on your shelf that tell you how to manage change, but how many do you see that tell you which changes you should be making?

Now, think about it. Which of these has the most impact on your ability to succeed?

I'm being a bit unfair—after all, how can some distant author know exactly what's best for you? But the point really matters. The current popularity of books about execution notwithstanding, making a good choice trumps implementing a poor choice well all day long. When it comes to being successful, wildly or otherwise, positioning yourself in the right business, in the good market, and with the hungry customers is far more important than managing that business superbly. Perhaps a hundred times more important. I'll say it again: A mediocre manager in a great market position will look like a genius compared to a top-notch manager in a lousy business. If you have the right answer to your business question, and you execute even moderately well, you will win hands down against a company that has the wrong answer, no matter how well it executes.

Let's look at the Fosbury Flop. Nobody dreamed of clearing eight feet in the high jump until Dick Fosbury turned the whole sport, well, on its ear with a radical new technique that he called the Fosbury Flop. Fosbury still recalls the debate that raged in the press over his radical approach to the bar. "There were some doctors who felt I was threatening kids' lives," he said. U.S. Olympic coach Payton Jordan added his voice to the naysayers, remarking at the time, "Kids imitate champions. If they try to imitate Fosbury, he will wipe out an entire generation of high jumpers because they will all have broken necks." The United Kingdom actually prohibited jumpers from using the Fosbury Flop for a time, presumably to protect their health.[1]

Despite these expert opinions to the contrary, floppers land on their shoulders, not their necks. Nonetheless, it took years before the flop began to dominate the sport. In 1980—twelve years after Fosbury's Olympic gold—only thirteen of the sixteen Olympic finalists were using the flop. Fosbury said:

> The problem with something revolutionary like that was that most of the elite athletes had invested so much time in their technique

and movements that they didn't want to give it up, so they stuck with what they knew. The revolution came about from the kids who saw it, and had nothing to lose. The kids who saw it on TV and said, "Gosh, that looks fun—let's do that." Grade school kids who didn't have coaches who would say, "No, you stick with the straddle."[2]

If you wanted to be an elite high jumper, what would be more valuable to you? Mastering the Fosbury flop (or the next breakthrough way to jump), or refining your straddle technique?

Champions of wildly successful initiatives relentlessly seek out the right solutions. They are congenitally dissatisfied with the conventional wisdom—especially when it strikes them as inappropriate for their situation or incomplete. They mine their networks to find partners who can provide better answers. They learn by trying, and they recognize that they don't have the right solution unless it's simple to understand and use. Finally, when they just can't discern the right answer, they start by building a platform to stand on that gives them a better view.

Upend the Given Wisdom

When Zack Duff, then thirty years old, considered taking on the Sim-Mole project, the evidence suggested that it couldn't be done. Others had tried to build such a simulator and had come up short. Some experts believed that a supercomputer would be the only way to handle the compute-intensive simulation programs, but its multimillion-dollar price tag certainly wasn't in the budget. But Duff had been "playing around," as he calls it, with parallel computing—linking small personal computers together so that they could share the computational burden of a hard problem. He was just intellectually feisty enough to believe that this approach would make a fine substitute for the unaffordable and potentially underpowered Cray.

Duff heard what the experts said. He listened to their logic and respected their experience. He just didn't believe they had it right. He gave more credence to his own capabilities and to the potential of technologies that had come along after the so-called experts had won their stripes. Skelton also took the high road. She insisted on starting with a white sheet of paper to make sure she got the best possible answers.

They were right to do so. The Sim-Mole that they built ran on hundreds of inexpensive microcomputers instead of one big honking machine. It worked. One of the reasons it worked was that Duff and his team were able to design and implement a way to divide up the computing workload among all the little machines and put the results back together effectively. Writ large, this is an innovation that rivals the development of effective assembly-line manufacturing.

Jim Schaefer similarly took an unheard-of approach to building back the volume of the Lima refinery: He sold gasoline to his competitors more cheaply than they could bring it to Ohio themselves. Regardless of the fact that BP ended up with the lion's share of the value from this approach, I'll bet you'd never find it in a strategy textbook. When BP's headquarters experts declared that Schaefer would never be able to run the factory at the volumes he sought, he was able to point out proudly that the plant *had already achieved* those volumes.

The high-school-educated operators who worked around Lima's overheated butane compressor faced off against eight years of engineering studies when they hypothesized that the cooler was just too small for the job. They did not believe that management would take the problem seriously, so they took it upon themselves to find the right solution.

Paul Monus took the same contrarian attitude. He knew that the plant would never return to its former glory if people kept doing things the same old way. He went out looking for something big that would help. His quest took him to MIT and the system dynamics crowd and to Peter Senge and organizational learning. While Monus found these ideas new and exciting, he wasn't completely satisfied. He needed something simpler and more practical—something that would work on the refinery floor, not just in a classroom. Enter Winston Ledet and the Manufacturing Game.

Although Ledet does have his Ph.D., he didn't come by his manu-facturing insights in a library; he learned them with his sleeves rolled up in the chemical plants of DuPont. As a DuPont employee, he worked with a small team of manufacturing engineers for more than three years to benchmark the maintenance practices and costs as well as the performance of seventy DuPont facilities and seventy compari-son plants from other companies. He explains,

> Maintenance is a significant part of the effort in manufacturing, especially in chemical plants. How well you maintain your plants is critical for performance, safety, and cost. During our study, Du-Pont was spending $1 billion per year on maintenance and the [corporate] profits for those years were also $1 billion, so you can see the magnitude of the impact.

By collecting three or four years worth of detailed operational data, Ledet and his DuPont colleagues gave themselves a fresh look at the facts. Over the next eighteen months, they were able to create a cause-and-effect model that linked a plant's approach to maintenance and its performance. This was not just a *theory* of maintenance; it was a new way of looking at how the process actually worked. Furthermore, it threw cold water on the accepted approaches for managing mainte-nance. It highlighted a new approach that would enable maintenance leaders to leave "best practice" managers in the dust.

Ledet explains how he and his colleagues upended the conven-tional wisdom at DuPont by starting with an open mind—Ph.D. and thirty years of experience notwithstanding—and working their way through the analysis:

> People in DuPont viewed maintenance like "the super." When something in the plant broke, you called the super and he came and fixed it. From our benchmarks, we found out there was a class of companies doing better than DuPont through an approach that we called "planned maintenance." The gist is simple: You fix

things before they break. This turns out to be much more efficient, so it reduces costs. And most organizations would understand this easily because they see their objective as cost cutting.

Planned maintenance is the most efficient way to work if you're just worried about cost cutting in maintenance as a separate budget bucket. You don't need to break down your functional silos in the plant to get the savings—you can keep the operational people separate from the maintenance people.

However, we found that the manufacturing people in Japan had a totally different concept: "total productive maintenance." Their idea was to prevent maintenance altogether by doing things in operations that avoid putting wear on the equipment in the first place. Of course, this requires that the operations people and the maintenance people work together. Well, this concept was hard for our manufacturing people to understand. They grew up believing that if you run the machine, it wears out and breaks.

We worked with the system dynamics people at MIT[3] to find the fundamental structure underneath the system. This kind of mathematical model shows what's really causing what and how you can intervene to improve the results. So we did a system dynamics model of maintenance. What did it show? That using a total productive maintenance approach would reduce manufacturing costs by a shocking amount. At DuPont, our model predicted that we'd save $2.5 billion over five years. I knew no one could swallow that, so I cut it down to a number they would believe.

In Ledet's world, the difference between getting it right and not getting it right was half a billion dollars a year at the bottom line. That's billion with a *b*. In other words, he found a way to increase the company's profits by 50 percent a year.

But Ledet and his team weren't finished. They had one more giant step to take before their stunning discovery would be useful to DuPont and eventually to Paul Monus. They had to find a way to get it into the heads and hearts of the people with their hands on the controls—the factory workers.

Make It Simple

The business landscape is littered with tools and approaches that are dead right. They may be analytically valuable, but they are so complicated and difficult to use that no one uses them. It doesn't matter how much benefit they *would* provide if they were adopted. What matters is how much benefit they *do* provide—almost none.

Getting to the right solution means that we have to come up with a good, new answer to a hard problem. But it also means that we have to make that answer simple to understand, simple to try, and simple to use. Why? Because if people can take the solution on board and make it their own, they may actually receive the benefits that it promises.

Making complex ideas simple isn't, well, simple. For example, the vice president of exhibits at Boston's Museum of Science, a highly regarded scientist by background, said that he had to unlearn everything he learned at MIT in order to discover how to lure casual museum visitors into the world of science. It doesn't work, he says, to tell people about the scientific method or to give them the mathematical equations that prove a theory. He has to create provocative and interesting experiences that lead people naturally to observe, to make guesses about what will happen next, and then to test those hypotheses. By the way, it all has to be fun.

Ledet and his team learned this lesson on the factory floor. Despite the fact that they were poised to bring their colleagues at DuPont $2.5 billion, their total productive maintenance program was met with everything from blank stares to active resistance. Ledet explains:

> We'd show the model results and even run the model live, but people would not understand the complexity. We wrote several articles to explain the concepts, but it still didn't work. People had

paradigms about how maintenance worked, and these paradigms kept them from seeing what we were saying.

We recognized that we had developed the new approach by creating the model ourselves, not by looking at something prefabricated. We had struggled through the process of creating our own mental model in order to "get it." That mental model is what enabled us to make the computer model in the end. We concluded that we had to let other people go through the same struggle to understand what was going on. We had to create an experience that would allow them to see the maintenance dynamic firsthand and create their own mental models. So we made a game.

When Paul Monus met Winston Ledet, he found both the yin and the yang of getting it right: a complex, fact-based analytical model underpinning a radical new approach to manufacturing maintenance, and a game that even the most inexperienced operator could play for one day to grasp that approach and begin to apply it.

The two-part harmony of powerful insights and simple interfaces shows up again and again in working wonders.

Finding Solutions

What if the right answer eludes us? As we know, it all seems so clear in retrospect, but at the time we have to make a decision, it is often daunting. This is especially true when we have big aspirations. Furthermore, the pressure to stop searching and just do something can be intense. Champions use a variety of approaches to get it right. They learn by trying; they engage colleagues, partners, and customers; and when the answers are not particularly pleasant, they face the truth.

Learn by Trying

Champions of wildly successful initiatives don't let the vision get in their way. Doesn't that sound odd? The management textbooks tell us that the vision inspires and motivates us. That's true. But if a conventional, well-planned approach is the only way we know how to move forward, a far-reaching vision can stop us in our tracks. How would we start? Where would we get the resources? Who could support such a massive undertaking?

Our heroes don't waste much time on these questions. Instead, they concentrate on taking a good next step. Stansylvania's Walter Matthews illustrates this point admirably. When he tried to convince his colleagues at the Revenue Agency that they should move the organization toward a taxpayer-centric paradigm, he got nowhere. They ignored him for years. How did he finally get the ball rolling? He launched the data study—a homely little project that didn't threaten anyone.

Carol Pletcher, former chief innovation officer at Cargill, cleverly launched a contest in an effort to help the company improve its level of innovation. Companies often have contests where employees submit their good ideas; this was totally different. Pletcher asked, instead, for employees to tell her about the innovations that they had *already* implemented. That way she could find out about the results too.

Of course, she and her team invited the folks with the most far-reaching innovations to an awards ceremony at which they had the opportunity to meet the company's CEO. Pletcher stresses, "Recognition of this sort delivers a critical message: *We* did this." In addition, Pletcher's group created an inventory of company innovation experiences from the submissions—now rated in terms of the results achieved. That solid starting point enabled the group to go back to the award applicants and find out exactly what factors distinguished between teams that were more innovative and those that were less so.

Pletcher's good next step accomplished exactly what she had hoped. Her group gathered plenty of evidence that innovation was already afoot, and it used this to give everyone in the company a sense of the possible. The team also learned what management levers mattered most for enabling breakthroughs.

Engage Colleagues

Ideas about the right answer are cheap. Everyone has them, and some are powerfully important. The trouble is, it's uncommonly difficult to separate the brilliant answers from the cockamamie ones.

Many companies invite all their employees to throw their ideas on the pile and then ask the smartest guys in the room to decide which ones to keep. However, the track record of this approach is abysmal. Even after extensive testing, most new consumer products fail in the market. The business landscape boasts many start-ups that are thriving with concepts that big companies decided to pass on. And the same executives who reject 90-some percent of the ideas their employees have offered—in order to select the best, of course—wonder why the new idea flow looks more like a trickle than a torrent.[4]

Jim Lavoie and Joe Marino, the founders of a Rhode Island software development company aptly named Rite-Solutions, recognized how dysfunctional this process was. Since their business depends on innovation every day, they set about coming up with a better one. The result? Mutual Fun.

If an employee wants to suggest a new product or a way to improve productivity, he writes up a brief description called an "expect-us" and then IPOs the idea on the company's internal stock market. If other employees find the idea appealing, they can help it along by pitching in with a little of their own effort—which also makes a share of the stock rise in value. Further, each employee gets to allocate $10,000 of her own faux capital among the ideas she believes have the most value—which taps the collective company perspective to push the most popular ideas higher on the market. Lavoie comments, "Having the same amount of capital as everyone else also makes people feel important and valued by the organization."

Lavoie explains how Mutual Fun differs from the usual corporate approach:

> Most companies have a funnel. The employees pour ideas in at one end, and executives apply a filter at the other to trap the small number of ideas they like. I used to be the big shot with the wallet, but I wasn't hanging around the water cooler where the employees were talking about what a dumb idea our new product was. With Mutual Fun, the senior people don't have to be omniscient. The

game removes all the hurdles associated with suggesting an idea. You don't have to prepare a business plan or calculate an ROI. Instead, people follow their interests, and informal networks naturally form around the good ideas without any management intervention. If your idea isn't receiving "adventure" capital, it's not because it was shot down by the boss. Your colleagues pay attention to the better ideas, and yours may still need work.

Even more importantly, ideas stay live on the company's real-time stock ticker until they are implemented. This keeps the informal network actively engaged until the idea turns into value for the organization. By the way, Lavoie and Marino share that value with the employees who backed the stock on its way up. Employees who contribute ideas and sweat equity through Mutual Fun receive a portion of the profits from the innovations they come up with.

Consider Rebecca Hosch, an administrative aide at Rite-Solutions and the mother of two. Although her role in the company was nontechnical, Rebecca had a good appreciation for the sophisticated pattern-recognition algorithms her colleagues produced to help the U.S. Navy spot enemy missiles. She thought these would make the basis for an engaging educational game for children. Hosch prepared an IPO for "Win/Play/Learn," a game that uses pictures and words to offer a stimulating framework for learning anything from farm animals to fractals, under the ticker WPL. WPL immediately captured the attention of other Rite-Solutions employees. Lavoie recalls, "We would have never connected those dots. But one employee floated an idea, lots of employees got passionate about it and that led to a new line of business."[5] Rite-Solutions spent $20,000 to develop the game, which landed it a $1 million contract with Hasbro.

Lavoie continues, "Most companies shy away from half-baked ideas. The stock market allows ideas to bake, using the collective genius of the employees. The ideas get better and better until they can hold their own in the normal priority-setting process." Tim O'Reilly, an open-source maven and the chief executive of O'Reilly Media, a computer book publisher, argues that the companies that set the pace in the future won't be the ones that snag the odd guru, but those that create the most effective "architecture of participation."[6] For Rite-Solutions, Mutual Fun is just that—a way to involve every employee in helping the company innovate and grow daily.

Seek Out Partners Who Have What You Need

How many of you would agree that no one organization has all the right answers, even with a compelling architecture of participation? Is it unanimous? One hundred percent of the wildly successful initiatives in my study involved a partnership somewhere along the line. Every single one of them.

UCE found Zack Duff and the team from Galactica. Paul Monus brought Winston Ledet and his Manufacturing Game to Lima. Unigamble would never have broken the code on manufacturing reliability without the scientists at Los Alamos National Labs. David Rose partnered with a pager company to bring his Ambient Orb to life. The Stansylvanian Revenue Agency partnered with DeYoung again and again over fifteen years.

Champions of wildly successful initiatives find ways to overcome the pernicious not-invented-here (NIH) syndrome. In its most obvious form, NIH keeps us pounding away in our cubicles on a hard problem instead of lifting up our heads and asking if anyone else has ever seen this issue before. NIH infests organizations in more subtle ways as well. It can also rear its devastating head as "only people like me are worth listening to" (OPLMAWLT). This unpronounceable variety of the disease keeps biologists from working with physicists, medical technologists from collaborating with clinicians, and engineers from consorting with social workers.

How do our heroes overcome NIH? They engage eagerly and honestly as colleagues. Let's call it the "Rudolph the Red-Nosed Reindeer" attitude. Most people think the main message in that song is how Rudolph saved the day. I beg to differ. I am completely charmed by the behavior of Rudolph's teammates. As you'll remember, they callously make fun of Rudolph because of his odd snout. That wasn't very charming. But when the red nose turned out to be critical for success, these same teammates dropped their attitude and pushed Rudolph to the head of the team. Does this happen in your organization?

The CEO of BioCo, a small biotechnology company, explains how he found Rudolph's teammates in a large, conservative pharmaceutical firm we'll call DrugCo.[7] In his description, the surprise he expresses at how his organization was treated reveals a great deal about this successful partnership and about his previous, not-so-sanguine attempts.

My company had developed a molecule that the pharmaceutical industry found extremely interesting. Several of the big players had approached us to talk about potential partnerships, and these relationships all started the same way: with a classic dog and pony show. On this particular day, we were going to tell [DrugCo] what we had and what we were thinking, and it was going to tell us why it would be a good partner.

At the very outset, the people from DrugCo said they wanted to understand what we were looking for. Then they actually tried to find out. They didn't come in with a preset idea of how this partnership was going to work; they convinced me they were actually trying to understand us.

In the next meeting, they came back and said: "Here's what we heard. Here's how our two companies might marry up." They clearly understood what we were trying to do. That was a great beginning.

They communicated expertly. They might say that they understood, but that they didn't necessarily agree. They didn't get themselves into the position of leading us on. They told us how they might want to structure the deal differently, but it felt very open. Through the course of the discussions, which got increasingly detailed, we were not getting huge surprises. Things were not shifting.

What really made this successful was that it wasn't a show. They actually meant what they said. They were really committed from the top of the organization to being a partner.

This partnership was especially difficult to structure because it violated the conventional wisdom about protecting a company's own intellectual property and market potential. In exchange for rights to its intellectual property, BioCo was asking DrugCo to teach it how to be a fully functional pharmaceutical company, not just an R&D boutique. In effect, DrugCo would be creating its own competition. But DrugCo realized that this kind of partnering would become ever more important to its own success, so it agreed and made a focused effort to make its new partner as effective as possible.

The result of this particular joint venture? Global sales of the drug they co-market have exceeded $2.2 billion over four years.

Surprisingly, not a few of the wildly successful initiatives involve a particular type of partnering: outsourcing. In some circles, outsourcing has a bad reputation. Politicians claim that it destroys the economy—well, the local economy. Individuals experience painful job loss. And no one appreciates a cheap, but poorly managed service experience, no matter where the agent happens to be sitting.

However, some executives have used outsourcing to drive radical strategic change in their organizations. In capable hands, outsourcing turns out to be a very effective tool. My study of seventeen examples of this sort showed that 82 percent achieved the strategic benefits they were after—almost always in record time. Even more telling, the companies that did not have this result failed for an unusual reason. Working with their outsourcing partners, they executed the strategy that they had laid out. In these cases, however, it turned out to be the wrong strategy. As a result, they didn't get the benefits they anticipated. In other words, they didn't get it right.[8]

The executives who used outsourcing in a wildly successful way shared an approach that violates outsourcing's conventional wisdom. Ordinary outsourcing initiatives usually begin by putting a company's core and noncore activities into their respective buckets. "Best practice" advises a company to consider outsourcing noncore functions, but *never* to allow a partner to take on core activities.

Executives who were wildly successful at outsourcing adopted a much simpler point of view. They considered what they had to accomplish to reach their strategic goals, evaluated what they could do themselves, then looked to partners to fill the gaps. They went looking for partners to provide whatever they needed that they didn't already have.

National Savings & Investments, an arm of the U.K. government that operates as a retail savings bank, outsourced all but 120 of its 4,500 people, including functions like information technology management, product development, and customer support.[9] A large high-technology equipment manufacturer outsourced its professional sales force when it wanted to make a strategic shift from selling boxes to selling solutions.

These aren't isolated examples. Instead of agonizing over a discussion of core capabilities, these companies went out and got what they would need if they were to succeed. They found good partners and treated them as such. As a result, they moved their own strategic mountains with a success rate that would make most capable managers drool.

Get Real Customers in the Game

Customers can't always tell whether the big ideas are right or wrong. I don't know of a single wildly successful initiative that crafted its goal from customer feedback. Jim Schaefer didn't ask the refinery's customers whether they wanted better prices; Frank, the banker we met in Chapter 5, didn't wait for the bank's customers to request a more strategic relationship.

Where customers can help is with a good next step. They vote with their feet; that's how we know we're moving in the right direction. The customers who served as guinea pigs for Frank's first strategic credit class gave the experience resounding applause. Some of them bought what the trainees were selling; others just invited a more intimate relationship. But senior bank executives could almost hear the éclat from their corner offices. That made their decision easy. The first training session had been optional, cobbled together among friends and colleagues. After that, it became mandatory for every junior credit officer.

Boots the Chemist, a U.K. cosmetics and drug retailer, found that its customers went even further to push an initiative that resonated with them. Boots had been eyeing a new market segment: ordinary, middle-aged citizens who wanted "get-healthy" products to repair the damage caused by holiday partying. Under the banner *DeTox,* Boots launched ten products that would "help protect from the dangers of free radicals, by-products of pollution and smoke [and] . . . refresh your detoxifying organs to leave you feeling revitalised and re-energized." Within a few weeks, Boots's manufacturing couldn't keep up with the demand.

Citing a need to understand the "well-being" market more closely, Boots's marketing management decided to open a fitness club. Instead of aiming for the Lycra and testosterone brigade, this club was positioned to appeal to professional middle-aged people who knew they should be getting more exercise but didn't have the discipline. At the time, no one else was offering fitness for the noncommitted.

The club was intended only as an experiment, but it was overwhelmed with membership. In an unexpected twist, it helped Boots make its new DeTox product line even more successful. A marketing executive explains:

> The club gave me 7,000 people who pay to join and who've pre-screened themselves to be my permanent focus group. We took them the healthy living program and asked them to help us pick the products to put on the shelves. In other words, we're asking the consumer directly to help select the merchandise we offer. We even get them to write the advertising copy. It's amazing how fascinated the consumer is by all this.

Boots executives chalk up the fitness club's unprecedented appeal to happy accident. But who opened the club as an experiment in the first place? Who took the DeTox products over to the club to see how the members responded? These executives had a good idea at the start, but they learned how to get it absolutely right by trying.

One unmistakable measure of their success? A new pub has opened up near Boots's corporate headquarters. Its name: Re-Tox.

Face the Truth

In the end, even right answers wrapped in simple interfaces can be hard to accept. In some cases, the hard work of engaging all the stakeholders will carry the day. William Althouse made it his business to tour all the touch points of the Stansylvania Revenue Agency to understand their information systems requirements. The managers in all those offices resoundingly agreed that it would be impossible to develop a single processing system for all types of tax. By diligently gathering all the requirements into a unified design, Althouse was able to debunk that belief.

In other situations, however, the obstacle to getting it right is not an interfering mindset or a poor grasp of the possibilities, but a big personal price to pay. Ian Whyte, the engineering manager at the Kinleith paper mill, confronted this issue and courageously faced the difficult truth.[10]

The Kinleith mill had been producing paper and pulp for one or another global forest products company for more than fifty years. In the early twenty-first century, however, as new mills in low-wage-rate countries with large tracts of forest came on line, price pressure intensified and margins shrank. Kinleith began to struggle to cover its cost of capital, let alone look like a good investment to its parent company. Its decades-long history of adversarial relations with its unions did not help matters.

Managers in the mill saw union members as inflexible, entitled, and even greedy. One manager explained that in a previous effort to improve productivity, "We reduced headcount. We believed that if we created a vacuum, the remaining people would move to fill it. That theory turned out to be wrong. The workers stayed where they were and created holes which we had to fill by recruiting. I found it quite soul-destroying."

The unionized workers saw things a little differently. They had watched a series of "revolving door" managers make decisions about how to run the mill that seemed shortsighted at best. They claimed that they did not take the initiative to improve the mill's performance because management cut them off from the authority to do so. That left them only one way to improve their lot—union solidarity. And the most senior and most skilled workers in the mill—the maintenance staff—stood squarely in this camp.

Historically, management had responded to union demands by "capitulating and adding something to the price of the product," according to one executive. However, continuing with this approach no longer seemed so smart.

In an October 2001 annual planning retreat, the mill's senior managers concluded that the future would be grim indeed if they didn't find a way to shatter the status quo. They agreed to do a zero-based analysis of the number of workers it would take to run the mill—assuming no change in the physical assets and no holds barred in resetting the staffing levels. As manager of engineering, Whyte had the responsibility for filling in the white sheet of paper for the right-sized maintenance organization. At the same time, ABB, an outsourcing services company, was asked how it would staff the operation if it were fully in charge of maintenance.

The senior managers got back together in early 2002 to compare their in-house analysis with the proposal from ABB. Whyte recalls, "Both analyses were remarkably similar. I could have taken exception to a detail or two in their work, but we both reached essentially the same conclusion: The mill could run more efficiently with about half the maintenance staff we had."

As often happens in these meetings, one executive voiced the frightening question that was on everyone's minds: "Should we right-size the maintenance staff ourselves or outsource to ABB to get it done?" Despite the fact that it was Whyte's organization that was on the block to be outsourced, he spoke up first. "ABB!" he said. He went on to explain, "Internally, we had a demonstrated track record of failing to implement our initiatives. . . . What we really needed was a change of culture, and ABB presented evidence that they could get it done."

The rest of the leadership team fell in behind Whyte on the decision to outsource maintenance to ABB. This wasn't the only challenge that Kinleith executives faced as they raised the mill's performance to world-class levels. But Whyte's personal courage in this situation reminds us that it may sometimes be difficult to recognize and accept the right answer when we come face to face with it. In this case, it meant that Whyte's job would be moved over to ABB. If he wanted to stay at Kinleith, he would have to find a new role. In all likelihood, he would no longer be supervising a staff of more than 300 people. Whyte says simply, "It was difficult for me to criticize my own department and my own performance, but it was still the truthful answer."

If You Still Can't See the Right Answer, Build a Platform to Stand On

You've questioned the conventional wisdom and engaged employees, business partners, and customers, but you still feel that the right answer is eluding you. What do champions of wildly successful initiatives do in this situation? They lay the foundation of the tower they aspire to build, then stand on it to get a better view.

For example, when Dr. Hsinchun Chen, head of the Artificial Intelligence (AI) Laboratory at the University of Arizona, began working with the Tucson police force, he envisioned using his lab's considerable AI expertise to help the cops nab the crooks. (We'll find out more about the software they developed in Chapter 10.) He pictured a project in which Ph.D. candidates would apply powerful computer logic to fragmented bits of information to discover the hidden patterns. But he had no idea just how fragmented the police department's data really were.

After coming face to face with Tucson's data—a cornucopia of separate files using every conceivable technology and format, including the gang database, motor vehicle records, fingerprint files, the sexual offenders registry, and so on—he decided that his team had better go back to square one. The team spent the first two years' worth of their grant money building a data warehouse, the only purpose of which was to corral the bits of data into a framework that would make them accessible.

No one would mistake this for academic-caliber work, and Dr. Chen had to endure pointed questions from his colleagues, his graduate students, the grant supervisor, and even his wife about why he was wasting his time on such pedestrian activity. He never skipped a beat, though. He was confident that organizing the data would make everything clearer. When Chen and his students completed the unglamorous data warehouse, they readily saw opportunities for AI contributions that the information mess had previously obscured.

If You Remember One Thing

Execution matters, but what you decide to execute matters ten times more. Wildly successful initiatives get it right. They find solutions that work, products that sell, and strategies that win.

CHAPTER 8

AIRNow

EPA Mavericks Show That Good Air Quality Has Grass Roots

The amazing thing about this project is that participation is completely volun-tary, and yet all fifty U.S. states and all ten Canadian provinces have embraced it. I haven't heard of many government programs that are voluntary *and* suc-cessful. It is a testament to Chet Wayland's quiet but effective leadership.

—Phil Dickerson, EPA environmental engineer

In August 2006, Chet Wayland, associate director of the U.S. Environ-mental Protection Agency's Office of Outreach and Information, flopped in his favorite easy chair and took a deep breath. He had just finished another briefing on the latest efforts by his staff to help Chi-nese government officials understand the EPA's unusual air quality initiative dubbed AIRNow. This had been one of many briefings by his staff in the past two years, as the team had traveled to China, Brazil, and Europe to promote the real-time data delivery program. Despite the challenges, his optimism remained intact.

"We've come a long, long way, since Phil Dickerson and I created AIRNow in 1998," Wayland reflected. The initiative had grown to provide the public across all the U.S. states and Canadian provinces with up-to-the-minute air quality data and one- to three-day forecasts. Although participation in the program was voluntary, air quality engineers across U.S. state and county governments, national parks, and Canadian provinces pooled their data every hour to produce color-coded maps (see Figure 8–1). People with asthma or heart problems, those who cared for young children, or those with regular exercise regimens could tell at a glance when to shift their activities indoors. They could also tune into The Weather Channel, check on the Internet, or pick up a copy of *USA Today* to find out whether they would breathe easy tomorrow.

Most recently, Wayland and Dickerson had been working through the EPA's office of international affairs to help other governments launch their own programs. Their team had traveled to China, Brazil, and Denmark and had met with air quality professionals from South

Figure 8-1. Ozone Eight-Hour Peak Air Quality Index for July 17, 2006

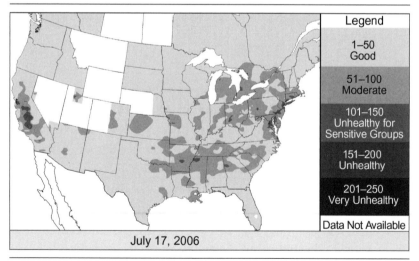

July 17, 2006

Legend

1–50	Good
51–100	Moderate
101–150	Unhealthy for Sensitive Groups
151–200	Unhealthy
201–250	Very Unhealthy
Data Not Available	

Source: www.airnow.gov.

Korea, Mexico, and the Netherlands to share their experiences, their learnings, their technology, their approach, and, in some cases, their help in getting funds.

From the beginning, Wayland and Dickerson had orchestrated the AIRNow initiative as a grassroots program, relying on voluntary participation and building its international scope one air quality region at a time. Eight years later, Wayland grins,

> I'm happy to report that we still haven't had to fit into the confines of "Project Management 101." Our initial goal was to get the fifty U.S. states on board with hourly ozone mapping, and we had no plan except to build from what we had. That bottom-up approach has allowed us to grow organically. Today all fifty states report fine particulate matter ($PM_{2.5}$) as well as ozone, and we're expanding into other pollutants and taking the program global [see Figure 8–2]. We just started AIRNow by making contacts and reassuring them: We're in this together. If we had planned it all out carefully, I'm convinced we never would have done any of it.

Figure 8-2. Particulate Matter ($PM_{2.5}$) Daily Twenty-Four-Hour Air Quality Index (Midnight to Midnight)

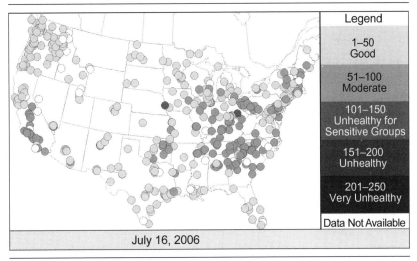

Legend

1–50
Good

51–100
Moderate

101–150
Unhealthy for
Sensitive Groups

151–200
Unhealthy

201–250
Very Unhealthy

Data Not Available

July 16, 2006

Source: www.airnow.gov.

Regulating Air Quality[1]

In 1971, President Nixon signed the first legislation designed to reduce air pollution—the Clean Air Act. It established National Ambient Air Quality Standards designed to protect public health and prevent damage to animals, crops, vegetation, and buildings.

Among other things, the Clean Air Act requires the U.S. EPA to monitor states' compliance with the National Ambient Air Quality Standards, the national targets for acceptable concentrations of six pollutants: ground-level ozone, particle pollution (also known as particulate matter), carbon monoxide, sulfur dioxide, nitrogen dioxide, and lead. Since the early 1970s, the EPA has tracked air concentrations of these substances based on hourly measurements of the ambient air at monitoring sites throughout the country. Two pollutants, ground-level ozone and airborne particles, pose the greatest threat to human health in the United States.

The EPA requires states to report ozone levels quarterly. These data are carefully collected, stored in the EPA data center, and used mainly to evaluate whether states are in compliance with federally mandated air quality standards. Phil Dickerson, an EPA environmental engineer, notes that when the data were processed and stored in a mainframe environment, "It was difficult for the public to get hold of the data in those days—they had to do a Freedom of Information Act (FOIA) request. And the data that we sent to them were hard to interpret." As a result, all but the most diligent citizens remained uninformed about ozone in their cities and neighborhoods, even when it reached potentially hazardous levels.

AIRNow Takes Shape

In 1994, progressive EPA environmental engineers in Maryland began a pilot program to map their state's ozone information. Hindered by poor computer capabilities and access to only one state's information, these early maps were limited and received little exposure. The pilot fizzled, but the idea survived.

Encouraged by growing interest in the Internet, the EPA's Region I, Boston, office picked up the baton in 1996. Managers there reasoned that they could pull data from multiple states and make them available to the public on a Web site. Dave Conroy, a manager in the Boston EPA air quality planning group, recalled,

> At the time, some states had toll-free numbers and sent some information to newspapers, but we felt we were not really getting the message about pollution levels out to the public. We pooled our money with Maryland through an association called NESCAUM [New England States for Coordinated Air Use Management]. NESCAUM let a contract to have the hourly ozone data from thirteen New England and Middle Atlantic states plus Washington, D.C., compiled into an animated map and posted on our Web site.

Lee Alter, the project manager for NESCAUM, who had been involved from the project's early days, continued,

> We had collected the data for twenty years, but no one ever looked at them. There was no easy way to share them; New York had to fax New Jersey to get its data. The regional EPA leadership backed the mapping project in order to build awareness about ozone, help people understand, for example, why vehicle inspections are important, and improve public health.

By May 1997, the software was up and running. Conroy summarized, "We achieved our objectives: We made the information available so that interested people could seek it out."

That first summer, EPA Region I posted ozone maps and forecasts three times a day on the Web, using information that the states contributed voluntarily. By the end of the 1997 ozone season, however, it was struggling to overcome the contentious organizational politics and technology hurdles that it faced in its bid to extend its reach to additional states. Despite its initial success, one participant reckoned that the team did not have the resources to continue to support the process through the next year.

EMPACT

Helping hands reached out from an unexpected source. As yet unaware of the Boston project, Chet Wayland and Phil Dickerson in the EPA's central planning organization were looking for a way to accomplish the same goal, but at a national level.

Wayland had just stepped into a new role as manager of the Information Transfer Group in the Office of Air Quality Planning and Standards, and he recalls, "I wanted to do a good job—something that would make a difference." Wayland's boss suggested that he take a look at a new Clinton administration initiative called EMPACT (Environmental Monitoring for Public Access and Community Tracking).

EMPACT had begun as a campaign promise, Dickerson explained, "When Clinton stopped in Kalamazoo in his reelection campaign, he promised people easier access to environmental data. Early in his second administration, he created the EMPACT initiative." EMPACT funded project proposals to bring people up-to-date, understandable information about local environmental conditions.

Wayland and Dickerson teamed up to develop a grant proposal. Their idea was simple: They wanted to bring timely air quality data to the public in a format that people could understand. Despite intense competition for the grant money, Wayland and Dickerson's application received a glowing response and was quickly approved. Wayland recalls,

> Phil knew Internet technology; he knew he could move data quickly. I knew that the information would be useful and people would want it. I am not sure we believed we could actually do what we said, but when the grant was approved, we knew we had to produce something. We figured, "Let's try it and see."

Wayland's direct supervisor gave him breathing room, saying, "I trust that you will do the right thing. Go ahead and take this as far as you can; I won't get in your way. As long as you keep getting external funding, I won't bother you. When you need my money, then we'll have to talk."

In the fall of 1997, Wayland and Dickerson looked around the country and discovered that EPA Region 1 had technology that allowed it to produce ozone maps. They went to Boston to meet with the regional air quality engineers and get their help on the initiative, which they had dubbed AIRNow.

"We were from headquarters," Wayland remembers, "but we weren't showing up empty-handed. We had the grant money, and we thought we would use it to help the regions build their monitoring infrastructure as an incentive for sharing their data." Dickerson went on,

Everything clicked. Region 1 was starting to groan under the weight of what it was doing, and it was running out of resources. We offered to take the project, bring it to headquarters, and try to expand it. Between that October and the following May, during the ozone off-season, we moved everything and tried to get it running with EPA headquarters in charge of it.

To satisfy the EMPACT objectives, Wayland and Dickerson needed hourly ozone data from the states. While the states already had monitors in place to comply with regulatory requirements that they submit data to EPA's Air Quality System (AQS), their infrastructures were not designed for consistent, high-quality, hourly data transmission. Dickerson continued, "The official AQS data go through an extensive quality assurance process before they are submitted to the regulators. Technically, the AIRNow and AQS data shouldn't be that different, but if a monitor is malfunctioning, AQS allows for correction." In contrast, the AIRNow data would go directly from the monitors to the mapping system at least once per hour.

"In the early days of the program," noted Ron Stockett, air quality monitor for the Missouri Department of Natural Resources, "some were concerned about sending in unchecked data." He continued,

> In our region, we insisted that they allow us to use two instruments at each site, just for quality control. If both instruments have the same data, then the numbers should be right. If one says 20 and the other says 80, you know something is wrong. That's our major method of quality control.

The states' concerns were also eased by the fact that both ozone levels and forecasts would be shown on maps as color bars rather than precise numbers. Wayland insisted from the beginning that the states agree on a standard ozone color key so that, for example, a "red alert" ozone day would have the same meaning across the country (see Figure 8-3).

Figure 8-3. Standard Ozone Air Quality Color Indicators

Air Quality Index Levels of Health Concern	Numerical Value	Meaning
Good	0–50	Air quality is considered satisfactory, and air pollution poses little or no risk.
Moderate	51–100	Air quality is acceptable; however, for some pollutants there may be a moderate health concern for a very small number of people who are unusually sensitive to air pollution.
Unhealthy for sensitive groups	101–150	Members of sensitive groups may experience health effects. The general public is not likely to be affected.
Unhealthy	151–200	Everyone may begin to experience health effects; members of sensitive groups may experience more serious health effects.
Very unhealthy	201–300	Health alert: everyone may experience more serious health effects.
Hazardous	> 300	Health warnings of emergency conditions. The entire population is more likely to be affected.

Source: www.epa.gov/airnow/.

Wayland and Dickerson used their EMPACT grant to offer seed money to states that wanted to join the initiative. This enabled the states to purchase the new hardware and software they needed to upgrade their data collection infrastructure. Some states needed additional monitors or data loggers to improve data quality. Others required faster modems to keep up with the hourly transmission deadlines. According to Stockett, "The EPA funding was critical to the success of this project. The states were willing to provide horsepower, but they didn't have the budget to provide hardware and software."

In addition, Wayland got his own chain of command to certify that the AIRNow data would never be used to evaluate a state's compliance with ozone regulations.

With Region 1's New England states already on board, Wayland and Dickerson tried to entice some of the other regions to join the collaboration. They quickly expanded AIRNow's reach down to South Carolina and into the Midwest. As the twentieth state eagerly signed on, Wayland and Dickerson's confidence grew. "We began to believe we actually could create a real-time national ozone map," Wayland chuckled.

Picking Up Steam

In September 1998, at the close of the ozone season, Wayland and Dickerson decided to move AIRNow's central data collection activity to the EPA's national data center in Research Triangle Park, North Carolina. They asked the EPA's IT outsourcing provider to supply post-processing, infrastructure, and an Internet Web site. They worked through the government's meticulous procedures for implementing a new application and went live in April 1999—just in time for the start of the 1999 season.

Dickerson recalls, "This was groundbreaking for the people in the computer center. They had never supported a public-access Web application or had the requirement to collect and process data hourly. It was all brand new to them. And in the middle of the transition, key technology people in Boston were moving on. We had to scramble."

With central processing stabilizing, the AIRNow program directors were able to increase the frequency of ozone maps to seven times a day. They also brought additional states on board. People like Mike Koerber, executive director of the Lake Michigan Air Directors' Consortium, were invited to meetings that Wayland convened to discuss how to expand the program. Koerber remembered:

> Each state had its own computer systems and databases, and we never had any luck trying to transfer mapping technology from one state to another. But all of our states were thinking about ozone action programs and how to make the data available. With AIRNow, the EPA was offering to provide a consistent system and make it as easy as possible to tie in. It was obvious to everyone that this was a good thing.

Lewis Weinstock, from Forsyth County, North Carolina, continued, "Being a small agency, we like innovation. When Chet called and asked us to participate in the forecasting program, he didn't have to twist my arm. North Carolina is one of the top ten states for air quality problems, so everyone realized this was a smart thing to do."

In an effort to expand the program, Wayland launched an annual AIRNow conference for all the initiative's participants and prospects. One environmental engineer recalled, "Chet would start by saying it was our program. He would have speakers talk about what they had accomplished, and then he would get up and ask us what we needed to take our programs to the next step."

Under Wayland's supportive leadership, more states and cities volunteered to participate. Sacramento, Los Angeles, San Diego, San Francisco, and the central California valley had been working with Sonoma Technology, a local contractor, for several years to map their own region. Wayland signed Sonoma up as the West Coast mapping center. Subsequently, Washington State, Arizona, and Texas joined the initiative. By early 2000, thirty-five states and a hundred cities were transmitting hourly ozone levels to the EPA.

As the AIRNow program expanded, it hit some technology bumps. For example, an early 2000 GAO audit of the EPA's security found serious issues. It threatened to shut down the EPA's connection to the Internet unless the agency implemented a strict firewall. On February 17, 2000, the firewall went up, and AIRNow went down. Dickerson recalls, "We came back from a conference and found that we were no longer connected to the Internet. There was no warning or lead time. It was a complete blow."

Over the next eight weeks, the AIRNow team reconfigured the data collection process so that states could drop off their ozone information to mirrored servers outside the firewall. The files would be picked up, encrypted, and brought inside the firewall. The team was less than thrilled with the fifteen-minute processing delay this introduced into their hourly cycle, but AIRNow was back in operation before the 2000 ozone season opened.

AIRNow Airs

As luck would have it, *USA Today* was redesigning its weather page in the spring of 2000. Lynne Perri, deputy managing editor, went looking for something that would make her paper distinctive. She explained,

> We needed something that our readers couldn't get either from TV or from a big city newspaper. We started talking to people, and the folks at the American Lung Association led us to Chet. There were some issues to iron out, but in the end, we decided to see if we could pull off daily air quality forecasting.

AIRNow's data did not match Perri's needs exactly. She wanted daily information for thirty-six key cities in the United States. AIRNow carried information on more than a hundred cities, but some of those on Perri's list, like Nashville and New Orleans, were missing. For those cities, Perri's paper ran "N/A" while the AIRNow team tried to pull the relevant environmental monitoring organizations into the community.

Wayland also opened up conversations with CNN and The Weather Channel.

To address lingering technology glitches, Wayland hired a new program manager, John White. When White arrived, he found FORTRAN programs, flat text files, and no data archives. Because of the increased media exposure and the need for overall data management, the team decided to upgrade AIRNow to an Oracle database system to increase reliability and to improve the team's ability to produce new products with the data. Despite the EPA's bias toward keeping systems work in-house, the team decided to work with an outside contractor. White enumerated the reasons:

> First, the contractors who run the in-house systems understand computers, but not weather or air quality. We wanted more scientific people who could help us actually understand the data and propose new ways to present the information. Second, an outside contractor turned out to be cheaper. Third, we could speed up our data turnaround process if we got outside the EPA firewall.

Sonoma Technology won the contract to develop the new MapCon software in early 2001, and when it delivered at the end of the year, it earned a three-year contract to run the system. Tim Dye, vice president of meteorological programs and public outreach for Sonoma, summarized:

> We bring two critical things to AIRNow. We are meteorologists, not computer technicians. So we know right away when the data do not look right. Second, we recognize the importance of reliability when we're feeding data to media outlets like The Weather Channel. We have an Oracle database running on redundant servers and hard drives. We have automated as much of the processing as possible to provide speedier, reliable service.

Dye asserted that strong communication and good coordination were the crux of the program. He continued:

AIRNow doesn't exist without the stakeholders. They are key to its survival. The program needs to figure out how best to serve the stakeholders so that they are overwhelmingly compelled to participate. How do we do it? We monitor things closely, and we have a few folks who are really good at communicating. For example, last week one of our meteorologists saw a strange reading from one of the monitors and sent out an e-mail. The stakeholder with the problem wasn't talking to a technician; he was talking to a colleague. We speak their language.

Once processing moved to Sonoma, new products and features were added regularly. For example, the program went to hourly updates of maps from a schedule of seven times a day (Figure 8-4 shows a technical schematic). The media were receiving their data feeds like clockwork. By this time, a total of forty-five states and more than a

Figure 8-4. AIRNow Data Flow Schematic

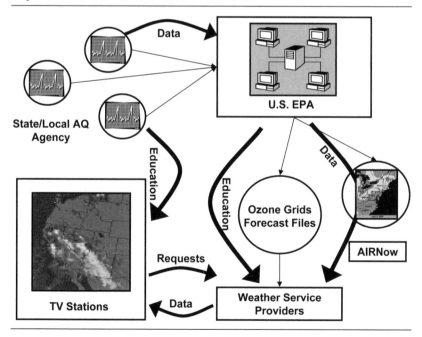

hundred agencies were contributing their data. This included Georgia, a latecomer among the southeastern states, which had gotten tired of explaining why it was grayed out on all the air quality maps. Sonoma's Dye noted,

> AIRNow has so much momentum that people now participate because their data and information really go places and are being used by the public. AIRNow is providing ozone maps and air quality forecasts that go to The Weather Channel, *USA Today*, and local TV. This year they're updated at thirty minutes past the hour rather than at forty-five minutes past the hour as was done last year. So we're closer to real time.

The AIRNow program brought air quality information out of the glass house and put it in citizens' living rooms. According to Forsyth County's Weinstock, the AIRNow initiative also significantly changed his role. He noted, "I manage an air quality monitoring group for a local agency in Winston-Salem. We are an analysis and monitoring section. We measure pollutants for the Clean Air Act. To put our group into context, the EPA sets expectations for maintaining ozone standards, but most air quality monitoring work is delegated to state and local agencies." Weinstock continued,

> We have a county of over 300,000 people, and North Carolina has a lot of air quality problems. Prior to AIRNow, we didn't interact much with the public; we saw our role as taking numbers and reporting them to the state and federal government. As the Internet grew and people's interest in air quality grew, everyone recognized that there was much more immediacy to the data and value to the public. We used to tell them six months later what they shouldn't have been doing on a particular day because of air quality conditions. Now we tell them three days ahead of time.
>
> We now see our role as being proactive, warning citizens and working with the media to make sure information is distributed

accurately and quickly. AIRNow has convinced most of the air quality people to come out from behind their computers and be ready to be in front of a camera.

By 2003, the EPA had developed a feature entitled "Where I Live" on www.epa.gov to provide tailored information to individuals. They also implemented AIRNow Tech, a private Web site for the stakeholders. This portal gave environmental agencies complete access to the ozone database and the ability to conduct their own analyses.

Making a Difference

It was hard to pinpoint health or environmental benefits that could be attributed directly and exclusively to AIRNow, although all would agree that it had made an impact. According to Boston's Conroy,

> We started a service in the region called Smog Alert Service, where people sign up on a list to receive notice by e-mail or fax when states are forecasting unhealthy air. There are about 2,000 organizations on our list—nurses, day camps, nursery schools. While we cannot quantify how these data help the public, sometimes we get replies like "Thanks for the service. It helps with an asthmatic child."

Another air quality forecaster noted that a football coach in California routinely cancelled practices when bad ozone days were forecast. Wayland added:

> We get tons of e-mail from the public. Someone who runs a daycare center can send the kids outside in the morning if air quality is forecast to be bad in the afternoon. Some proactive cities like Washington, D.C., make the buses free on ozone action days. We have cases in Baltimore where companies voluntarily shut down certain manufacturing processes on a bad day. UCLA did a study

that showed that hospital admissions for children with respiratory problems declined 4 to 7 percent on days when air quality forecasts were for unhealthy levels. People with asthma and heart problems know to stay indoors and rest so they won't end up in the emergency room.

Susannah Fuchs, senior program and air quality director of the American Lung Association of Eastern Missouri, noted that companies often take steps to reduce pollution during ozone season, especially if a bad air day is forecast. She pointed out, "A company's transportation coordinator might coordinate car pools or even provide bus passes." Some firms voluntarily changed their work hours to avoid adding to rush hour ozone levels. Others delayed using gasoline-powered lawn mowers until air quality improved. Supporters hoped that these voluntary measures would add up to enough air quality improvement that the state would ultimately avoid EPA sanctions. One state official remarked, "We'd rather not have the EPA enforcers watching over our shoulders."

Forsyth County's Weinstock added,

I can't document that I have saved anyone's life, but people appreciate the product and tell us so. And the alerts in North Carolina have gotten state legislators to pay more attention to power plants and cars. Legislators who never would have voted for increased air quality regulation will do it now because of the code orange and red alerts.

Chet's group deserves the credit for demonstrating why this is important. They don't like to take credit for themselves, but they shield people from red tape and encourage collaboration. People love to work with them, and that's not typical of the local-state-EPA relationship. Chet has often asked us to present at his conferences, and he helped us win an EPA national award. We don't have to do this, but it's fun and innovative, and our boss loves it.

Dye went further:

> This program has something for everyone. Getting meaningful air quality information out there helps people to take action to improve their own health. In addition, this program enhances the capabilities of the air quality agencies that participate. They're providing a clear public service, and when they see their work on TV, it makes that agency stand out. For myself, I'm a scientist. I used to be content to sit at my computer and do my research. With AIRNow, for the first time, I'm doing something that really makes a difference for people. It changed my life.

Time to Declare Victory?

By the end of 2003's ozone season, the AIRNow team had reached a plateau. Almost all the U.S. states were contributing data, and the few that were not had so little ground-level ozone that they didn't even run monitors. Was it time to close down the growth initiative and put AIR-Now on a maintenance diet?

Absolutely not.

According to LADCO's Koerber, AIRNow's success created high expectations for air quality efforts in general. He remarked, "Public awareness is high. Policy makers, the media, and the public want to know, if we can do ozone, why we can't we do particles and other pollutants?"

Wayland, Dickerson, White, and Dye recognized that monitoring and forecasting particulate matter ($PM_{2.5}$) would involve a year-round reporting schedule and a great deal more effort. While 1,300 ozone monitors were operating in the United States, only 280 $PM_{2.5}$ monitors were in place. In addition, many agencies were not staffed for year-round forecasting. Their professionals used the ozone off-season to take care of other responsibilities. Finally, EMPACT had provided $4 million through 2001, but that money had run out, so the team had to find other sources of funds. Wayland explained, "By the time we turned to the EPA for funds, we had so much momentum that it couldn't imagine stopping the program." In addition, Wayland was always on the lookout for new funding sources to keep spending below his own management's radar, remarking, "We were never a huge drain on the budget. The bosses would not have gotten much from cutting it, so they let it go on."

Privately, the team members also wondered whether it might be time to shift to more formal, disciplined, deadline-driven project management. They had been extremely successful using their contrarian, all-volunteer, organic method, but the EPA leadership continued to question this distinctly nongovernmental approach.

The AIRNow team pushed ahead in spite of the issues. The team members decided to continue in a collaborative way, reasoning that they had always had more success by engaging their colleagues in the regions than by demanding compliance. By October 1, 2003, the team began to report and forecast air quality year round, including $PM_{2.5}$.

Surprisingly, monitoring $PM_{2.5}$ brought the last few states into the fold. Montana did not even monitor ozone but was concerned about particulate matter. Over the next year, AIRNow filled in the remaining U.S. states and Canadian provinces and went national with particulate matter. Some skeptics argued that PM monitoring was unnecessarily expensive, but the evidence of health effects at the current ambient standard was mounting. In September 2006, based on a massive body of scientific evidence, Congress cut the allowable concentration of $PM_{2.5}$ in the air almost in half. "Now those skeptics have a bigger problem," Wayland remarks, "and they're glad we have begun to educate the public."

Always looking for ways to make the program more vibrant, the team began tracking other pollutants for researchers, collecting meteorological data at each monitoring site for the National Weather Service and expanding its scope internationally (see Figure 8–5). These new audiences and partners also helped on the funding side. Wayland sought grants from NASA, NOAA, and the World Bank as well as the EPA to continue building AIRNow capabilities.

Figure 8-5. Key Events in AIRNow's Development

1994	U.S. state of Maryland begins ozone mapping.
1997	U.S. EPA Region 1 takes responsibility for ozone mapping and expands it to thirteen New England and Middle Atlantic states and Washington, D.C.
1997	President Clinton announces the EMPACT program.
1998	EPA headquarters takes over the ozone mapping program and names its initiative AIRNow.
2000	EPA firewall improvements make it difficult for states to upload their ozone data to EPA data center computers.
2001	Sonoma Technology is awarded the contract to run the AIRNow data collection and reporting systems. EMPACT grant runs out.
2003	AIRNow maps most U.S. states' ozone levels hourly.
2005	Fifty U.S. states and ten Canadian provinces send data to AIRNow hourly. Particulate matter mapping launched. AIRNow goes global. Team visits China, Brazil, and Europe and meets with South Korea and Mexico.
2006	Nationwide particulate matter levels reported hourly. U.S. Congress cuts the allowable $PM_{2.5}$ standard almost in half.

Responding to expressions of interest from other governments, the AIRNow team visited with officials from China, South Korea, Mexico, and Brazil, in addition to giving the EU advice about how to develop a European AIRNow. Wayland explains, "We provide the know-how and the technical guidance. We help them secure funding, and we are even developing software for some of the countries. But we don't want to run anyone's program for them; we need to teach them to do their own."

After living with AIRNow for eight years, Wayland and Dickerson still crackled with energy and optimism. Dickerson explained, "People tell you to plan things in advance. But with AIRNow, if we had planned up front, I'm not sure we would have done as well. We would have come up with a different answer. As it was, we just had a spark that turned into a bigger and bigger fire."

Wayland continued, "We were trying to get people engaged. They don't want a big design; they want you to show them something that will help them. AIRNow was not full of bureaucracy or pie in the sky; it was not some big design on how it *could* work—it *did* work."

Sidebar: Ozone and Particulate Matter, Well, Matter[2]

Ozone is a gas that occurs both in the Earth's upper atmosphere and at ground level. Ozone can be good or bad, depending on where it is found. "Good" ozone occurs naturally in the Earth's upper atmosphere—six to thirty miles above the Earth's surface—where it forms a protective layer that shields people from the sun's harmful ultraviolet rays. "Bad" ozone is formed in the Earth's lower atmosphere when pollutants emitted by cars, power plants, industrial boilers, refineries, chemical plants, and other sources react chemically in the presence of sunlight.

Because ground-level ozone forms more readily in the hot, sunny conditions of summer, it tends to be a seasonal problem, approaching hazardous levels in the United States between May and September. It also travels easily. A summer ozone plume generated by Boston's automobile and industrial exhaust can be in Maine's Acadia National Park in a matter of days.

Breathing ozone can trigger a variety of health problems, including chest pain, coughing, throat irritation, and congestion. It can worsen bronchitis, emphysema, and asthma. "Bad" ozone can also reduce lung function and inflame the linings of the lungs. Repeated exposure may permanently scar lung tissue. Ground-level ozone also damages vegetation, leading to reduced crop and forest yields, reduced growth of tree seedlings, and increased susceptibility to disease and harsh conditions. In the United States alone, ground-level ozone is responsible for an estimated $500 million in reduced crop production each year.

Unlike ozone, particle pollution (also known as particulate matter) in the air is a year-round challenge. It includes a mixture of solids and liquid droplets, some of which are emitted directly, while others are formed in the atmosphere when other pollutants react. The EPA regulates particles less than 10 micrometers in diameter—smaller than the width of a single human hair—because these can get into the lungs.

According to scientific research, fine particles—those less than 2.5 micrometers in diameter—present particular health risks. These particles are so small that they can be detected only with an electron microscope. Sources of fine particles include all types of combustion, including motor vehicles, power plants, residential wood burning, forest fires, agricultural burning, and some industrial processes. High levels of so-called $PM_{2.5}$ have been linked with respiratory problems such as decreased lung function, asthma, chronic bronchitis, irregular heartbeat, nonfatal heart attacks, and premature death in elderly people or those with heart or lung disease.

The Clean Air Act requires each state to develop a state implementation plan (SIP) that describes the programs that the state will use to achieve and maintain good air quality. For example, to address an issue with ozone, a state could install vapor recovery nozzles at gasoline station pumps to reduce refueling emissions, adopt strict NOx emission limits for power plants and industrial sources, limit solvent usage in factories, or tighten vehicle inspection programs.

The Clean Air Act places on states the responsibility for establishing and operating a network of ambient air quality surveillance monitors and for reporting the data hourly to the EPA. The compliance schedule gives state monitoring organizations the opportunity to review their data for accuracy before reporting them. The EPA uses data from these hourly reports to determine whether an area is complying with the standards, and if not, what enforcement actions are required.

CHAPTER 9

Secret #4:
Energize People

What makes a regional air quality engineer put himself out to make sure his hourly data flow to headquarters never hiccups when the whole thing is optional to begin with? What makes a group of people continue striving to improve their plant's performance when they have been told that the bulldozers will show up in a few months? What makes a bunch of hotshot, twenty-something engineers bury themselves in a simulation lab and give up their nights and weekends for years to build a tester for mining equipment? What makes a group of corporate employees invent and implement a new currency in Zimbabwe so that they can keep their company's cotton pipeline flowing?

The knee-jerk answer that most of us would give is "passion." Employees go beyond the proverbial call of duty when they are passionate about what they are doing.

But check your own pulse. What are your individual passions? Where would ensuring an uninterrupted supply of information about ozone fall on your list? How about making a better mining system?

Now, an even ruder question: Which one (or ones) of your personal passions has motivated you to achieve wild success?

Most people would have the same reaction you have. We all have personal passions, but, for many practical reasons, most of us do not end up individually changing the world as a result. So *individual* passion may be an ingredient in wildly successful initiatives, but it's definitely not the whole story.

To dig a little deeper, let's look at an example. About thirty years ago in Lexington, Massachusetts, a Boston suburb (and, yes, the site of one of the first skirmishes in the American Revolution), an English teacher in the public high school decided to start a debate club. He reasoned that it would be an engaging way to help the students develop skills in research and public speaking as well as an interest in the societal issues of the day.

By luck or by talent, as Zack Duff might say, the club got off to a good start. It had some strong debaters, and within a few years it became a contender for the state championship. From that standing start, for the next thirty years, it never lost a state championship. How? Among other things, the coaches, student participants, and parents created a strong emotional field that ignited the effort and energy of the team.

Why is this remarkable? We're not talking about some expensive private school that can recruit particularly talented individuals. It's a public high school, and the club accepts whoever walks through the door.

We're not talking about some sport where the whole town turns out to cheer. Policy debate involves a lot of fast-paced, back-and-forth, fact-based argument on weighty topics such as whether the federal government should increase its control over tribal lands. With debaters hammering through detailed positions at 300 words a minute— average speech runs at about a fifth of that rate—all but the most avid fans find it difficult to follow.

We're not talking about graduate students. The team members are normal teenagers who, in order to compete, must master graduate-level research skills, have an intimate knowledge of public policy topics, and develop professional-caliber public speaking abilities. And they have to spend much of their free time either doing research in the library or practicing with the team.

So why do they do it? Moreover, why do they do it at an elite level, year after year? The architects of the program used a set of emotional levers that kicked off and then sustained a strong emotional field. It draws students into the fray, compels them to engage, and pushes them to excel. We'll use the debaters' own words to describe how these levers work.

Emotional Levers

Winning

Because the team participates in an interscholastic league, the students have the opportunity to compete and win. One former Lexington debater, now a Harvard Law student, explains the effect:

I'm a competitive animal at heart. I liked the competition in debate for all the same reasons kids with a different body type like football. (In high school, I was 5′11″ and 130 pounds.) You get beaten or you beat them. When you win, you get the ego reward that comes with victory.

Striving

The former debater also stresses,

> Winning is important, but the process of winning is an even bigger deal. Debate is similar to any competitive activity that involves strategy—like chess. The fun is not just in winning, it's in figuring out the strategies you have to employ to win. Sometimes it is more fun to lose an intellectually challenging round than to beat someone who never should have been there.

Belonging

A high school senior on the debate team varsity points out the social fabric that the program's creators deliberately engineered:

> Lexington has a unique system whereby the older varsity members tutor the novices from the start. Usually high school seniors wouldn't give freshmen the time of day. But on the debate team, the seniors take the freshmen under their wing. Each varsity member is assigned to work with a pair of novices. We show them the ropes. Not just the rules, but the way it really works. That draws them into the social atmosphere and motivates them to make an effort. At least, that's the way it worked for me.

Another debater adds,

> High school is full of cliques. If you're not athletic, you're nowhere on the social ladder. I won't tell you that you can get the social status of a football player by being on the debate team; that will never happen. But people know who we are, and they're proud of what we can do. We're not nobodies anymore.

The social connection doesn't stop when students leave high school. A former debater says, "The kids graduating are leaving the team, but they stay in touch. They may be doing debate in college or they're acting as assistant coaches, working in summer programs, or acting as judges. The connection to the team just doesn't go away."

Choosing

Even teenagers—maybe especially teenagers—want to feel a sense of control over their lives, and the debate program gives them the opportunity to make their own choices. It doesn't recruit students; they volunteer to join the team. The coach plays an uncommonly nondirective role. One varsity debater explains:

He spends a lot of time on administrative things—like making sure we can get into the school on Saturday to practice. He's not really up-to-date on all the policy issues, so that means we have to do our own research on the topics and come up with our own arguments. That's good because it gives you more freedom in what you do.

Another debater continues,

The coach is a facilitator. He teaches you the fundamentals, then backs off and does all the organizational work to get you to the tournaments, make sure you get in rounds, tell you about little tactics, give you some intelligence about what the other teams will be running. He isn't like a football coach, calling the plays; we are self-directed.

Creating

By the time May rolls around, debaters are pulling their accumulated research around on dollies because it weighs so much. And part of everyone's job is to share what she has found in the library with the other members of the team, so that everyone has access to the same body of research. Synthesizing reams of material into compelling arguments is where individuals add value, though. One debater enthusiastically explains,

We're all starting with the same huge pile of material. That's where hard work, brains, and a certain amount of creativity come in. My partner and I came up with a way of looking at the topic that no one else had thought of. We not only won our competition hands down, but other kids on the team started coming to us when they needed better strategies.

Defending or Protecting

The stakes get higher every year the team extends its string of state championships. Even if debaters didn't get excited about winning, they would certainly not want to lose. One says, "There's a tradition of winning here. I sure wouldn't want to be part of the team that lost the state championship after thirty straight years on top." This would not have been an emotional hook in the early days of the team, but it certainly is now.

Contributing—a Sense of Doing Something Meaningful or Important

Students feel the pull of another lever that has become increasingly powerful over time. One debater relates:

> I was drawn to the program from the first because of its reputation and sense of tradition. I knew about it even in grade school. It was in the newspaper—courtesy of the coach. He always made sure it was well publicized. The older kids in the neighborhood talked about it—it was everywhere.

The high school took it seriously. A debate parent explains,

> In Lexington, debaters had classroom time every day for debate— it's just like an honors class with honors credit. We once had a debater from Virginia Beach staying with us during a tournament. His team had only six members and a total budget of $2,000. The Lexington debate budget is $70,000 or $80,000. When the Virginia Beach team's coach left to take another job, the team evaporated. That just couldn't happen here.

In the Lexington debate program, the combined effect of these emotional levers creates and sustains an emotional force field that students can find almost irresistible. They use the language of addiction when they describe the debate experience. One says: "I went through the first-year program and *got hooked.*" Another remarks: "Lexington debate is like crack cocaine. Once you get started on it, you can't give it up." More than just the words, we see concrete evidence that something powerful is at work. One high school senior and varsity debater, who had already received his admittance letter from Dartmouth and might otherwise be joining his classmates in a relaxed senior spring, says: "I can't wait for spring break so I can have an uninterrupted week in the library doing research for debate."

Those of you who don't have teenagers or don't remember how challenging your teenage years were for your parents might wonder what the example of the Lexington debate team has to do with organizations full of adults. After all, the work of business and government should be driven by rational decision making, not by so-called emotional fields.

Perhaps this assertion is true for ordinary initiatives, but it is dead wrong for wildly successful ones. The same seven emotional levers show up in every initiative I have studied.

Making the Emotional Hooks Work

There are two important aspects of the emotional hooks that are worth stressing. First, each hook has both a positive and a negative form. When it's positive, it acts as an attractor, pulling the group in a particular direction. For example, the pull of winning makes the participants in any contest work harder. The negative form of winning is, of course, losing. And anger over losing also pushes contestants to work harder. So when initiative champions use this particular hook effectively, both the positive and the negative forms of winning can add strength to the emotional field (see Figure 9–1).

It's worth thinking for a minute about what it feels like to be part of this strong emotional field. It's intense, if not always happy. It's full of highs and lows, not peaceful contentment. Remember Zack Duff's Sim-Mole team? How would an individual feel when he had to report that he had not done what he promised and another team member was given the responsibility for his deliverables? He would be angry and perhaps disappointed at his personal loss. If he stayed—and most of

Figure 9-1. Working Wonders Push Forward by Using Both Positive and Negative Emotional Hooks

Lever	Positive Form	Negative Form
Winning. The powerful pride that comes from earning the top spot.	Joy of victory. De-Young's Black won the work for Stansylvania.	Refusal to lose. The new leader of the sales office that unfairly fell to the bottom of the rankings convinced his people to meet the inequitable targets anyway.
Striving. Emotional commitment from facing adversity and overcoming challenges.	Exhilaration of facing a challenge. Becker would rather start a company than work as a drone.	Anger over being barred from trying. Lima refinery workers keep improving even after the plant closure is announced.
Belonging. A strong sense of identity and affiliation with the group.	Commitment that comes from being part of something. Wayland's annual AIRNow conference energizes participants.	Determination not to be excluded. When Sainsbury's wouldn't buy Jacobs Creek wine, the company took out a billboard on a main road saying "Jacobs Creek, available everywhere but Sainsbury's."
Choosing. Independence of choice that requires and inspires commitment and ownership.	Excitement over directing your own work. Unigamble's engineers followed their noses, not the rules, to solve the reliability challenge.	Refusal to comply with others' poor choices. Paul Monus refused to allow union resistance to derail the Manufacturing Game.
Creating. Motivation that comes from developing new ideas and solving problems.	Joy of invention. Ted Graham's inspiration for the media-influence map drove the initiative forward.	Anger at having ideas rejected. The Lima workers took the compressor problem into their own hands.

Figure 9-1. Continued

Lever	Positive Form	Negative Form
Defending. Strength of will that comes from protecting the group's livelihood, position, and future.	Resolve to preserve the group's well-being. The Kinleith management team fought hard to make the mill economically viable.	Determination not to fail. The Stansylvanian Revenue Agency rolled in behind Althouse when Y2K loomed.
Contributing or Giving. Investment and satisfaction that helping others generate.	Gratification from making a difference for others. The people who made COPLINK possible wanted to and did prevent countless crimes.	Frustration at having contributions blocked or devalued. Rose refuses to allow people like the Sphincter to get in his way.

them did—the situation would require him to deepen his commitment to the team's goal. That's the addictive emotional field at work.

The negative emotions often exert far more force than the positive. I'll illustrate with a real example, although the names have been disguised. In a large professional services firm, the executive in charge of one of the practices had a problem employee. Let's call the boss Mr. Goatfob and the employee Sarah. Sarah was good at her job and highly productive, but she came from a different background from Goatfob. Goatfob didn't spend time with Sarah or try to understand her substantial contributions; he just concluded one day that Sarah had to go—she just wasn't the right material for Goatfob's organization. Over the coming months, Goatfob maligned Sarah to others in the company, gave her backwater assignments, and refused her requests to meet to discuss the situation.

Clever Sarah saw what Goatfob was doing and got angry. An optimist by nature, she decided to turn her anger to her advantage. She reasoned that engaging in Goatfob's game of political infighting would become a sinkhole for her effort and talent. Instead, she used her anger to energize her free-time efforts to launch her own company. By the time, Goatfob had engineered Sarah's termination, she had her enterprise off the ground and poised to grow. The following year, her income tax payment exceeded Goatfob's salary.

Perversely, Goatfob did Sarah a big favor. Without him in the picture, she might have been content to keep working away in the shadow of others. As it was, she became wildly successful in her own right.

The second important aspect of the emotional hooks is that they are tools like any other. Someone must deliberately use them in order to make them work. The way a team member frames or interprets what is going on in an initiative has a great deal of influence over how other participants feel.

A seasoned sales executive whom we'll call Matt learned this lesson firsthand. At the time, he was a new manager in a well-regarded sales branch of a high-tech company. Because of a mistake at headquarters, the office was asked to increase sales by 50 percent in one year—more than twice the rate expected of other sales groups. When the company's leadership would not admit its mistake, the group's respected director resigned, a dozen of its best salespeople left to join a competitor, and the morale of the remaining staff plummeted. The office ranked next to last among its peers in "percentage of quota" that year.

Matt was tapped by headquarters to turn the office around. He gathered the survivors and told them how fortunate they were to be given the opportunity to meet a higher sales target than the other branches because it would require them to develop a new kind of selling. Rather than just taking orders, they would have to learn how to create demand. As one of his first acts, he mounted a ship's bell outside his office door. When one of the team members made a sale, he invited that person to ring the bell to convene an impromptu meeting, say a few words about what she had accomplished, and bask for a moment in the limelight. Matt explains, "It was a deliberate attempt to make us feel like winners. Our numbers still put us in the cellar for a while, but we stopped dwelling on that." Within two years, this branch not only had returned to the top of the percentage-of-quota ranking, but also had grown at double the rate of the next best office. And when the business environment turned tougher for the company, individuals from this sales office bubbled quickly to the top of the organization.

Before the new sales manager showed up, the salespeople felt that they were being treated unfairly by being given quotas that were impossible to achieve. This feeling created a strong emotional field, all right, but one that was so negative that the whole team was dispirited. There was no striving, no choice, no opportunity to contribute, and definitely no winning.

The new sales manager did not change the quotas appreciably. Instead, he changed the way the salespeople looked at them. He convinced the members of his team that they had been given a unique opportunity to learn how to actually sell products rather than just taking orders, and that when the market became more competitive, they would be the heroes. Together, they all went to work to master this high art. This sales manager did not change the facts of the situation; he just changed how the salespeople felt about it. As a result, he created a strong *positive* emotional field and the most successful sales team in the country.

Let's see how Chet Wayland, Phil Dickerson, and their colleagues at AIRNow used the hooks at their disposal to create a strong emotional field.

Take Volunteers

Wayland and Dickerson invited their colleagues in the regions to volunteer—to *choose* to help, to *belong* to the team. Wayland also used the EPA naysayers' negativity for an additional push. He explains, "When someone would throw an obstacle in the way, that would spur me on. It was personal. I didn't want to be told it was impossible. Proving those people wrong became part of the fun."

Do Things for the First Time

When Wayland and Dickerson wrote their proposal for the EMPACT grant, they knew that this would obligate them to produce something, but they did not know how they were going to pull it off.

In February 2000, when Wayland and Dickerson were off at a conference, a congressional flap over Internet security caused the EPA to shut down its Web site—including the AIRNow data feeds. Our heroes had just finished announcing that their program was poised to go national; meanwhile, back at headquarters, the plug had been pulled. Dickerson, ever the optimist, refused to give up. Wayland explains, "Our workaround was the klugiest thing you can imagine, but it worked. And it was up and running on May 1."

When they agreed in 2003 to provide *USA Today* with air quality status and next-day forecasts for the thirty-six cities that were of interest to the paper, some of the cities were not even participating in the program. Two weeks before the go-live date, three cities let it be known that they weren't going to be able to do the forecasting. The team scrambled to bring them back into the fold.

Don't (Just) Pay for Performance; Sing Praises

As the initiative grew, Wayland and Dickerson launched an annual AIRNow conference to give the participants an opportunity to meet and learn from one another. In addition to giving team members a feeling of *belonging*, Wayland planted other emotional hooks from the podium. One regional engineer recalls, "Chet would start by saying it was *our* program." Wayland was renowned for singing people's praises at these meetings. If he didn't invite them to present their accomplishments as part of the program, he would ask them to take a bow from the floor. He also had a habit of reading effusive e-mails he had received from day-care centers, individuals with asthma, and people who cared about the environment. One attendee tells us, "He has this way of making all 350 people in the room feel like a million bucks, no matter how large or small their contribution."

If You Don't Have Enemies, Make Some

Since the strongest emotional fields involve a combination of positive and negative forces—obstacles to overcome as well as encouragement for doing so—champions of wildly successful initiatives take great advantage of enemies or even create them. Wayland and Dickerson used the deadline inherent in ozone seasonality as their foil. (Because ozone is produced when the climate is hot and sunny, it is monitored between May 1 and September 1.) In its early days, the AIRNow program used the off-season to build new capabilities, recruit new regions, and improve its technology. As a team, it could race against the clock to get all the monitors, procedures, and systems buttoned back up by May 1, when the real-time data flows relentlessly began again.

These emotional hooks fly in the face of conventional management wisdom about how to staff and motivate a team. Normally, we look for people who have experience doing what we have in mind—the closer their experience is to exactly what we're asking for, the better they look. And we pay a lot of attention to performance metrics and individual bonuses for meeting them. These factors don't even come up in most wildly successful initiatives.

Instead, champions use the emotional hooks to create a group dynamic that multiplies individuals' motivations. Different people may respond more readily to one emotional hook or another, and a healthy dynamic has something for everyone. In the aggregate, the group's tangible commitment and obvious enthusiasm draws others into its field. As these new recruits contribute their skills and effort, the capacity and capability of the organism expand. This creates energy and momentum that fuels the work that people must do to accomplish their initiative.

Robert Cialdini, in his amazing book *Influence: The Psychology of Persuasion,*[1] explains the social psychology behind this dynamic:

> Social scientists have determined that we accept inner responsibility for a behavior when we think we have chosen to perform it in the absence of strong outside pressures. A large reward is one such external pressure. It may get us to perform a certain action, but it won't get us to accept inner responsibility for the act. Consequently, we won't feel committed to it (p. 93).

He goes on to illustrate this point with examples from Chinese prison camps and college fraternities, both of which engineer personal ownership of behavior to achieve deep and lasting commitment from their "members."

The Interpersonal Foundation

In wildly successful initiatives, we see evidence of critical interpersonal capabilities that set the stage for emotional commitment, not just of individuals, but among the group: playfulness, trust, and realistic optimism. Without these, a manager may plant the emotional hooks, but she will not get the same collective, addictive effect.

Playfulness

Wildly successful initiatives cultivate a lighthearted work environment that invites cockamamie ideas and defuses tension. Someone on the team becomes the resident wit, wrapping painful messages in humor to make them easier to swallow and taking the edge off of high-pressure deadlines with fun. When the Stansylvanian Revenue Agency's Althouse committed to finish the new tax-processing system before Y2K made the agency's current system inoperable, he asked a lot of his team. Its members took on a short deadline with fatal consequences if it were missed. Althouse recalls, "I provided free coffee. And when things got tense, I would go sit with the programmers and make them laugh."

Humor helps managers put a productive emotional tension into performance processes as well. Drew Phelps, a customer delivery manager with the network services company NWN, was on the hook to improve the company's dismal track record of responding to one very important customer's network alerts. Instead of punishing his engineers every time they missed the service level, he created a game. If the engineer on duty caught an alert in under five minutes, he won a six-pack of beer. If the response came in between five and fifteen minutes—NWN's internal goal—the engineer earned one bottle of beer. For a response in between fifteen and thirty minutes—the promise to the customer—the reward was "you'll get nothing and like it." Anything after thirty minutes meant that the engineer bought Phelps a six-pack. Within a week of launching the game in September 2005, average response time dipped to less than five minutes and stayed there. Perhaps as important, the engineers enjoyed the improvement process and were eager for more.

Trust

The second critical interpersonal capability, trust, forms the foundation for commitment. Honest and transparent relationships let the feelings flow, keeping the emotional field strong and present. In an environment of trust, the feelings are catching. This contrasts sharply with a team that is characterized by closed and distrustful relationships, where hidden agendas or political posturing keep people emotionally separate.

Integrity in both words and action is also critical. For example, Jim Schaefer and his management team inspired trust by devoting their effort and keeping their word. Perhaps even more importantly, they started the ball rolling by trusting others first. They listened to the operators in the plant and gave them the latitude to exercise their judgment. They joined the operators in Ledet's Manufacturing Game, leaving their titles outside the door and working together to find the path to breakthrough performance.

Wayland and Dickerson showed up in EPA Region 1's Boston office in 1996 saying, "We're from headquarters and we'd like to help." In most organizations, this would guarantee that they left empty-handed. That didn't happen here. Why? Because Wayland and Dickerson presented themselves as trustworthy partners and colleagues—joining with the region, not taking over.

Optimism

Playfulness and trust benefit from the third interpersonal capability that is important to a strong emotional field, optimism. It's often easier to see the obstacles, risks, and costs than to see the upside opportunity in an initiative. However, where individuals like the Sphincter see roadblocks at every turn, champions of wildly successful initiatives naturally see possibilities. Encouraging this mindset so that it infects the entire team buoys the emotional field during the inevitable setbacks.

Optimism expresses itself readily. It sounds like this: "Let's give it a try"; "There must be a way"; "We're going to be better off because this happened."

Ambient Devices' David Rose explains the critical role that optimism plays when he talks about creating a product that is new and unexpected. Four pieces of the business model have to fall into place: a product that customers want, a team to develop and build the product, money to pay the employees, and customers to buy the product. Of course, the pessimist would say that it's impossible to make a product without workers, impossible to get workers without money, impossible to get money without customers, and impossible to get customers without a product. The optimist, on the other hand, convinces the workers that they will get paid even though the coffers are empty at the moment. And convinces the customers that there will be a product, even though it's currently just a sketch. And convinces the investors that the customers will buy the product, even though their commitments are conditional and tenuous. In this way, an optimistic outlook leverages confidence in the possibilities to make them come true.

Champions start with a foundation of playfulness, trust, and optimism and build a strong emotional field around their initiatives. But even the most addictive interpersonal environment hiccups from time to time.

Managing the Emotional Field Over Time

Ask a project management expert how to get good results and you are likely to hear something about time boxes. By keeping the project short, clear, and crisp, the team has a better chance of getting it done before something changes or its members lose interest.

Oddly, wildly successful initiatives play out over years. The Stansyl-vanian Revenue initiative took fifteen years. AIRNow has been thriving for a decade. The refinery in Lima began its turnaround in the early 1990s, and it continues to log performance improvements today. Many things change along the way, but the teams do not seem to lose their appetite for pressing on.

This doesn't mean that participants experience the same high level of emotional intensity every day. Like any journey, an initiative will have its ups and downs, stops and starts, engaging in frenzied, focused activity at times and blundering around at others. The path will circle back upon itself, perhaps many times, and the strength and character of the emotional field will shift over time. What's unique to wildly successful initiatives is that the participants find ways to manage the emotional transitions and reinvigorate the team again and again over the years.

Let me stress that keeping an initiative's emotional field vibrant is not a job for just one person, or even for a few leaders of the initiative. Everyone who participates in the initiative contributes to its energy in one way or another. Optimists, enthusiasts, and people with big aspirations energize others; pessimists, misanthropes, and curmud-geons do the opposite.

New People

One of the most obvious ways to boost the energy in an initiative is to welcome new participants into the community. Ambient Devices' Rose admits that even as the founder of a start-up, he can sometimes lose his enthusiastic edge. When he feels this happening, he goes looking for recruits. He explains,

I'm such a people person that I always get reengaged when new people with new perspectives come in—especially people from very different backgrounds. People *not* like me. Because our new-est employee came from Kodak's technology licensing office, he sees Ambient as a valuable technology platform that other large companies will covet. Because of his background, the new employee brings a new lens to survey the opportunity landscape. That gets me energized again.

Because of their strong emotional field, people in wildly successful initiatives have a unique ability to hand off control. In conventional projects, handoffs are dangerous. No one cares for a "baby" like its parent does, and critical commitments often fail to carry across the transition. Wildly successful initiatives don't seem to have this problem. One team member who has carried the ball as far as possible will readily pass it laterally to colleagues. These individuals take up their responsibility with renewed energy.

Wildly successful teams open themselves to new participants without much regard for organizational boundaries. They go where they will and find what they need. The AIRNow team spans multiple U.S. government agencies, nonprofits such as the American Lung Association, and private-sector companies such as Sonoma Technology, and reaches into other governments on several continents.

New Problems

Wayland and Dickerson are continually searching for ways to keep the AIRNow program vibrant, adding new challenges as well as new benefits to keep people from becoming complacent or, worse, indifferent. In the early days of mapping ozone levels, the team faced plenty of obstacles. Once that process was running smoothly, the team took on a new pollutant—particulate matter. It had to put a new network of monitoring equipment in place as well as find sources of funds to support its efforts. Through its IT partner, Sonoma Technology, the team continues to add features to the system that will appeal to its network of data contributors. Wayland comments,

Now that we're nationwide in the United States, we have shifted our focus. We are helping our counterparts in other countries and working on some other pollutants that U.S. researchers would like to get real-time information about. We are also adding meteorology because we can. At each monitoring site, we are collecting data that can be used by the National Weather Service and other agencies to supplement their data networks—and at no cost to them. We built our capability, and now we are finding other uses for it—moving beyond public awareness to research. That gives us a new audience and another way to keep the program vibrant.

New Punch

Just as abject failures do, some wildly successful initiatives go through dark days. People lose confidence; some abandon the initiative, and others quietly withdraw their commitment. But every successful initiative ultimately has a group of diehards at its core. At least one of them will stand up for the effort—in words and in behavior—and drag others back to a positive perspective. In Lima, Berger and Schaefer never stopped looking for a buyer for the refinery. The operators raised their own flag over the parking lot and took ownership of the plant's performance—this when their headquarters executives had already announced that the facility would be torn down.

In New Zealand's Kinleith paper mill, a small group of managers laid out a radical plan for putting the plant on a sound financial footing. It involved outsourcing the maintenance function, a move that brought plant management face to face with ugly union recriminations. Furthermore, the conflicts weren't limited to the workplace. The paper mill was located in a rural area; almost all the workers, both hourly and salaried, shopped at the same stores and sent their children to the same schools. When the architects of the outsourcing arrangement began receiving threats to both their own health and that of their families, their resolve wavered. Again and again, one member of the team took the floor in their group meetings to remind them all why they had started down this path. The only way to keep the mill viable was to cut costs, and outsourcing promised to do just that. If management gave in to the union demands, the mill would close, and everyone would be out of a job. Together they renewed their commitment and decided to hire bodyguards and continue what they started.

The managers' commitment saw them through the process of outsourcing, but that wasn't the end of the emotional upheaval. Once ABB won the outsourcing contract, its newly installed on-site director of maintenance, Juergen Link, had to find a way to reset his organization emotionally.

Link had stepped in to supervise 200 unionized maintenance workers whose ill will toward the company and its management had festered for years. They had bitterly fought against being outsourced, and they had lost. Link recognized that his new organization would never learn to create value together unless he found a way to heal these wounds.

Link explains, "When you are taken over, you feel you are not good enough. But it is always the system you are in that prevents you from doing well. We had to clear away the resentments." Link and his managers arranged an "emotional journey" for the workers. They all took off for two days in the woods of New Zealand's north island. The team was scattered about the forest in small groups, with nothing but a compass to help them find their way to a rendezvous point. That evening, around the fire, Link pointed out how important it had been for them to value and rely on one another to reach their destination. He went on to say that this was how his new maintenance organization at Kinleith would operate—with experienced, capable people relying on one another to create value.

The forest experience was only the first example of Link's art of creating a strong emotional field. He recognized how vitally important it was to begin his work there by kick-starting a positive relationship.

Ordinary, tidy initiatives often face challenges when they shift from the planning phase to development and from development to institutionalization. Wildly successful initiatives are not immune to these transitions—different emotional hooks come into play more strongly. For example, the opportunity to create new solutions may give the team an emotional boost early on. When it comes to delivering the goods, striving to meet a deadline comes to the fore.

The most dangerous time in a wildly successful initiative comes when it moves out from under the radar and becomes an official endeavor. You know what happens. Professional management rears up and claims authority. The illegitimate, or at least nonstandard, management approaches that propelled the initiative toward wild success must be "cleaned up." Momentum slows; fun evaporates; the initiative becomes ordinary. This isn't terrible. It's just a little sad—especially for the people who remember what it was like to work in the strong emotional field.

Galactica's Karl Schmidt worked on several Sim-Mole improvements after helping to build the original simulator. "The experiences that followed were less spectacular," he explains.

> I have worked on and off on the system over the years, but building it for the first time was the best. Doing something no one had ever done before with marginal hardware and no blueprint; well, that was something. The next challenges became to do it faster or cheaper or to incorporate different hardware. It hasn't been the same thrill in later phases.

If You Remember One Thing

Evoking powerful emotions is the everyday work of people who are wildly successful.

CHAPTER 10

Coplink

An Unconventional Collaboration Revolutionizes Law Enforcement

Tucson recently had a series of incidents in which a white male and a black male were enticing young girls into their car. All the police knew about the car was that it was a yellow Cadillac with an "R" in its tag. They put these fragments of information into Coplink, and within two minutes, it came up with the suspects. Before Coplink, the leadership would have told the officers to do more drive-bys at the schools, but that probably wouldn't have solved the problem.

–Mike O'Shea, Program Manager, National Institute of Justice

Hsinchun Chen, the director of the University of Arizona's Artificial Intelligence Laboratory, considered his operation one of the bright spots in the academic community. Unlike most of his computer science colleagues, he belonged to the School of Management, and he had a taste for real problems. "The academic data-mining literature is boring because everyone is trying to get a 3 percent improvement on the same old hypothetical problem. In my lab, we work on real applications. They are so much more challenging." He was looking for knotty problems for which he and his graduate students could pull associations and concepts out of messy, unstructured data.

Brad Cochran, a close-to-retirement Tucson police sergeant who was responsible for the crime analysis unit, was pursuing his bachelor's degree in information systems at the University of Arizona. In his day job, he struggled to support both the officers on the street and his chief with information scattered across disparate databases on different platforms. "We couldn't get data without running two or three routines and getting piles of paper," Cochran complained. "You could take weeks to sift through all that to find the nugget you wanted. In many cases, we just didn't have the time."

When Cochran took a course from Chen, he began to connect the dots. He knew Chen's national reputation in search capabilities, and he had been scanning the grant databases for one that might fit what he had in mind. He spotted a National Institute of Justice (NIJ) grant opportunity to create a collaborative system that would support both law enforcement research and practice. With this in hand, he approached Chen about the possibility of their working together. Chen recalls the meeting with Cochran and Jenny Schroeder, a young police officer who was also in Chen's class at the time: "The three of us were brainstorming. Old cops and young. Brad was about to retire; Jenny had only been on the force for a few years. We were talking about the possibilities of the technology and how important it could be for them." The officers were so passionate to put the technology to use on their problem that Jenny developed the grant proposal in three days.

At this meeting, Coplink was conceived (see Figure 10-1 for an overall timeline of the events associated with Coplink). Initially, the trio envisioned a data warehouse system that would collect all the scattered information in a local police department's files into a single location. Because resource-strapped police forces often looked for grants to develop systems, they tended to focus on one kind of information at a time. Furthermore, the highway patrol, the sheriff's office, and the Tucson police all worked within their own silos, developing their own

Figure 10-1. Timeline of Events

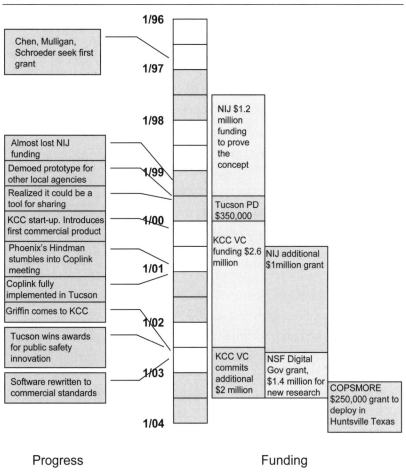

Progress   Funding

systems. The result was a veritable garden of disconnected databases. For a local police force, these might include administrative files, the gang database, the mug shot database, the sex offender database, the parole database, and others.

Schroeder explains that police work often starts with making associations among people, places, and cars. Schroeder, Cochran, and Chen envisioned a system that would make it easier to round up all the information about a situation, no matter which database that information came from. They reasoned that this would potentially help officers identify relationships among the snippets of data that were hidden by the disarray.

In the fall of 1996, when Schroeder and Cochran took their proposal to their chief, Doug Smith, he was extremely supportive. "We're a 'load' city," Smith explained.

> Marijuana and cocaine are smuggled across our border, and then the smugglers are paid off in product. They're looking around here to find someone to sell it to, so we have the violence and property problems that result. Our closure rate on cases is only 8 or 9 percent, which is terrible. With 20 percent of the criminals committing 80 percent of the crimes, I can save myself fifteen burglaries by getting a burglar in jail fifteen days faster.

Smith had had previous experience working with the law enforcement grant-funding agencies: COPS MORE, local law enforcement block grants, and the National Institute of Justice, all of which fell under the office justice program.[1]

NIJ's grants tended to support research rather than actual law enforcement tools; COPS MORE did the opposite. Needing both, Smith worked with a friend from the COPS MORE office to have funds from its side moved to NIJ to support both aspects of the Coplink project.

In July 1997, NIJ awarded Chen and the Tucson Police Department a $1.2 million, two-year grant to develop a proof of concept prototype. They called it Coplink.

Building the Prototype

Chen pulled together a team of graduate and undergraduate students. Schroeder volunteered to represent the Tucson Police Department on the development team, and Sergeant Cochran agreed. Cochran also invited another woman who had extensive experience with the records management system to participate. Describing himself as a practical person, Cochran explains that his superiors gave him a great deal of latitude in managing the project because of his longstanding reputation for getting things done.

At the outset, Chen had a vision for the project that included sophisticated analysis of disparate information nuggets based on social network theory. However, he knew that the team had to build and populate a technically ordinary data warehouse first. Chen explained:

> Most of us researchers develop things and write papers. And most of the prototypes are never used again. I was ignorant about law enforcement when we started the project, but I wanted to give them something useful. In the first two years, we couldn't publish anything because everything we were doing was too basic from a technology standpoint.

Chen's team of Ph.D., master's, and undergraduate students built the data warehouse prototype. Guided by Schroeder, they concentrated on integrating data from a few key sources: the records management system, the mug shot database, and the gang database. Throughout the process, Schroeder taught the students about law enforcement. She recalled, "To fulfill the first grant, we just needed a proof of concept. But we liked the prototype so well that the university worked out a way to apply it to our real database and deploy it in our department." Schroeder trained fifty fellow officers on the Tucson force.

During one of the user trials with an early prototype of Coplink, ATF [the federal Bureau of Alcohol, Tobacco, and Firearms] called from Phoenix because it was searching for a homicide suspect. The agents didn't know his name, but they knew that his sister's boyfriend lived in Tucson, and they had *his* name. We were able to find their suspect's name in five minutes. Not only that, but we told them that he was already in jail. Without Coplink, it would have taken us weeks to find this information. We probably would not have had the resources to do it.

—Jenny Schroeder, Tucson police sergeant

Funding Fears

As part of the NIJ grant process, an administrator visited the team for a project review about six months after work began. Cochran recalls that the system's interfaces had been built, but they were not linked to the actual database. Chen was swamped with his university obligations and was unavailable to meet with the NIJ reviewer. Cochran said he could handle it, but the demonstration failed to convince the NIJ that Coplink would provide distinctive new value. "They didn't understand where we were going," Cochran remembers painfully. "They only saw where we were."

The reviewer's evaluation reported that Coplink did not make any relevant new contributions to research, and he recommended discontinuing the funding. Grants and funding are awarded through an expert-driven peer review process that is similar to the way academic research articles are approved for publication. Chen explains,

> When reviewers see a proposal or a result, they evaluate it both on scientific merit and on its broader impact. The balance is usually 80 percent science and 20 percent impact. Coplink's value was the reverse—a bit less scientific contribution, but massive social impact. It's just so different from what they normally see.

Richard Miranda, Cochran's supervisor at the time, would not accept this result, Cochran recalls. "He said, 'I don't care what you do. Go to their symposium in Atlanta and kiss butt if you have to, but don't lose the funding.'" Cochran got plane tickets for Chen and himself, packed a demo laptop, and took off for Atlanta, where the NIJ brain trust was holding a conference.

Chen was able to convince the NIJ that the Coplink team was on to something big. Ultimately, NIJ did renew the grant in mid-2000 for $1 million. To cover Coplink in the interim, the Tucson Police Department anted up $350,000 in bridge funds. Schroeder notes, "The Tucson PD had developed a good relationship with the university. We did not want to lose the cohesiveness of the team."

In the meantime, another critical piece of the puzzle fell into place. Joe Hindman, the technology administrator for the Phoenix Police Department at the time, was registering his daughter for school at the University of Arizona. He was told that a group of criminal justice professionals was having a meeting there, so he invited himself to sit in. Cochran, Schroeder, Chen, and law enforcement agents from all over the state of Arizona were discussing how the Coplink concept could be extended to meet their needs. Intrigued by what he saw, Hindman recalls, "I thought that the data-mining tools might be a strong enough incentive to get the police and the sheriff's departments to share data. I told Brad that I wanted to play."

In the world of law enforcement, Tucson was a medium-size operation, with about 1,000 sworn officers and 300 to 400 civilian crime analysts. Phoenix and its six sister communities in the Salt River Valley dwarfed it. Remarks a member of the intelligence community, "Phoenix is the kingpin for us; Tucson is the second city. For Coplink to be truly valuable, it must succeed in the Phoenix area, with its well-established records management system, its sophisticated use of data, and its 2.5 million people—lots of whom are criminals." Like Tucson, Phoenix was struggling with violent and property crime rates that both exceeded the national average and appeared stuck at an unacceptably high level.

In mid-2000, the Coplink team demoed its system to a well-attended meeting of the Phoenix Police Department brass. Shortly thereafter, the Phoenix police chief agreed to Hindman's proposed implementation plan. Chen and the Tucson team linked Hindman up with the NIJ to secure the funding to expand the Coplink concept and demonstrate that it could scale up to include multiple large agencies. Cochran recalls, "I knew Phoenix didn't have the money for all this in its budget, but NIJ got more excited about it as we took on bigger partners. The agency knew this would give it more impact in the criminal justice community, so it came through with more money."

The Tucson gang-unit supervisor brought in an individual as a suspect in a homicide. For some reason, a friend of his came along with

him. When the supervisor asked this second guy for some identifica-
tion, he presented a valid Arizona driver's license. But something
seemed wrong to the supervisor. The guys were talking, and he over-
heard one of them refer to the other one's mother as "aunt." He ran
this through Coplink, which has mug shots, and found out the second
guy's real identity. It turned out he was wanted in connection with
another homicide.

—Jenny Schroeder, Tucson police sergeant

Becoming Bulletproof

Coplink was conceived and born through the early collaboration between Chen's AI lab and the Tucson police, but in 2000, the system
was still a quirky prototype. It had been built to prove a concept rather
than to support the day-to-day press of police business, and it was continually under construction by an ever-changing cast of graduate students. In addition, the Coplink visionaries were just getting started.
They could now see the potential for a much more powerful system
with improved data analysis capabilities and linkages across justice departments' jurisdictional boundaries. "Criminals are like great white
sharks," one officer notes. "When they have eaten all the food in one
area, they move on." The team began rallying support for intercon-
nected regional nodes so that the police in the Phoenix area could both
work together and follow criminal leads to Tucson and beyond.

When Jenny Schroeder was promoted to sergeant, Tucson officer
Linda Ridgeway took her place on the team and worked with the graduate students to push Coplink's analytical capabilities forward. Coplink
Connect—the ability to integrate databases—was well established. The
team turned its attention to Coplink Detect—the ability to find criminal
associations (see Figures 10-2 and 10-3 for technical schematics).

Meanwhile, Chen launched Knowledge Computing Corporation
(KCC), a private firm designed to bring Coplink fully into the commercial realm. With $2.6 million of venture capital funding, Chen began
the process of rewriting Coplink's code to make it robust, reliable, and
commercial-grade. Chen also began working with the University of

Figure 10-2. Schematic of Tucson Coplink Implementation

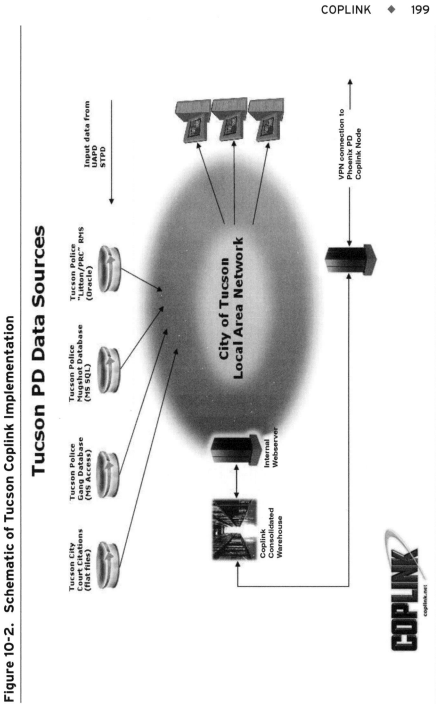

Tucson PD Data Sources

Figure 10-3. Schematic of Coplink Regional Architecture

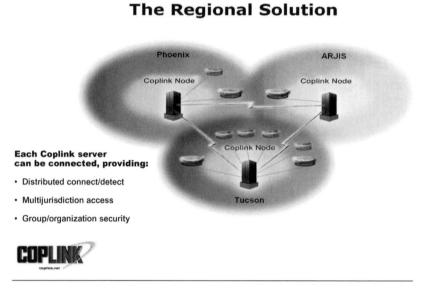

The Regional Solution

Each Coplink server
can be connected, providing:

• Distributed connect/detect

• Multijurisdiction access

• Group/organization security

Arizona's Office of Technology Transfer to sort out an intellectual property licensing deal. "I call it the 'office of preventing technology transfer,'" rails Chen. "It often takes so long to work things out with it that
people just give up, and the technology gets stuck in there forever."

Two Steps Forward, One Step Back

KCC did not make as much progress as Chen had hoped over the next
two years. While the company did finally acquire a license for the
Coplink software from the university, it did not land any additional
customers. Chen and the board hired an experienced CEO from a large
company, but this individual's lack of start-up experience led to a series
of bad decisions. For example, he priced the product at $1,000 per seat
with a $1 million minimum. This price tag not only put off cash-
strapped police departments but aroused a negative reaction from the
NIJ. The NIJ reasoned that the software should be free to law enforcement agencies because its development had been funded by the government. Chen counters,

For the most part, NIJ funds bulletproof vests and devices that puncture tires; it has no experience with software. So it has a problem with the commercial pricing that you need to provide reliable code and ongoing support to offer a product that actually works in the real world of law enforcement.

At the same time, in the post-9/11 environment, the National Science Foundation (NSF) decided to try to make a more direct contribution to the defense of the nation. In order to make an immediate impact, the NSF worked with the NIJ to identify existing grants that could be redirected toward increasing intelligence effectiveness and given stronger support. The NSF added its financial weight to Coplink by providing its own grant to Chen's university lab.

> We had a series of robberies at chicken fast-food places. The suspects at different locations appeared to be the same people. During one of the incidents, a witness thought he recognized one of the robbers as a person called "Peanuts" who lived in a certain part of town. There must have been over 100 people called Peanuts in our files, but by using Coplink, we found a mug shot of the suspect and included it in a photo lineup. He was identified and arrested. Without Coplink, there's no telling how long it would have taken our investigators to find the right one.
>
> —Detective Tim Petersen, Coplink officer,
> Tucson Police Department

By mid-2002, KCC had burned through all its angel money, Phoenix was still struggling to implement the system, and Tucson remained committed. It was unclear how Coplink could succeed until Bob Griffin arrived. Griffin recalls,

I had been named Washington, D.C.'s, 2001 Entrepreneur of the Year and met the dean of the University of Arizona. At a lunch meeting, the dean introduced me to a few professors who were teaching a course on entrepreneurs, and they invited me to become a guest lecturer at the business school. During one of our sessions, the dean said that Tucson has two big challenges: finding senior management talent and doing technology transfer out of the university. He described the situation at KCC and asked me if I would be willing to meet with the professor who founded the company to talk about its challenges.

When Griffin looked under the covers, he found a company with a few basic problems. He summarized, "There was no adult supervision, no direction or leadership, no money, few qualified prospects, and no commercial product." He concluded, however, that KCC had the key ingredients for a successful company: talented people and great underlying technology that provided excellent commercial potential. He recalled, "There were clients who raved about Coplink, and it solved a real problem." He agreed to step into the CEO's role to turn the company around.

Building Buzz

Griffin raised an additional $2 million from KCC's original investors to give him some runway. He focused the organization, got the right people in key jobs, and started trying to build buzz. When the sniper shootings started in Maryland's Montgomery County in 2002, Griffin learned that one of his senior executives, Doug Smith,[2] had trained with the county's police chief, Charles Moose. Smith called Moose and offered him the Coplink software for free. In addition, he convinced the NIJ to pay for the server and Microsoft to provide a $250,000 SQL license. With all the politics, however, it took two weeks to get five critical data sources pulled into Coplink. As a result of the delays, the Coplink implementation was too late to identify the snipers. Just to put the system through its paces, however, Smith demonstrated what it would have shown. In one short run, it brought up seven suspects, including Lee Boyd Malvo and John Muhammad. "Within minutes of a shooting, we could show that they ran a red light," Griffin pointed out. "They were questioned about sleeping in a rest area. After one shooting, they were stopped at a roadblock. Why is the same car showing up at opposite ends of the state within minutes of shootings? That's not a coincidence; that's a pattern."

Undaunted, Griffin and his organization continued to visit police forces around the country to demonstrate Coplink. They did encounter predictable resistance. Some police organizations expressed reluctance to share their data. One detective remarked,

> Imagine if you had been following a case for eighteen months. Your reports are out there, but you don't have enough evidence to make an arrest. Someone in another department picks up your information, adds the last detail, and arrests your suspect. Not only does that department get credit for the closure and accolades from the press for two days of work, but it gets all the asset forfeiture funds.

Some officers were also unwilling to credit Coplink with helping them solve cases because they believed it depreciated their own professional contribution. This attitude interfered with KCC's drive to get public exposure for the product.

By mid-2003, however, KCC had signed up ten police departments across the nation: Des Moines and Polk County, Iowa; Boston, Massachusetts; Huntsville, Texas; San Diego County, California; Redmond and Spokane, Washington; Ann Arbor, Michigan; the state of Alaska; and Henderson County, North Carolina. Coplink had also received positive press from *Time*, *Newsweek*, CBS television, and CNBC. The CIA and the FBI were both evaluating Coplink, and it was being demonstrated in Canada, the United Kingdom, Singapore, and Hong Kong.

Loosening the Academic Ties

Chen's Coplink grants were wrapping up. The NIJ and NSF had worked hand in hand for years to support Coplink, with the NIJ funding the "cop" side of the effort and the NSF providing money for the academic side. This unusual collaboration had been a "new twist" for the NIJ. NIJ program manager Mike O'Shea remarked, "We usually fund projects on our own, but in this case, we had an excellent experience working with Valerie Gregg and Larry Brandt's digital government program." Chen's NSF grant would expire in mid-2004.

The NIJ's official position was that Coplink should begin to stand on its own two feet. While O'Shea continued to be a strong advocate for the system, public safety departments that wanted to implement it had to look elsewhere for money. Huntsville, Texas, used a COPS MORE grant. Des Moines and Polk County, Iowa, funded their projects with enhanced 9/11 money. Some others used drug forfeiture money.

> Two weeks ago, the Tucson police found a guy who had been shot, set on fire, and buried under a mattress. He was disfigured beyond recognition. But we ran the information we had about him, including a tattoo. It narrowed our search down to four potential people, and the police were able to identify him through dental records. They also got a list of six of his associates so that they could begin looking for his killer.
>
> —Bob Griffin, CEO, Knowledge Computing Corp.

Chen, who remained a board member at KCC, mused, "The research is at a critical moment. Now we are asking research questions of the data that no one else can ask." Chen's NSF funding was due to expire in six to eight months. He had a proposal under review by the Department of Homeland Security and was expecting to partner with the California agencies to extend Coplink research. He was pursuing other uses for the software as well, such as applying it to border safety. He argued that research of this kind required long-term funding.

Members of the intelligence community outside of Tucson were watching Coplink's progress with interest. Some hoped that its most effective algorithms could be applied by other research programs to catch terrorists. One researcher remarked,

We have some policy issues to solve, but Coplink has put three critical elements in place: It has academic credibility through the University of Arizona, it has a good working partnership with actual police officers, and it has substantial support from other parts of the U.S. government. The connection between real problems and academics makes it most valuable to us. Most academic research is done on toy problems, but real problems are much harder, and Chen's lab is brilliant at solving them. In addition, there's no one in control—no chief of the whole thing. All police departments hate each other, and someone has to spend time keeping everyone from walking out on the project. This is very difficult, and the Coplink people have successfully developed that capability. Maybe it's because they're from a school of management.

Tsunami

By August 2003, Coplink's value had not yet shown up in crime statistics, but evidence of its worth was accumulating. An independent NIJ study showed that Coplink users improved leads 65 percent over users of a standard records management system. Word of Coplink's value was spreading across the fraternity as more police departments signed up to implement it. KCC counted twelve real customers and had turned the corner to profitability. Griffin had repriced the product so that it would be cost-effective for a small sheriff's department as well as a large police force. For the first time, KCC was facing a "tsunami of interest."

The Phoenix, Tucson, San Diego region was pushing ahead. Coplink was not yet live in Phoenix, and the individuals who had originally launched and supported the project had left, but the department remained committed to making the system work. A regional association of crime fighters in the Southwest and California had scored its own NSF grant to implement Coplink in San Diego County and the Tucson sheriff's office. A total of nineteen agencies in the region had signed letters of agreement to implement Coplink. The federal customs and border patrol had also expressed interest.

NIJ program manager O'Shea, asked in 2000 to pass judgment on whether Coplink had any practical value, had also become an evangelist. In his role of communicating interesting new technologies to state and local public safety departments all over the United States, he had a unique platform for spreading the word about Coplink. "Everywhere we show this, they want it," he grinned.

> It's easy to use. They don't have to send anyone to six months of training or change any of their current systems. And people like the fact that they can interface with other agencies. As the system grows, they'll be able to follow a criminal across the country. It's an incredible tool.

In 2003, Coplink's ability to connect the public safety organizations across a region was already being implemented in Des Moines and Polk County, Iowa. Six city and county law enforcement agencies were collaborating to get a broad array of public safety data brought together through Coplink. According to Smith, all the fire departments in the area used a de facto standard system called Firehouse. In addition to police files, the region's Coplink system would integrate Firehouse data and Department of Transportation information that was important to federal emergency management association (FEMA) directors.

> The Tucson police found a guy face down in the street. He had been shot, his throat had been slashed, and he had been run over by the car when the perpetrators were leaving the scene, but he was still alive. All he could say was, "Shorty did it." Now, Shorty is a common street name; there must be hundreds of them in Tucson. He was also able to tell them that he thought Shorty might have "Caesar" tattooed on his arm. They put this in Coplink and found one person who had been paroled twenty-four hours earlier. From the time they found the victim to the time of the arrest was five hours. He's now doing sixteen years. Without Coplink, it could have taken them days or weeks to find the right Shorty.
>
> —Bob Griffin, CEO, Knowledge Computing Corp.

Policy roadblocks to information sharing were being cleared away. Each state, each public safety agency, and the federal government had unique legal requirements that governed who could view criminal record information. Detective Tim Petersen, the Tucson Coplink officer who took over from Linda Ridgeway, explained,

> We have entered into letters of agreement with all agencies participating in Coplink. These are legal documents approved by the agency's counsel or administrator that agree to restrict access to the same people who can get the information through other means. That lets us tap the certification infrastructure that is already in place.

Coplink's Connect and Detect capabilities were attracting interest, and the developers promised regular new releases. KCC was working on a wireless version that could be used in a police car. It was also eager to roll out Coplink Agent. One Coplink project manager explained: "If someone searches on a suspect named 'Bill Jones,' that person can flag him. If someone else adds information about Bill, the first person will be alerted by e-mail, cellular phone, or instant messaging over the Web. Then they can talk to each other and hopefully collaborate to solve the case together." Added Joe Hindman, now Coplink administrator in Scottsdale, "I would make the system more proactive. Any time a detective gets a case, he should also automatically get what the computer thinks about the case." With Coplink's development focus shifting from the lab to KCC, these officers were eager to participate in a user group to help influence the system's future direction.

On a Roll

By early 2007, KCC had landed the Los Angeles Police Department (LAPD), its fourth California jurisdiction and the third largest police department in the United States, with 9,300 sworn officers and 3,000

civilian employees. Winning the LAPD put six of the seven largest police jurisdictions in the country in the Coplink camp, including Chicago, Houston, Phoenix, and San Diego. Altogether, it created the
largest information-sharing initiative for law enforcement in the world,
with the LAPD alone managing 11 million records. Bob Griffin, still
CEO of the enterprise, remarks, "Coplink's rapid national expansion
continues to be fueled by leading law enforcement agencies like LAPD
that are spearheading intelligence-led policing efforts."[3]

Like the other 349 jurisdictions participating in Coplink, LAPD
funded its project through a grant. In its case, the U.S. Department of
Homeland Security's Urban Area Security Initiative provided more
than $28 million to the Los Angeles urban area to improve its ability
to prevent, respond to, and recover from acts of terrorism.[4]

Coplink would act as the intelligence core, linking many public
safety agencies and departments together.

The U.S. military had deployed Coplink in Iraq to track down insurgents. It had been successful in locating one highly placed terrorist,
who was subsequently arrested and publicly brought to justice.

KCC continued to push the envelope on Coplink's technical capabilities. The newest release included an intelligence module that constantly panned the growing information network for new leads on
current investigations and alerted the relevant law enforcement agent
when it had discovered a pattern of interest. A new GIS analyzer gave
users the ability to array data bits spatially to help identify geographic
patterns.

Chen remained on the board of KCC, but his University of Arizona
AI lab had turned its attention to bioterrorism. Scoring funds from
DHS, the CIA, the Corporation for National Research Initiatives, and
its sustaining sponsor, the NSF's digital government program, the center turned its taste for real-world problems to border safety and terrorist
networks. By 2007, its unparalleled expertise in the technologies of
fuzzy association among disparate data nuggets had won it worldwide
recognition.

Individual police commissioners still occasionally dug in their heels when it came to sharing information. They still worried about who would get credit for the collar. They sometimes threw up false obstacles to Coplink to keep from losing "control" over their jurisdictions. However, as Coplink expanded, their interest in sharing information in order to catch the bad guys gained momentum. When KCC implemented the Orange County, California, jurisdiction, it found 55,000 "common criminals" who also appeared in the Minnesota and Tucson databases. Griffin says simply, "Today's crooks are highly mobile."

And the crime rate in Arizona? For the first time in recent history, Arizona began to gain ground relative to the rest of the nation in terms of crime. Between 2002 and 2004, Arizona reduced its property crime rate by 8.7 percent, compared to the national average reduction of 3.1 percent. It dropped its violent crime rate by 9.1 percent, while the national average fell only by 5.8 percent.

It's difficult to put a dollar value on this improvement, but some rough figures won't hurt. If we ignore violent crimes and just look at property crimes, the improvement from 2002 to 2004 gives us 510 fewer crimes per 100,000 people. With 5.7 million people in the state, that's a total of 29,000 property crimes that never happened. Researchers estimate the average total cost impact of a property crime at as much as $20,000, counting the effect on housing prices and tourism. Even if we use only $1,000 per crime, however, Arizona's performance improvement saved its citizens $29 million in 2004 alone.

No one would argue that Coplink was solely responsible, but people certainly agree that it helped.

One grant monitor summarized the nature of the accomplishment:

This initiative has been a success because all the elements came together—against all odds. It had a research lab, venture capital, a private firm, state support, regional support, support from the NSF, support from the NIJ, support from the intelligence community. The detectives love it because it's intuitive, but it's really hard to make a system like that. You have wildly different records management systems in different departments. They are doing completely different things with their databases. You have to take these very different databases and fuse them together so that they look exactly the same. The input going in may be variable, but what comes out is standard. That's really hard to do. But if all the world's cops had it, they'd have a common language. Then the criminal couldn't move from one place to another and escape the system.

CHAPTER 11

Secret #5: Spiral Up

Trans – for – ma – tion, oh, yeah, yeah! Can you hear the beat? Can you feel the heat?

Nine times out of ten, when executives launch substantial organizational initiatives, they are explicitly looking for a transformation. If you call a consultant, you are guaranteed to learn that your enterprise needs to be torn down to the nub and utterly remade because some aspect of your organization is completely unacceptable—for example, your culture lynches innovators or you can't squeeze any more growth out of your wizened markets.

Whether by ourselves or with the help of the pros, we take on the task of big change fast. We dutifully articulate our aggressive vision and our three-year plan to achieve it through (fill in the blank) diversification/innovation/globalization/acquisition. We structure initiatives with top-level visibility and strong ROIs, and we cram activities into task plans in a way that will complete the work before the organization loses interest or, worse, faith in the executives who sponsored the thing in the first place.

Two-thirds of the time this doesn't work.[1] When the dust settles, the consultants, M&A professionals, and lawyers have done what they promised, and the employees have put in long hours, but the organization has actually destroyed value. It is worse off than it was before.

Wildly successful initiatives take a completely different route. They do not aim for transformation. Frequently they achieve it, but that is not their reason for being. Instead, they set out to make a particular kind of contribution. They succeed over the long haul not by trying to vault to Paradise, but by spiraling up one valuable step at a time.

The Confidence Game

Wildly successful initiatives start the spiral with an approach that I call the "confidence game," optimistically bringing the elements of a viable business model together. They create plateaus of accomplishment and use each of these plateaus to take a fresh look at what is possible. They take advantage of accelerators such as luck and forcing functions to build momentum. They explicitly avoid conventional progress measures. And finally, they do not declare victory and close the initiative; they keep spiraling up.

For example, Wayland and his team would say that they never let the vision get in their way. They rounded up states to participate in AIRNow over years, not months. He says, "Every step was a positive. We said to ourselves, even if it ends in New England, with only fourteen states, it's a contribution. It's cool. There were no huge goals we had to meet. Deep down we may have had a big vision, but every step was a success."

Let's look at how this works from the start. Coplink provides an excellent example. Wildly successful initiatives begin with the four business model elements David Rose points out in Chapter 9: a product idea, a customer, someone to build the product, and someone to pay for the work. A "confidence artist" (in the best and most positive sense of the term) can weld these interdependent elements into a working model by convincing each player that the others will fall in line. To the customers: We are building this product that meets your needs, and we hope you will buy it. To the investors: Customers will buy this product if you invest so that we can build it. To the employees: If you build this product, it will succeed and you will be rewarded.

That's how interesting initiatives get off the ground: They levitate. Imagine four people holding hands with their feet not quite touching the ground—like group skydiving, but in the other direction. As the elements begin to work together, they inform one another, improve the solution, and increase their respective confidence in its merits.

How did Coplink achieve liftoff? Brad Cochran was no stranger to the grant process. As a Tucson police sergeant, he knew how to find money. He had a glimmer of an idea about what he wanted to accomplish, but he had no access to people who could do that kind of work. Hsinchun Chen had plenty of technology talent in his lab and an appetite for research on real-world problems, but he had no idea what kinds of challenges the police force was facing. He had the AI workers, but no product idea, no way to learn about a product, and no money for this activity. The National Institute of Justice had money for academic-quality research, but not for software systems. That would potentially satisfy Chen, but not Cochran. The COPS MORE grant program had money for software systems, but not research. That could help Cochran, but it would leave Chen out. And without Chen, Cochran could not pursue the idea he had in mind.

Here's how the confidence game worked. (Please keep in mind that I'm using this term to describe a very positive entrepreneurial dynamic.) Cochran convinced Chen that he could get the money if Chen could build the product. To satisfy both Chen's research goals and his department's performance goals, he convinced two granting agencies to work together to fund a more valuable solution. Chen convinced Cochran that his lab could build the product, but only if the police department assigned someone like Schroeder to work with it full time. That turned out to be critical for building a product that would actually work. Chen also convinced the graduate students who worked in his lab that working on the Tucson police project would further their academic careers. That's how this team put together a product idea, the people to build the product, a customer who wanted the product, and investors to pay for it.

Ambient Devices' Rose emphasizes that this process requires "baby steps." This is a critical difference from conventional organizational initiatives, most of which must lay out a great leap forward in order to get the executive attention and resource commitments that they think they need. The entrepreneurial confidence game (remember, this is positive) nudges each of the critical elements forward. Chen, Cochran, and Schroeder applied for a grant that would cover only their first two years' worth of work. They expected to be able to go back to the well when that ran out. In other words, they did not wait to begin their journey until they had lined up everything they needed to get all the way to the end. Instead, they collected enough to make a good step forward and planned to find the rest of the resources as they went along.

This mindset epitomizes the confidence game. It applies not only to money, but to people, partners, tools, and so on. Paul Monus went looking for a breakthrough paradigm to change the way the people in Lima managed operations. He didn't stop until he found one. Jim Schaefer encouraged his folks to spend money on improving productivity, even though he did not have sufficient budget to cover it. He believed that the savings would offset their spending over time.

Make no mistake. These people did not simply wish for resources to fall into their laps. They relentlessly sought them out. When they found one source blocked, they pursued another. Ambient Devices' Rose thought he needed a partnership with a large telecommunications company like Sprint or AT&T to broadcast the stock market and weather data that his devices would display. However, all the telcos he approached gave him the proverbial cold shoulder. Ever the problem solver, Rose cut a deal with a pager company—an organization that was hungry for growth opportunities and eager to collaborate. Ambient's customers ended up better off too because the pager company offered very attractive rates.

Cochran, Chen, and Rose had the wherewithal to bring their own organizations in behind them. Everyone needs partners, but at least they could rally their own resources. In some cases, wildly successful champions need help even with this step.

Let me tell you about Ted Graham, a manager at Hill & Knowlton (H&K), a $300 million PR business owned by the global advertising giant WPP. As an ambitious and high-performing global knowledge management lead in a public relations firm, his story starts in 2003 with a less-than-stellar performance review. His wife, a busy and successful corporate lawyer, had just given birth to twins, and the combination of sleep deprivation and family responsibilities had appropriately diverted his attention from his job outside the home. "In a global role like mine, you have to travel to stay top of mind," he explains. "I had lost a couple of steps." His boss, a family man himself, acknowledged how challenging it is to be a parent for the first time. Graham recalls, "That kick-started me. I realized that, at the end of the day, it's not your charming personality or even the amount of time you put in on the job that creates success. It's the power of your ideas."

At a time when the future of knowledge management (KM) was a question mark for many firms, including H&K, Graham attended a professional KM conference looking for something fresh. Amidst the buzz of provocative ideas, Graham had an insight. "It was one of those things you don't see unless you're hungry," he recalls. He explained that, at the time, every PR company was spending countless hours trying to map the network of media influencers. If you could figure out which reporters were getting their ideas from which pundits, you could target your PR campaign directly at the central figures instead of strewing press coverage everywhere in hopes that something would hit. Mapping these idea flows was extremely slow, time-consuming, error-prone, and expensive for the client. At the conference, Graham concluded that he could apply the technology of social network analysis through a high-throughput computer search of articles on the Internet and media databases and produce a influencer network map that would blow customers away. Not only would it be virtually instant—and inexpensive—but it would be much more comprehensive as well as more accurate.

Graham had learned the lessons of the PR professionals well; he knew the importance of the confidence game. After all, that's a PR firm's stock in trade. He recognized that he did not have the personal credibility he would need in order to rally H&K's resources to bring his idea to market. He knew he would have to carve out space to develop a working demo and to attract the attention of the geographic and practice leaders who controlled access to the resources and the clients. He needed help to get the confidence game rolling.

Graham called Christopher Solheim, an H&K senior executive from the United Kingdom whom he barely knew. Solheim was not in Graham's reporting line or geographic business unit. He was, however, uniquely credible in the company because of his past accomplishments, which included developing some business intelligence products. Graham explains, "He had this track record of taking a seed investment and making something salable. He took risks, too. He had left H&K and had launched his own successful business, then came back after he sold it. People felt that if we followed his lead, we would be well served."

Graham started selling. With passions flying, Graham was able to convince Solheim to add his considerable credibility to the new product effort, and the game was afoot. With Solheim's imprimatur in place, Graham's boss was willing to allow him the free time to push his prototype forward, and Graham's KM colleagues were willing to pick up the slack in his day job. Graham and Solheim were also able to win the confidence of H&K's chief marketing officer, Tony Burgess-Webb, an inveterate and effective proselytizer of good ideas in the company. As a result, other H&K staffers threw their own free-time effort onto the pile. Citing Solheim's ability to make the case, Graham and his skunk works ultimately got a little money from the CEO's discretionary budget to build the prototype.

Graham's network media map achieved liftoff when it resulted in a visible client win. Somewhat dissatisfied with the results it was getting for the $100,000 it had spent on identifying media influencers, the company's largest client decided to hold a PR bake-off, potentially moving this part of its budget to another firm. Scrambling for great answers that would win the day, the client team called Graham. (Doesn't this remind you of Dancer, Prancer, et al.?)

Graham recalls,

> The business was ours to lose. We were pitching against a pure secondary research company, and everyone expected that we would lose. The client had given us the names of five key influencers who were important to its business. In five days, we put together an influence map for these five plus others that were even more important. We showed the topics these individuals were tied to, who the key journalists on these topics were, and their attitudes about the issues. The client was blown away. At the end of the presentation, the people attending asked for forty more influence maps on other issues.

H&K's global CEO got wind of the win. He invited Graham to talk to key people in each of the offices about how to push the new capability. He also set aside a slot on the agenda of the June 2006 worldwide executive committee meeting for Graham to explain how the influence-mapping product could set the firm apart from its competitors. With sixty clients already signed up, Graham recalls, "It went so well that we ran over my time by forty-five minutes discussing all the clients who could use this. Then we chose two clients from every single region and every single practice group to target. That set out the next wave."

Create Plateaus

Managers normally divide their ordinary projects—especially those with big goals—into phases. First we'll complete the design of our new office area. Then we'll have the interior designer plan the layout and order the furniture. Then we'll have the contractor come in and construct the cubicles. Finally, we'll move all our belongings to the new space. Ordinary project phases such as these certainly divide up the work and make it more manageable, as they are intended to do. But they don't help the project spiral up—that is, increase its scope, importance, or attractiveness over time.

Wildly successful initiatives grow and evolve by moving from one plateau to the next. Here's the test. If you stopped our little office project at the end of one of the phases—say we have a design and a furniture layout, but no way to construct the cubes—would we be "stuck in the middle" or standing on solid ground and better off than before? Let's ask the same question about Graham's media-influence map. If he had stopped in June 2006 with a working system and sixty clients, but hadn't rolled the product out across the company's geographies, would he have been on solid footing? That's a plateau. Graham did not just complete a piece of work; he put it into use.

For the AIRNow team, for example, the ozone seasonality was a lifesaver. Wayland emphasizes,

> If we had tried to run the program year round from the beginning, we would have failed. We couldn't have built it fast enough. For ozone only, we had the off-season to catch our breath, talk to partners, learn from our mistakes, and decide what new features we could add. By 2003, when we started running year round, we were just adding another pollutant; the infrastructure was already solid. That let us start small and work our way up. That downtime allowed us to think and to add bells and whistles that made the program more appealing.

Plateaus trump ordinary project phases because they show results and attract adherents. They also have another benefit that turns out to be critical for some initiatives: When champions stand on a plateau they have created, they can see farther than before.

Recall that wildly successful initiatives have big aspirations, but that these aspirations may also be a bit fuzzy. The team often lacks a road map for achieving them. Instead of waiting for clarity, however, it takes a good step forward and gets to a plateau. By building good foundations, learning along the way, and accumulating confidence and credibility, new possibilities open up.

Duff and Skelton did not have the organizational muscle to start the Sim-Mole development using actual hardware. Even though the emulation software they used did not become a permanent part of the system, it gave the team a way to show what it could do. Some might surmise that it won the team enough credibility to get the hardware it needed.

The first two years' work on Coplink did not involve a single bit of artificial intelligence logic. For Chen's lab full of experts, it meant going back to information technology ABCs. Chen's university colleagues even asked him why he was wasting his time. However, by pulling together all the data fragments—and working directly with police officers such as Schroeder to learn how to make sense of what they were looking at—Chen and his students created a new platform for asking interesting questions. It was not until they had built this new environment that the team actually recognized how important Coplink could be.

Working wonders wannabes might conclude that a plateau is the same thing as a quick win in an initiative—a very popular technique for buying the time a project needs to begin to pay off in earnest. Beware. These are not at all the same. Managers score a quick win when they are able to produce a big result for a little effort. They leverage the halo effect that this creates to get the time and resources to dig into the dirty underbelly of the problem and fix it fundamentally. What often happens, however, is that the organization is so satisfied with the results of the quick win that it loses the motivation to do the rest of the job. It never goes back and addresses the root cause of the issue.

In contrast, wildly successful initiatives build up from the fundamentals to create their plateaus. If Chen, Cochran, and Schroeder had opted for a quick win in Coplink, they would have applied AI logic to a single database to show the power of the technology instead of spending their time building the comprehensive data platform. If the Stan-sylvanian Revenue Agency had wanted a quick win, the IT team would have started by building a glamorous online tax filing system that ap-pealed to taxpayers but operated like a glorified fax machine. Instead, they tediously built the back-office processing system first.

Whether wildly successful initiatives are getting to the first plateau or pushing toward the next one, they are always on the move. Champi-ons deliberately use accelerators to build the forward momentum that they need if they are to spiral up. While these tactics are also available to ordinary initiatives, they are not normally incorporated in the plan.

Use Accelerators to Build Momentum

As we know, champions of wildly successful initiatives are not working inside a tightly planned project structure with dedicated resources, must-meet deadlines, and detailed task plans. Their landscape is more like an open space. They motivate effort with aspirations and a strong emotional field. In addition, they use three specific techniques to boost momentum, increasing the initiative's mass and its velocity.

Take Advantage of Luck

In a recent study of change management in social security organiza-tions, we asked the managers of forty successful change initiatives what role luck played in their projects. Less than a third reported that luck was an important factor. However, when we contrasted those ini-tiatives that were highly successful with those that were average, we found a surprising result: Luck and wild success seem to go together.

Lest you conclude that *being* lucky is what accounts for wild suc-cess, let me tell you the story of Jacobs Creek wine and how Chris Roberts *used* luck to create the largest-selling branded wine in the world.

The setting is mid-1980s Australia, one of the best wine-producing regions of the world. With McKinsey & Company trotting around the world advising CEOs to "stick to their knitting," the company that employed Roberts decided to shed its "noncore" assets. One of these was the Orlando winery. Orlando Wine marketed locally, but its products were virtually unknown in the United Kingdom, the biggest wine-importing country in the world. Roberts, the head of a different business unit at the time, recalls,

> I knew the Australian wine industry was on the cusp of being able to expand internationally. It had 100 years of experience—much more than the French—and an economic advantage. Money was flying around cheaply; paper millionaires were everywhere. I was just a salaried employee. I thought I would see if I could buy it myself.

Roberts rounded up three colleagues and some outside financial backers and presented the board with a leveraged buyout proposal.

Shortly thereafter, he had his first bit of luck. "The timing was fortunate," he explains.

> The tender went out in August 1987 and closed in November 1987. A famous crash occurred in the middle: October 19, 1987, saw a worldwide decline in stock values of about 23 percent. At that point, many of the other people bidding for the business dropped out. All my market studies showed that even after crashes, people continued to drink, so we charged forward. We did have the opportunity to drop our bid by 40 percent.

Roberts and his team won the bid and immediately set about expanding into the lucrative U.K. market. They created a new brand name, Jacobs Creek, reasoning that U.K. customers wanted something that they could actually pronounce. They positioned the brand as simple, cocky, and thoroughly Australian with the tagline "Nothing flows faster in Australia than Jacobs Creek."

Sales took off. When Roberts tells the story, he claims that the wine's phenomenal success was "due to good luck." He ticks off five factors that went his way and helped pry open shelf space in critical U.K. distribution channels as well as the hearts and minds of the nation's wine drinkers:

◆ Australia won the America's Cup race—the first time in more than 100 years that another country had taken the cup away from the Americans. According to Roberts, that gave all things Australian a positive glow.

◆ The Australian dollar was devalued, giving Jacobs Creek an advantageous cost position.

◆ The Chernobyl nuclear disaster made consumers skeptical of wines from European vineyards.

◆ Trade with South Africa, traditionally a strong wine-exporting region, was under a boycott because of apartheid.

◆ Austria had been accused of doping its wines with glycol and had been slapped with a two-year trade moratorium, leaving a big hole in the market.

Do you buy Roberts's explanation? A little digging on the Internet will reveal a key bit of information that Roberts failed to mention when he asserted that his success was due to luck: All five of these "lucky" events took place *before* he and his colleagues bought Orlando. Roberts recognized the market opening and positioned his brand to take advantage of it. The luck was available to anyone; Roberts and his team were clever enough to use it.

Create Forcing Functions

In a classically entrepreneurial move, champions of wildly successful initiatives sign up for things they don't know how to deliver. Making a promise of this sort forces the team to stretch to reach it. That stretch propels it forward.

We talked about this technique before in terms of the strong emotional field, but it's worth mentioning briefly here as well. This approach flies in the face of a well-ordered project plan because it takes things out of order. Instead of arranging activities in step-by-logical-step order to ensure that the team is fully prepared to take on the next task, forcing functions leap ahead.

Wayland and Dickerson wrote a grant proposal that promised results they had no idea how to deliver. That didn't stop them from promising. Duff and Skelton took on a problem that others had dubbed "impossible to solve" and gave themselves about a year to get to the first plateau. Althouse and his colleagues at the Stansylvanian Revenue Agency decided *not* to make their existing tax processing system Y2K-compliant and used the unavoidable deadline to force the organization to cooperate on completing the new system. Paul Monus invited the schoolteachers of the workers' children to participate in the Manufacturing Game to embarrass the union into engaging.

Leverage a Heartbeat or Natural Rhythm

Conventionally managed projects work under the mechanical assumption that they start, run at a consistent pace, and finish. There's no allowance for highs and lows, bursts of speed and slow points. The most important thing is to finish before the players get burned out or lose interest.

Wildly successful initiatives make a more organic assumption. Champions don't just recognize that there will be fits and starts, dark days and exhilarating peaks; they embrace these. As a result, they have to worry not only about sustaining momentum as their initiative heads for one plateau but also finding ways to revitalize and reenergize the team to ready it to take on the next stage.

Managers everywhere—whether wildly successful or not—use what I call a small heartbeat to keep teams moving. Project leaders often use a daily or weekly status meeting as their metronome, depending on the pace they have set. Cisco salespeople have weekly quotas that they must achieve. Duff and Skelton asked team members to make weekly commitments for deliverables. Effective CEOs try to touch their key people regularly in this way.

Unlike leaders of conventional initiatives, champions of wildly successful initiatives also use big heartbeats to help their teams spiral up. These periodic surges of new oxygen to the team may come quarterly or annually. What differentiates them from small heartbeats is their purpose. Champions use them explicitly to revitalize the initiative rather than simply to sustain forward progress.

In the early years of AIRNow, Wayland and Dickerson used the ozone season to catch their breath and decide which new features they would add to the system to attract more states to the collaboration. They also ran an annual AIRNow conference that pulled together the team so that it could share its energy and accomplishments. Remember the way that air quality engineer described the experience? He said, "Chet would start by saying it was our program. He would have speakers talk about what they had accomplished, and then he would get up and ask us what we needed to take our program to the next step."

Both Coplink's Chen and the Lexington debate team used the heartbeat of the school year to pump fresh thinking into their initiatives. The outsourcing partnership in New Zealand's Kinleith mill used its annual contract review the same way—as an opportunity to look together toward the next plateau. Jim Schaefer's Maumee missions served the same purpose. These sessions were not conventional status meetings where the boss held people's feet to the fire. They were collaborative gatherings in which colleagues infectiously renewed their energy and volunteered their effort.

What happens when the big heart beats? It's definitely not a performance review.

Measuring Progress

Not surprisingly, champions of wildly successful initiatives use detailed performance metrics in a unique way as they spiral up. In conventional projects, measures play a central role in making performance judgments. Superiors use the numbers to decide who gets a promotion and who needs to be reassigned. Falling to the bottom of the rank order justifies a negative decision—as we saw with the Lima refinery's statistics, for example, which justified headquarters' decision to close the plant's doors.

Champions of working wonders don't use performance measures the same way at all—to dole out rewards and punishments. That is simply the wrong mindset. Instead, they use the customer satisfaction index, hydrocarbon loss, productivity statistics, and sales levels to stimulate improvement. Jim Schaefer explains:

> We very much wanted to improve our mean time between pump failure from thirteen to nineteen months. (We actually got to fifty-eight.) We kept close track of the improvements and publicized their effect. That was part of my role in cheerleading—I always cited where we were making progress, and I tried to be as fact-based as I could be. BP headquarters did things a little differently. It published "league tables." These were much like baseball standings. The league table might show that Lima was the worst in BP for hydrocarbon loss. This really discourages anyone at the bottom. It would have been much more encouraging if these tables had also showed how much each refinery had improved.

We see the distinction between measuring performance and managing outcomes very clearly in effective strategic outsourcing relationships. In contrast to less effective partnerships, where the outsourcer draws penalties for failing to meet operational targets, the client company does not even measure the service levels its outsourcing provider achieves. Instead, the outsourcing provider measures itself. When the provider identifies an issue, it addresses the problem and keeps its client in the loop. What other kinds of performance questions do the companies tackle together? Whether they are on the right strategic path together.

Ted Graham knows exactly how many customers have signed up for Hill & Knowlton's new media-mapping product. But he doesn't confuse hitting a sales goal with the fundamental purpose of his initiative. Wildly successful initiatives have bigger aspirations that defy concrete metrics. How would you measure whether the public was more engaged with the quality of its air? Could you set tick marks on your ruler that told you the extent to which your refinery had become the "queen of the fleet"? How about the extent to which you had created "Zen-simple, glanceable computing"?

As we have already seen, making headway on beyond-reach aspirations defies the traditional management mantra of smooth, predictable results. The process is more like real life—bursty and nonlinear. To keep this uneven, lurching pace from getting in the way, champions keep the scorecard measures in perspective—as feedback, not as conclusions. They aggressively resist boiling their aspirations down to specific measurable targets. That would be limiting. Instead, they inform and encourage their upward spirals with stories of the impact they have made, both small and large.

In the annual AIRNow conference, Wayland reads e-mails from day-care center directors and people with heart disease thanking the team for making their life a little easier. What does Jim Schaefer highlight when he talks about the Lima refinery? He talks about the personal phone calls he got on Thanksgiving from people in the plant, expressing gratitude for his efforts on their behalf. He talks about the celebration that Lima's Mayor Berger held to welcome the refinery's new owners and the standing ovation he received from the people of Lima for his contributions.

Don't Declare Victory

Perhaps the most surprising characteristic of all in wildly successful initiatives is that they do not end. In this respect, they couldn't be more different from ordinary projects. Conventionally managed projects end, even when they are not finished. The deadline has arrived, and the budget has been spent—notice the use of the passive voice here to obscure accountability—so victory is declared. It matters little whether the intended outcome has been achieved. Most organizations never bother to look. Sometimes it doesn't even matter what got done. The project scope gets revised to cover what can actually be delivered, and the project is wrapped up as a success.

We've probably all been part of projects like this. They aren't failures. In fact, they are more the rule than the exception. Things get done, then teams disband, and people go on to the next priority.

Wildly successful initiatives don't work this way at all. They just keep going. They spiral up for years. The AIRNow team has been making a bigger and bigger contribution each year since 1998. Sim-Mole has been serving UCE for the past fifteen years. The Lima refinery continues to produce, and Coplink continues to help police nab crooks.

What's the difference? Ordinary projects—and ordinary project management—focus on completing the tasks. For wildly successful initiatives, the tasks are only a means to an end. These champions are pursuing an outcome. And they set their sights high so that no matter how much they accomplish, there's always more to be done.

CHAPTER 12

Working Wonders

Putting the Pieces Together

At the outset of this book, we talked about two legitimate ways to manage work: the conventional, deliberate approach for projects where we wanted predictable results, and the wildly successful approach for venturing into the upside. Let's take a moment and recap the differences. For working wonders:

Reach Beyond Your Grasp

◆ *Don't choose your objectives rationally; make them personal.* Ultimately, every highly successful initiative has at its core a deep sense of purpose. These initiatives succeed by igniting wildfires of meaningful work.

◆ *Don't aim for a target that's within reach; go for something you don't know how to accomplish.* The conventional wisdom says that successful projects should have crisp goals and a clear road map for achieving them. This clarity persuades the organizational stakeholders who must support the initiative to buy in. But most wildly successful initiatives involve a leap of faith of some sort.

Make Space

◆ *Don't wait for the normal organizational channels to line up; carve out the space to explore.* Give yourself and your team the option of finding your own way through the open field. This liberates everyone's time and energy. All you will need are some broad boundaries and a focus on removing the occasional obstacle.

◆ *Don't make space for failure; insist on progress.* Knute Rockne, the legendary Notre Dame football coach, famously said, "Show me a good and gracious loser and I'll show you a failure." Making a contribution that has no impact is a waste of time. Why would we bother?

Get It Right

◆ *Don't accept the "good enough" solution; hold out for the right answer.* Engage your brains. Executing the wrong solution superbly doesn't make it the right solution. Involve your partners and your customers, and learn by trying until you get it right.

◆ *Don't get enthralled with complex technical features; use simplicity to bring others on board.* The word *simple* finds its way into every story of remarkable success. Leaders of these initiatives recognize that simple is the gateway to useful. And if our results are not useful, they can never be valuable.

◆ *Don't get tangled up in measuring performance; look at impact.* Conventional project managers report status brilliantly. They tick off the tasks that have been completed, highlight the ones that are overdue, and focus attention on the deficiencies. Wildly successful teams don't see the merit in this. They look instead for snippets of evidence that they are creating the outcomes they are after.

Energize People

◆ *Don't draft people who have done similar projects previously; ask for volunteers to take on something they have never done before.* What could be more promising than an initiative staffed by veterans? One that is littered with first-timers. Make no mistake, effective innovation teams feature extremely competent people. But two counterconventional characteristics stand out. First, team members are often self-selected, rather than drafted. Second, the team members are plowing new ground, not familiar furrows. The experience of choosing to take on a challenge one has never faced before adds creativity and energy to the process. And it shows up in the results.

◆ *If you don't have enemies, make some.* Innovators put emotional fields in place with appealing goals, opportunities to engage, recognition for contributions, and strong team bonds. They also convert negative forces in the environment from obstacles to foils. By framing the opposition deliberately, they unleash the team's competitive spirit and bond team members in adversity.

◆ *Don't (just) pay for performance; sing praises at the top of your lungs.* Community recognition and public visibility fan innovative sparks into hair-on-fire motivation much more effectively than that annual 3 percent pay increase. The heroes in successful initiatives are made, not born. Leaders spend their time giving credit for accomplishments to others. They run internal contests to make winners and help team members win external awards as well. They fuel their engines, and those of their teammates, not with financial incentives, but with public acclaim. As a result, team members feel that they belong to something important and are making a difference. These feelings increase commitment and build momentum.

Spiral Up

◆ *Don't manage through a detailed, disciplined task plan; coordinate the activities you can see and keep your options open.* To achieve predictable results, managers lay out all the tasks the team must accomplish and relentlessly monitor their status. Wildly successful initiatives don't work this way. Instead, they use an approach that one executive calls "ready, aim, steer."

◆ *Don't let the vision get in your way; create plateaus of accomplishment.* Big ideas are great, but what really inspire people are results. Wildly successful initiatives get things done and move on to the next challenge.

◆ *Don't wait until you have secured the resources you need; find what you need as you go.* A common refrain among project managers is that they did not receive the resources they needed to succeed. In fact, teams that are involved in highly successful initiatives almost never have claims on enough resources to do what they promise at the outset. Instead, they find ways to attract what they need.

◆ *Don't work away at a steady pace; create bust-out momentum.* Wildly successful initiatives play out over years, not months, and seesaw through ups and downs, setbacks and forward progress. Champions use forcing functions and leverage luck to ratchet up the intensity when energy flags.

◆ *Don't close the books and declare victory; keep the initiative alive to take on new challenges.* Ordinary projects have an explicit end. Declaring victory allows the team members to move on to their next assignment with honor. In contrast, highly successful initiatives do not seem to end. Leaders and team members do not tally up their winnings and move on. Instead, they expand the scope of the initiative and aim for an ever-larger contribution.

The Dynamic

Actually, talking about the pieces of the working wonders approach doesn't make much sense. You will have noticed that this book talks in circles. No matter how hard we try to divide up the key elements of a wildly successful initiative, we never get to a bill of materials or a manufacturing work order. There is no set of enumerated instructions such as "First put tab A in slot B."

Wildly successful initiatives are not manufactured step by step from talent and money and tasks the way conventional projects are. That is entirely the wrong analogy. (It's probably the wrong analogy for almost everything people do, but that's the subject for another book.)

Working wonders is more like creating a thriving community. These initiatives are composed in real time out of the interaction of the participants in the situation. They circle back, grow, and evolve in rich interplay, not linear determinism.

For example, the strong emotional field affects a team's ability and willingness to spiral up, and vice versa. The Kinleith management team's rock-solid commitment to making the mill viable enabled it to stand up to the union. Its success at outsourcing maintenance spurred it on to make other staffing improvements in the mill. Similarly, identifying the right answer opens up space, and vice versa. By bringing the Manufacturing Game to Lima, Paul Monus helped the refinery's management and operators tap wholly new opportunities to improve the plant's results. Equally, inviting workers to form action teams to deal with the problems *they* believed were most important highlighted solutions that management had overlooked.

You get the idea. Each of the five aspects of working wonders fuels and influences the others. They are neither separable nor lined up in a time sequence. As in the confidence game, there is no sign on the board that says "start here." You can start anywhere.

Many of the people featured in this book start with an idea that they are reaching for or a nasty problem that they are trying to solve. But that doesn't have to be the first ball in the air. Helen Greiner started with know-how and the voice of the customer. Early in her career, Greiner, co-inventor of the Roomba robotic vacuum cleaner, was at MIT. When she told people she was working with robots, they frequently said something like, "Will it clean my house?" So she started a company that would make robots to clean the house.

In *Good to Great,* Jim Collins suggests that the best approach is to start with the team, then work out what to do together. None of the examples in this book took that exact route, but we can easily imagine how it could happen: Wayland would grab Dickerson and Dye to take on a new challenge.

Regardless of the starting point, working wonders involves putting the dynamic in motion and keeping it there. When the complementary forces begin to kick in—the customers want the product or service; the employees are eager to contribute; the investors line up to play—the initiative gathers momentum. As we have seen, its ability to fuel itself may be so powerful at this point that it becomes virtually unstoppable.

Roll Up or Roll Out

Malcom Gladwell would call the point at which an initiative becomes unstoppable the "tipping point." After that, it's all downhill. Champions of wildly successful initiatives experience this point quite differently. They see it as a critical juncture and an opportunity for careful decision. When the initiative becomes unstoppable, it has gathered enough momentum, support, and resource attractiveness to carry on with ordinary project management. It no longer requires a working wonders approach to proceed. Conventional managers, with their task lists and performance measures, can readily roll the initiative out across the relevant organizational landscape.

However, if the initiative's champions choose this route, they must recognize that they are standing on the final plateau. The spirals are over. Let's look at two contrasting examples to illustrate this point.

In 2004, when the AIRNow team added the last relevant U.S. state to its ozone system, the champions hit a Rubicon. Should they begin managing the AIRNow system as a traditional operation, or should they continue with their contrarian, working wonders approach? Was efficiency now more important than growth? Wayland recognized that, if they chose the former approach, just about everything in the initiative would change. Meeting service levels, driving down costs, and managing the annual budget cycle would become the order of the day, instead of attracting new participants to the activist air quality community.

Wayland and the team resisted the pull of "good management practice" and kept their initiative pushing the envelope. As a result, they were able to extend AIRNow to begin tracking particulate matter and other pollutants as well as to begin to influence other countries' governments to launch similar air quality programs. It is unlikely that the team would have added these significant accomplishments to its list if it had set its sights on cost control.

In contrast, the engineers at Unigamble who saved their company billions with their manufacturing reliability initiative took a different course. They engaged the problem, found an entirely new solution, demonstrated its impact, and developed effective methods for communicating the new mindset their approach required. After implementing the new approach in some of the global company's manufacturing facilities, they hit the same Rubicon. Should they continue with a working wonders approach or shift to a structured rollout methodology? They chose the latter. The initiative's evangelist explains,

> It's a mistake to use good planning until you know exactly what you have to do. You get the first third of the organization to follow you based on their passion and the brilliance of the idea. You get the second third when you learn how to package up the idea and communicate it simply and clearly. But you don't get the last third until the project is well organized. We didn't deliver a billion dollars to the bottom line because a few manufacturing lines figured out a new way to manage reliability. We delivered because most production systems adopted our method.

Neither rollup nor rollout is the right answer for every situation. Champions must treat the so-called tipping point as a critical decision point and choose the best approach for their initiative. It does make a difference. Wayland would admit that AIRNow's growth has been remarkable, but its efficiency could have been improved. Unigamble's reliability team drove its solution across the manufacturing organization but has had less success starting up a new business based on its reliability expertise.

The People

This book started off by asserting that you wouldn't be reading about Jack Welch. I have nothing against Dr. Welch (did you know he has a

Ph.D. in chemical engineering?), but he is one of the "rock star" business leaders that we hear a lot about. He's a celebrity and larger than life. In 2006, he began teaching a course at MIT on the heady topic of conversations with, guess who, Jack Welch.[1]

The people in these pages are not organizational rock stars. Who, then, are they? Do they have common characteristics that make them uniquely well suited to working wonders?

First of all, they are real people—everyday people who have jobs and homes and families. They are not polished personas created by someone's marketing department. They are, however, accomplished. Along with their teams, they actually did the things described here, personally.

In terms of their backgrounds, wildly successful champions cover the map. Lee Skelton is a hard-as-nails program manager, and Zack Duff is a brilliant physicist. Chet Wayland is an environmental scientist with a flair for marketing, and Phil Dickerson is an information technologist. Jim Schaefer and Paul Monus are engineers with MBAs. David Rose is a serial entrepreneur with a degree in psychology and a doctorate in education. Hsinchun Chen is a professor and a noted expert in artificial intelligence; Brad Cochran and Jenny Schroeder are police officers. In terms of working wonders teams, these are only the tip of the iceberg.

Champions also work their wonders in a wide variety of organizational settings. We have seen their tracks at a paper mill in New Zealand and an oil refinery in Ohio, at a retail banking organization and a grocery store chain in the United Kingdom, at U.S. start-ups in packaged software and glanceable computing, and in government departments ranging from justice to environmental protection.

Champions of wildly successful initiatives do, however, have a short list of personal characteristics in common. First, they are optimistic. Where others see obstacles, they see opportunities. This makes it easier for them to reach beyond their grasp, to commit to an initiative they don't know how to accomplish, and to spiral up.

Champions infect others with their enthusiasm. They use their upbeat attitude and interpersonal skills to energize their colleagues and associates. Their ability to energize others makes them influential and attractive. As a result, they are more likely to have extensive social networks, and they are more often central to these networks. Perversely, the higher up an individual is in the hierarchy, the *less* likely it is that others will experience him as an energizer.[2] The implication? The company's higher-ups often don't know how to create the strong emotional field that our champions use to draw people into their initiatives.

Leading from the middle, then, not the top, champions of wildly successful initiatives don't delegate, they collaborate. They are as generous in sharing the limelight and in crediting others' contributions as they are humble about their own roles. Not only do they work well with other people, but they hold very positive assumptions about the people in their world.

For example, Mike Winch, who brought self-service checkout to the U.K.'s Safeway grocery chain, based his innovation on the assumption that customers would ring up the items in their carts fairly and honestly. They did. Jim Schaefer assumed that the refinery workers had good ideas about how to improve operations and wanted to help make the plant more effective. They did. Dr. Chen assumed that police officers had something to teach Ph.D.s about connecting the dots. They did. Olga Patricia Roncancio Mendoza assumed that even competitors would work together if you gave them the space to create good business opportunities. They did.

Finally, and perhaps related to their affinity for working with other people, champions of wildly successful initiatives have a taste for crossing boundaries. Zack Duff describes himself, humbly, as filling in the cracks. He gathered a team of brilliant scientists, programmers, and engineers and says, "Whatever they didn't know how to do, I did myself." When Jim Schaefer took over as the general manager at Lima, Mayor Berger reached out a welcoming hand, asking Schaefer in their first meeting, "How can I help you?" Juergen Link, the German-born site manager for the Kinleith mill's Swiss outsourcing provider, is delighted to find himself managing a team of 200 New Zealand maintenance workers.

Champions of wildly successful initiatives repeat their successes. When asked to describe their working wonders, they often answer, "Which one do you want to hear about?" Their other skills and talents notwithstanding, these people have mastered an approach that works again and again.

The One Great Person Theory

We are left with two very important questions. First, is working wonders possible only because a few very exceptional individuals have this unique blend of capabilities that positions them to succeed utterly? Are we on the trail of some rare bird such as the corporate track record in Jim Collins's *Good to Great*: Only eleven companies in fifty years were able to turn in the kind of performance that made his cut?

No. Champions of wildly successful initiatives are everywhere. In my absolutely nonrandom survey, I found that almost half of the people I contacted could describe an initiative that either was already wildly successful or was on its way to becoming so. If we count only those that have already delivered results, the total is more than 12 percent. In other words, if you get together with seven colleagues and associates in your organization, one of you is likely to have had the experience of working wonders.

If you are not convinced, you can conduct your own poll. Ask your colleagues, friends, and family to tell you about their wildly successful initiatives. Let me know what you find: info@progress-board.com.

The second question stems from an even more indelible mindset we share about how great accomplishments happen. Can we point to one central figure for each wildly successful initiative—a single individual who attracts all the others and makes everything possible?

Again, no. Special people are part of every working wonder. Jim Schaefer, Paul Monus, Dave Berger, Zack Duff, Chet Wayland, William Althouse, and Hsinchun Chen would certainly fall into this category. But they do not stand alone. In not one single wildly successful initiative can we identify a lone individual on whom the initiative depended. We always see several heroes, and sometimes many more than that.

Skeptics might say that the real heroes are just passing around the credit; the accomplishment still belongs to them, no matter how much they try to give it away. That *is* one of the things champions do that attracts people to their initiatives. But we have to ask ourselves, where would Chen be without Cochran and Schroeder? Where would Cochran and Schroeder be without Chen? What about Griffin? Not to mention people who played smaller roles with dramatic impact: Cochran's boss, who told him to get on that plane and win that grant; the dean of the University of Arizona, who brought Griffin into the picture; Linda Ridgeway, who worked tirelessly to cleanse the data warehouse so that early Coplink results would be reliable.

Consider AIRNow. Wayland and Dickerson kicked off the initiative by applying for the EMPACT grant. But the EPA engineers in Region 1 welcomed them and gave them a running start with both software and cooperation. No one would say that Sonoma Technology was *the* key to the AIRNow initiative; it wasn't even part of the initiative for the first few years. But would AIRNow be successful today without those folks? Can we really discount their contribution by crediting Wayland and Dickerson for attracting them to the project? Where does Lynn Perri of *USA Today* fit in? Because she took a chance on AIRNow when it was clearly not quite ready for prime time, she gave the initiative its first taste of national attention. Are we comfortable taking her contribution out of the picture by crediting Wayland and Dickerson with convincing her?

Paul Monus puts it best:

> Simonelli, Griffith, Schaefer, Berger, Ledet. These are tremendous people. We have to include the union leaders, too. They had been so hurt by management. They had taken so much disappointment, but they were willing to change their minds. There were twenty heroes. If any one of them had been missing, things would have been different.

The idea that we can find one central individual who was responsible for each of these initiatives should remind us of the way preheliocentric stargazers tried to make sense of planetary movements.[3] They constructed theoretical explanations, but these did not fully fit the facts. In the end, they had to question their fundamental assumptions. We must do so as well.

Let's give up the hierarchical assumption that having one key person in charge is essential for wild success. Let's say instead that every working wonder needs multiple heroes. We don't really know all the answers when we start out. We don't have a crystal-clear picture of where we're going or how we're going to get there. We don't know all the people who are going to play an essential role. All we do know is that we are not going to make a mark alone. How does that change the way we approach our aspirations?

For starters, it creates a clear self-test. Take your own pulse—the pessimists will feel stymied, and the optimists will be freed up to begin. Fill in the blanks in the following sentences to get a running start:

I would feel exceptionally proud to _____.

When I am collaborating with _____, _____, and _____, great things happen.

When we are doing _____, time flies.

I would be happy to do without other things in my life if I could only _____.

We try to put _____ out of our minds, but it won't go away.

The Way We Organize (or, You Are What You Eat)

Collective intelligence; collective will; collective leadership; contrarian management approach—there's one more conclusion to explore. Stepping back for a moment from our focus on *championing* wildly successful initiatives, we have to acknowledge some common characteristics lurking in the content of the solutions as well. The same five paradigms come up again and again, not in how the initiatives are managed, but in what gets implemented.

1. *System dynamics.* Winston Ledet's Manufacturing Game was built on a system dynamics approach that eliminated the need for maintenance. Unigamble's breakthrough in manufacturing reliability also derived from system dynamics. The early results from Ted Graham's media-influence-mapping venture reveal a similar dynamic underpinning the process of influencing public opinion.

2. *Open, nondeterministic solutions.* Coplink, Mutual Fun, AIRNow, and Sim-Mole have an important characteristic in common. As Zack Duff puts it, "There's no ground zero." None of these solutions drives users toward a predetermined right answer. They all take in an ever-changing array of inputs and react with an ever-fresh response.

3. *Parallel or networked processes.* Networked information flows loom large in Ted Graham's media-influence mapper, as they do in Duff's Sim-Mole. As Coplink expands from jurisdiction to jurisdiction, it leverages this effect dramatically to compile data fragments about crooks from their many haunts. AIRNow is nothing if not a massively parallel network of sensors.

4. *Multidisciplinary foundations.* Olga Patricia Roncancio Mendoza helped entrepreneurs find business opportunities in the spaces between their industries. Duff and Skelton would never have been successful without bringing together geologic, petrologic, signal processing, and computer science information. Rite-Solutions' Win/Play/Learn combined principles from education and pattern recognition.

5. *Simple interfaces.* The champions of wildly successful initiatives took great pains to provide the tools and technologies they built with simple interfaces. Skelton demanded that the Sim-Mole's controls work just like the Mole's so that the simulator could be used for training in addition to testing. Mike Winch worked with Symbol Technologies on a handheld device that had three big buttons

so that even the most technophobic shopper would find it wel-coming.

These five principles embedded in the hard science and technology underpinning working wonders should sound familiar. They closely parallel the management "system" that led to their design, implementation, and use. A wildly successful management approach is dynamic, not mechanistic; open and responsive, not tightly planned; parallel, not linear; diverse, not narrow; and simply communicated, not convoluted. Could it be that, in order to be effective, organizations must make sure their management approaches line up with the fundamental paradigms in the tools and technologies they are using?

We've heard this before. For example, Baldwin and Clark advise companies to organize modularly to produce modular products.[4] In our seminal work on business models, Sue Cantrell and I went even further. We found that organizations modeled on a fluid paradigm were uniquely able to offer products and services that responded dynamically to customers' changing needs.[5]

If management approaches must parallel technology paradigms, we have some work to do. Conventionally trained managers must take the time to understand the principles that underpin the powerful new tools and technologies they would like to use. Then they must translate these principles into new management mindsets. Working wonders is clearly one approach that points the way.

What Difference Does Working Wonders Make?

My unbelievable husband is working away on a wildly successful business initiative. He has asked me to save its story for the second edition of this book, once his handiwork has indelibly demonstrated its value. But I can't help describing the impact of working wonders in terms of some of the experiences he is living through. A year ago, as he launched a company on the path to dramatic growth, he spent a lot of time with strategic business partners such as Cisco and Microsoft to explain what he intended to do. They listened politely. A year later, the company has achieved the growth targets he set, and more. His business partners are stunned by the company's performance. What does that tell us?

They are accustomed to hearing happy talk. They may not be as cynical and negative as the Sphincter or Goatfob, but they have learned to discount their partners' well-meant promises. In their experience, what partners *say* they will do far exceeds what they *actually* do—so much so that they are shocked when someone actually meets his stated goals.

Champions of wildly successful initiatives set high goals, then meet them. This seems like a simple equation, but it makes the ground under the skeptics tremble. This kind of performance begins to establish an utterly different kind of expectation, not just for the initiative teams themselves, but for others. In this environment, cynicism fares poorly and commitment thrives.

We'll never eliminate the Sphincters and Goatfobs in our organizations. We wouldn't really want to; as enemies of the upside, they play a very valuable role. But we can surely influence our colleagues who are sitting on the fence. We can pull them into an organizational world where saying means doing, where people never give up and wonders are worked. Just think what we could accomplish together.

Notes

Chapter 1

1. See John McCarthy, "BPO's Fragmented Future," *Forrester Research*, August 2003, p. 6; and Standish Group, "Project Success Rates Improved Over 10 Years," *Software Magazine*, January 15, 2004, http://www.softwaremag.com/ L.cfm?Doc=newsletter/2004-01-15/Standish.

2. Amrit Tiwana and Mark Keil, "The One-Minute Risk Assessment Tool," *Communications of the ACM* 47, no. 11 (2004), pp. 73–77.

3. Susan Cantrell and James Benton, "Harnessing the Power of the Engaged Workforce," *Outlook*, no. 1, February 2005.

4. "Engaged Employees Drive the Bottom Line," ISR Research, http://www.is rinsight.com/pdf/solutions/EngagementBrochureFinalUS.pdf.

5. Jane Linder, Rob Cross, and Andrew Parker, "Charged Up," *Business Strategy Review* 17, no. 3 (2006), pp. 25–29.

6. Jane Linder, "Continuous Renewal: Managing for the Upside," *Outlook*, no. 2, April 2005, pp. 39–43.

7. Frank Gehry, Pritzker Architecture Prize Jury citation for 2003, www.pritzker prize.com/2003annc.htm.

Chapter 2

1. "Dan's Sohio Timeline: A Great Ohio Institution Is Built and Destroyed," www.dantiques.com/sohio/timeline.htm.

2. Not his real name.

3. The Manufacturing Game is a registered trademark of Ledet Enterprises, Inc.

4. Wikipedia. http://en.wikipedia.org/wiki/John_Browne,_Baron_Browne_of_ Madingley

5. Hans Houshower, "A Voyage Beyond the Horizon and Back: The Heartland Refinery's Continuous Improvement Story," an unpublished learning history, July 1, 1999.

6. Joel Podolny and John Roberts, "British Petroleum (A2): Organizing for Performance at BPX," Stanford Graduate School of Business case study no. S-IB-16A2, 1998, revised April 2, 2002.

7. J. D. Griffith, D. Simonelli, and P. Monus, "A New American TPM: Leadership Requirements for Breakthrough Change," presented at the NPRA Maintenance Conference, MC-99-95, May 27, 1999.

8. "Clark Announces Agreement to Purchase BP Lima, Ohio, Refinery," PR Newswire, July 1, 1998.

Chapter 3

1. *A Guide to the Project Management Body of Knowledge (PMBOK) 2000 Edition* (Newtown Square, Pa.: Project Management Institute, 2000).

2. Joseph Ellis, *Founding Brothers* (New York: Knopf, 2000).

3. Constitution of the United States of America.

Chapter 4

1. The names of the country and the individuals have been disguised.

Chapter 5

1. A famous saying by Mont Phelps, CEO of NWN Corporation.

2. Robert Cialdini, *Influence: The Psychology of Persuasion* (New York: Quill William Morrow, 1984), pp. 129–136.

3. Jane Linder, *Outsourcing for Radical Change: A Bold Approach to Enterprise Transformation* (New York: AMACOM, 2004).

4. Gary Anthes, "Easi-Order," *Computerworld*, March 20, 2000, http://www.computerworld.com/news/2000/story/0,11280,41911,00.html.

5. Matthew Boyle, "IBM Sets Sights on Retailers," *Fortune*, November 17, 2006, http://money.cnn.com/magazines/fortune/fortune_archive/2006/11/27/839 4323/index.htm.

Chapter 6

1. The Capability Maturity Model (CMM) is a set of software development process recommendations commissioned by the U.S. Air Force and developed by the Software Engineering Institute at Carnegie-Mellon University. It was first published in 1989. It categorizes software development practices into five levels of maturity, with level 1 being the most ad hoc and level 5 being the most disciplined and repeatable.

Chapter 7

1. Pat Bigold, "The Flop That Flabbergasted," *Honolulu Star Bulletin*, February 13, 1999, http://starbulletin.com/1999/02/13/sports/story2.html.

2. Ibid.

3. System dynamics is a mathematical modeling approach invented by Jay Forrester at MIT in the 1950s. An electrical engineer by training, Forrester applied engineering feedback concepts to model and diagnose the knottier problems he found in management. Some would say that system dynamics has never fully reached its potential because it is complex and difficult to communicate to the uninitiated. Peter Senge's *Learning Organization* is built on a system dynamics theory of organization.

4. See "Innovation 2005," Boston Consulting Group, 2005 (for more information, contact ITCSurvey@BCG.com); and Gordon Wyner, "Got Growth?" *Marketing Management*, March/April 2005.

5. William Taylor, "Here's an Idea: Let Everyone Have Ideas," *New York Times*, March 26, 2006, http://www.nytimes.com/2006/03/26/business/yourmoney/26mgmt.html?ei=5090&en=0d90ed5116e769d0&ex=1301029200.

6. Ibid.

7. The names of the companies in this story are disguised at their request.

8. For more about this amazing story, see Jane Linder, *Outsourcing for Radical Change: A Bold Approach to Enterprise Transformation* (New York: AMACOM, 2004), Chapter 2.

9. Ibid., Chapter 1.

10. Jane Linder, "Clean Skin at the Kinleith Mill," Chapter 20 in *Global Outsourcing Strategies: An International Reference on Effective Outsourcing Relationships*, ed. Peter Barrar and Roxane Gervais (Hampshire, England: Gower Publishing, 2006).

Chapter 8

1. Information in this section was excerpted from material on the U.S. EPA's web site, www.airnow.gov.

2. Information in this section was excerpted from material on the U.S. EPA's Web site, www.airnow.gov.

Chapter 9

1. Robert Cialdini, *Influence: The Psychology of Persuasion* (New York: Quill William Morrow, 1984), pp. 92–96.

Chapter 10

1. These Department of Justice grant programs were designed to support community policing and advances in law enforcement and administration of justice.

2. This is the same Doug Smith that had helped find funding for Coplink when he was the chief of police in Tucson. He left that job in mid-1998. After spending two years running an operational intelligence center for the Hight Intensity Drug Trafficking Areas program (HIDTA), he retired. Chen called him in 2001 to join KCC.

3. "LAPD Deploys COPLINK® to Support Crime Reduction, Gang Interdiction and Counter-Terrorism Initiatives," October 16, 2006, http://media.prnews wire.com/en/jsp/tradeshows/events.jsp;jsessionid=8EA988E849AEEF3116 6706D57DE4A443.tomcat1?option=tradeshow&beat=BEAT_ALL&eventid=1002203&view=LATEST&resourceid=3315577.

4. Letter from William Fujioka, Los Angeles city administrative officer, to the mayor of Los Angeles, October 4, 2006, http://clkrep.lacity.org/councilfiles/03-2569-S7_rpt_cao_10-4-06.pdf.

Chapter 11

1. See Frederick M. Zimmerman, *The Turnaround Experience* (New York: McGraw-Hill, 1991), p. 72; and John Kotter, "Why Transformation Efforts Fail," *Harvard Business Review*, March–April 1995, pp. 59–67.

Chapter 12

1. www.rockymounttelegram.com/biz/content/shared-gen/ap/finance_general/w, published September 27, 2006. In September the seventy-year-old Welch began his first classroom job, teaching an eight-session weekly course at MIT's Sloan School of Management. The course is titled "Conversations with Jack Welch."

2. Jane Linder, Rob Cross, and Andrew Parker, "Charged Up: Managing the Energy That Drives Innovation," *Business Strategy Review* 17, no. 3 (Autumn 2006), pp. 25–29.

3. According to Wikipedia, http://en.wikipedia.org/wiki/Copernicus, astronomers articulated heliocentric theories as early as the seventh century BC. Copernicus added his weight to the growing belief that the Earth revolved around the sun about 1,000 years later. During this time, some skeptics used Ptolemy's geocentric system of spheres, epicycles, and eccentric orbits to explain away odd planetary movements in order to preserve the basic assumption that the Earth was the center of the universe.

4. Carliss Baldwin and Kim Clark, *Design Rules*, Vol. 1, *The Power of Modularity* (Boston: MIT Press, 2000).

5. Jane Linder and Susan Cantrell, "It's All in the Mind(set)," *Across the Board*, May/June 2002, pp. 38–42.

Index